Editorial project:
2019 © **booq** publishing, S.L.
c/ Domènech, 7-9, 2º 1ª
08012 Barcelona, Spain
T: +34 93 268 80 88
www.booqpublishing.com

ISBN 978-84-9936-219-9 [EN]
ISBN 978-84-9936-379-0 [DE]
ISBN 978-84-9936-714-9 [IT]

© Editions du Layeur
Dépôt Légal : 2019
ISBN : 978-2-915126-61-7

Editorial coordinator:
Claudia Martínez Alonso

Art director:
Mireia Casanovas Soley

Editor:
Cayetano Cardelús

Layout:
Cristina Simó Perales

Printing in Spain

On April 28, 2019, U.S. explorer Victor Vescovo set the record for immersion aboard his bathyscaphe in the Mariana Trench. To his surprise, 10,928 meters above the surface, he not only found fascinating abyssal species, but he was also able to see how the human footprint had arrived before him to one of the least accessible corners of the planet in the form of scrap metal or plastic.

This disturbing discovery, together with the multiple signals coming from all corners of the planet, represents a new warning for the awareness of the need to promote global policies that protect the environment in all areas. In this sense, the responsibility of architecture with society acquires a special protagonism.

The projects presented in this book, coming from nineteen countries on four continents, illustrate the multiple possible approaches that architecture uses around the world in search of sustainable and environmental preservation strategies and their application in the design and construction of single-family homes. With the support of the most modern technology or using traditional resources and techniques, the small scale of the domestic environment becomes a fantastic test to develop tools aimed at promoting energy efficiency, recycling and reuse of materials, social sustainability, respect for nature and the harmonious integration of architecture in a natural environment increasingly punished.

Am 28. April 2019 stellte der US-Forscher Victor Vescovo den Rekord für das Eintauchen an Bord seiner Bathyskaphhe im Marianengraben auf. Zu seiner Überraschung fand er in 10.928 Metern Höhe nicht nur faszinierende Abgrundarten, sondern konnte auch sehen, wie der menschliche Fußabdruck vor ihm in Form von Schrott oder Kunststoff in eine der am wenigsten zugänglichen Ecken des Planeten gelangt war.

Diese beunruhigende Entdeckung, zusammen mit den zahlreichen Signalen aus allen Teilen der Welt, stellt eine neue Warnung für das Bewusstsein dar, dass globale Politiken zum Schutz der Umwelt in allen Bereichen gefördert werden müssen. In diesem Sinne erhält die Verantwortung der Architektur gegenüber der Gesellschaft eine besondere Protagonistie.

Die in diesem Buch vorgestellten Projekte aus neunzehn Ländern auf vier Kontinenten veranschaulichen die vielfältigen Möglichkeiten, die Architektur weltweit auf der Suche nach nachhaltigen und umweltschonenden Strategien und deren Anwendung bei der Planung und dem Bau von Einfamilienhäusern nutzt. Mit Unterstützung modernster Technologien oder unter Verwendung traditioneller Ressourcen und Techniken wird die kleine Dimension der häuslichen Umwelt zu einem fantastischen Testfeld für die Entwicklung von Instrumenten zur Förderung der Energieeffizienz, des Recyclings und der Wiederverwendung von Materialien, der sozialen Nachhaltigkeit, des Respekts vor der Natur und der harmonischen Integration der Architektur in eine natürliche Umgebung, die zunehmend bestraft wird.

Le 28 avril 2019, l'explorateur américain Victor Vescovo a établi le record d'immersion à bord de son bathyscaphe dans la fosse Mariana. À sa grande surprise, à 10 928 mètres au-dessus de la surface, il a non seulement trouvé des espèces abyssales fascinantes, mais il a aussi pu voir comment l'empreinte humaine était arrivée avant lui dans l'un des coins les moins accessibles de la planète sous forme de ferraille ou de plastique.

Cette découverte inquiétante, conjuguée aux multiples signaux provenant des quatre coins de la planète, constitue un nouvel avertissement pour la prise de conscience de la nécessité de promouvoir des politiques globales qui protègent l'environnement dans tous les domaines. En ce sens, la responsabilité de l'architecture avec la société acquiert un protagonisme particulier.

Les projets présentés dans cet ouvrage, provenant de dix-neuf pays sur quatre continents, illustrent les multiples approches possibles de l'architecture dans le monde à la recherche de stratégies de préservation durable et environnementale et leur application dans la conception et la construction de maisons unifamiliales. Avec l'appui des technologies les plus modernes ou en utilisant les ressources et techniques traditionnelles, la petite échelle de l'environnement domestique devient un banc d'essai fantastique pour développer des outils visant à promouvoir l'efficacité énergétique, le recyclage et la réutilisation des matériaux, la durabilité sociale, le respect de la nature et l'intégration harmonieuse de l'architecture dans un environnement naturel toujours plus puni.

El 28 de abril de 2019, el explorador estadounidense Víctor Vescovo batió en la Fosa de las Marianas el récord de inmersión a bordo de su batiscafo. Para su sorpresa, a 10 928 metros de la superficie no solo encontró fascinantes especies abisales, sino que también pudo comprobar cómo la huella del ser humano había llegado antes que él hasta uno de los rincones menos accesibles del planeta en forma de desperdicios de metal o de plástico.

Este inquietante descubrimiento, unido a las múltiples señales que llegan desde todos los rincones de planeta, representa un nuevo aviso para la toma de conciencia hacia la necesidad de promover políticas a nivel global que protejan el medio ambiente en todos los ámbitos. En este sentido, la responsabilidad de la arquitectura con la sociedad adquiere un especial protagonismo.

Los proyectos presentados en este libro, procedentes de diecinueve países de cuatro continentes, ilustran las múltiples aproximaciones posibles que alrededor del mundo utiliza la arquitectura en búsqueda de estrategias sostenibles y de preservación del medio ambiente y su aplicación en el diseño y construcción de viviendas unifamiliares. Con el apoyo de la más moderna tecnología o utilizando recursos y técnicas tradicionales, la pequeña escala del ámbito doméstico se convierte en un fantástico banco de pruebas para desarrollar herramientas destinadas a fomentar la eficiencia energética, el reciclaje y reutilización de materiales, la sostenibilidad social, el respeto por la naturaleza y la integración armoniosa de la arquitectura en un entorno natural cada vez más castigado.

AKA ARCHITECTS

AKA delivers site-specific designs responsive to people, climate and place. We provide socially, economically and environmentally responsible design whatever the purpose or application.
AKA has successfully worked across a range of scales and building types with a focus on people-centric design and community projects.
Our design solutions respect the connection to place: site, landscape, and climate. We design for people, with people in mind. Working collaboratively as part of a team we value input from our clients, consultants and builders.
Incorporating passive solar design principles and sustainable practices we create humble but comfortable spaces with a focus on thermal performance. Materials are selected to be durable, economical, and beautiful —celebrating the contrast of the rough with the refined.
We aim to create projects that perform and work well without costing the earth.

AKA liefert standortspezifische Designs, die auf Menschen, Klima und Ort reagieren. Wir bieten sozial, wirtschaftlich und ökologisch verantwortliches Design für jeden Zweck und jede Anwendung.
AKA hat erfolgreich mit einer Reihe von Größenordnungen und Gebäudetypen gearbeitet, wobei der Schwerpunkt auf menschenzentriertem Design und Gemeinschaftsprojekten lag.
Unsere Designlösungen berücksichtigen die Verbindung zum Ort: Lage, Landschaft und Klima. Wir entwerfen für Menschen, mit Blick auf Menschen. Wir schätzen die Zusammenarbeit im Team und den Input unserer Kunden, Berater und Bauherren.
Mit passiven solaren Designprinzipien und nachhaltigen Praktiken schaffen wir bescheidene, aber komfortable Räume mit dem Fokus auf thermische Leistung. Die Materialien werden so ausgewählt, dass sie langlebig, wirtschaftlich und schön sind – und den Kontrast zwischen dem Groben und dem Raffinierten zelebrieren.
Unser Ziel ist es, Projekte zu schaffen, die gut funktionieren, ohne die Erde zu belasten.

AKA propose des conceptions de sites spécifiques qui répondent aux besoins des personnes, du climat et du lieu. Nous fournissons une conception socialement, économiquement et écologiquement responsable quel que soit le but ou l'application.
AKA a travaillé avec succès sur une gamme d'échelles et de types de bâtiments en mettant l'accent sur la conception centrée sur l'homme et les projets communautaires.
Nos solutions de conception respectent le lien avec le lieu : site, paysage et climat. Nous concevons pour quelqu'un, avec cette ou ces personne(s) à l'esprit. Travaillant en collaboration au sein d'une équipe, nous apprécions l'apport de nos clients, consultants et constructeurs.
En incorporant les principes de conception solaire passive et les pratiques durables, nous créons des espaces humbles mais confortables en mettant l'accent sur la performance thermique. Les matériaux sont choisis parce qu'ils sont durables, économiques et beaux - et célèbrent le contraste entre le brut et le raffiné.
Notre objectif est de créer des projets qui fonctionnent bien et, cela, sans coûter cher à la planète.

AKA ofrece diseños específicos para cada lugar que responden a las necesidades de las personas, el clima y la localización. Ofrecemos diseño social, económico y ambientalmente responsable sea cual sea el propósito o la aplicación.
AKA ha trabajado con éxito en una amplia gama de escalas y tipos de edificios con un enfoque en el diseño centrado en las personas y en proyectos comunitarios.
Nuestras soluciones de diseño respetan la conexión con el lugar: sitio, paisaje y clima. Diseñamos para la gente. Trabajando en colaboración como parte de un equipo, valoramos las aportaciones de nuestros clientes, consultores y constructores.
Incorporando principios de diseño solar pasivo y prácticas sostenibles, creamos espacios sencillos pero confortables con un enfoque en el rendimiento térmico. Los materiales son seleccionados para ser duraderos, económicos y hermosos –celebrando el contraste de lo áspero con lo refinado.
Nuestro objetivo es crear proyectos que funcionen bien sin que ello suponga un coste para la tierra.

APPLE CRATE SCHACK

The project follows a design that is guided by needs, not desires. A modest footprint but a generous volume satisfies all spatial and functional requirements. Circulation is efficient: strong connections extend the spaces to interact with the surrounding landscape.
The house is both experimentation and an investigation of ideas: the aesthetics of the "apple crate" refers to the local fruit industry. A limited palette of materials speaks of durability and economy.
The project develops passive solar design principles and encourages sustainable practices through elements such as photovoltaic panels, reverse-cycle heat pump, rainwater collection tanks, reuse of building materials and equipment, and the use of local materials.

Das Projekt ist eine Erforschung der Angemessenheit: Das Design orientiert sich an den Bedürfnissen, nicht an den Wünschen. Eine bescheidene Standfläche, aber ein großzügiges Volumen erfüllt alle räumlichen und funktionalen Anforderungen. Die Zirkulation ist prägnant und effizient: Starke Verbindungen erweitern die Räume für die Interaktion mit der umgebenden Landschaft.
Wohnen ist auch Experimentieren und Erforschen von Ideen: Die Ästhetik der „Apfelschachtel" bezieht sich auf die lokale Obstindustrie. Eine begrenzte Palette von Materialien spricht für Langlebigkeit und Wirtschaftlichkeit.
Das Projekt entwickelt passive solare Gestaltungsprinzipien und fördert nachhaltige Praktiken durch Elemente wie Photovoltaikmodule, Inverse-Cycle-Wärmepumpen, Wasserrückgewinnungstanks, die Wiederverwendung von Baumaterialien und Installationsausrüstung oder die Verwendung lokaler Materialien.

Le projet est une exploration de l'adéquation : la conception est guidée par les besoins et non les désirs. Un encombrement au sol modeste mais un volume généreux permet de répondre à toutes les exigences d'espace et de fonctionnalité. La circulation est succincte et efficace : des liens forts prolongent les espaces pour interagir avec le paysage environnant.
Le logement, c'est aussi l'expérimentation et la recherche d'idées : l'esthétique de la « boîte de pommes » fait référence à l'industrie fruitière locale. Une palette limitée de matériaux parle de durabilité et d'économie.
Le projet développe des principes de conception solaire passive et encourage les pratiques durables à travers des éléments tels que les panneaux photovoltaïques, les pompes à chaleur à cycle inverse, les réservoirs de récupération d'eau, la réutilisation des matériaux de construction et des équipements d'installation ou l'utilisation des matériaux locaux.

El proyecto es una exploración de adecuación: el diseño se guía por necesidades, no por deseos. Una huella modesta pero un volumen generoso satisface todos los requisitos espaciales y funcionales. La circulación es sucinta y eficiente: las fuertes conexiones extienden los espacios para interactuar con el paisaje circundante.
La vivienda es también experimentación y una investigación de ideas: la estética de la «caja de manzanas» hace referencia a la industria frutícola local. Una paleta de materiales limitada habla de durabilidad y economía.
El proyecto desarrolla principios de diseño solar pasivo y fomenta las prácticas sostenibles mediante elementos tales como paneles fotovoltaicos, bomba de calor de ciclo inverso, tanques para recuperación de agua de lluvia, la reutilización de materiales de construcción y de equipos de instalaciones o el uso de materiales locales.

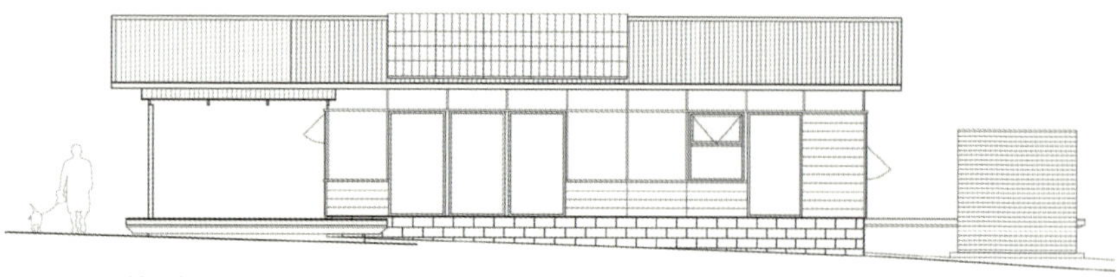

North elevation

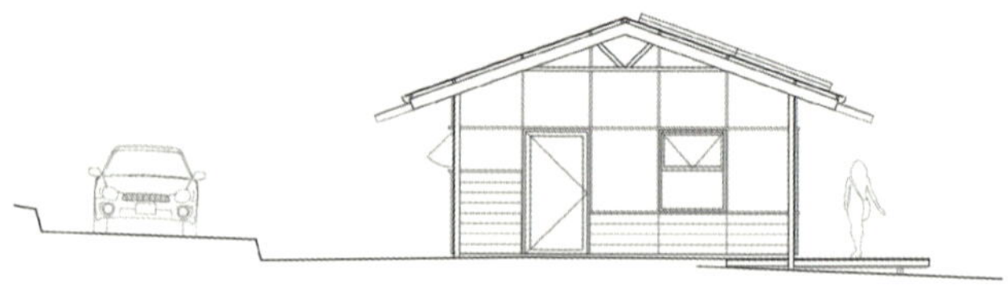

East elevation

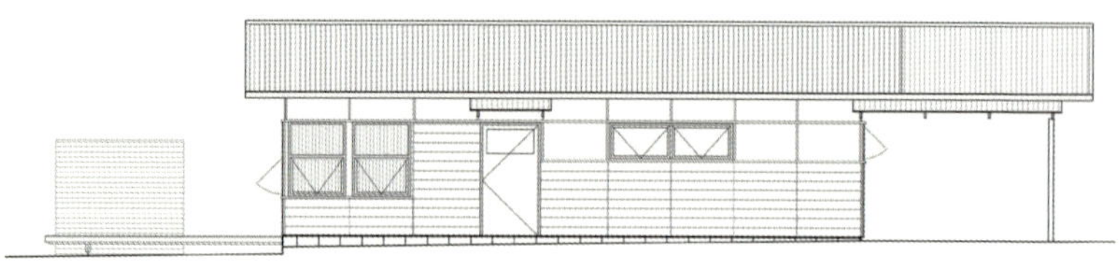

South elevation

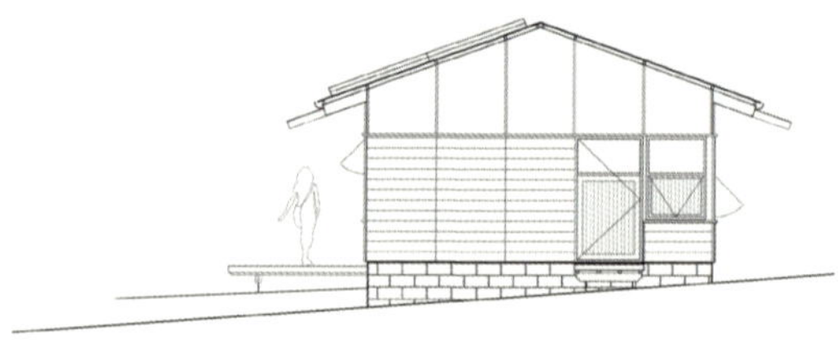

West elevation

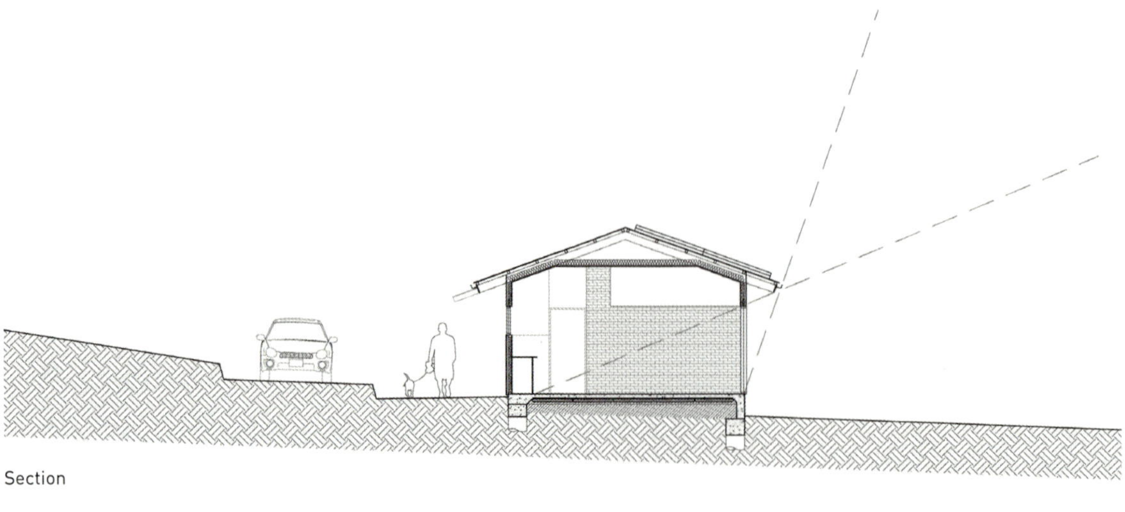

Section

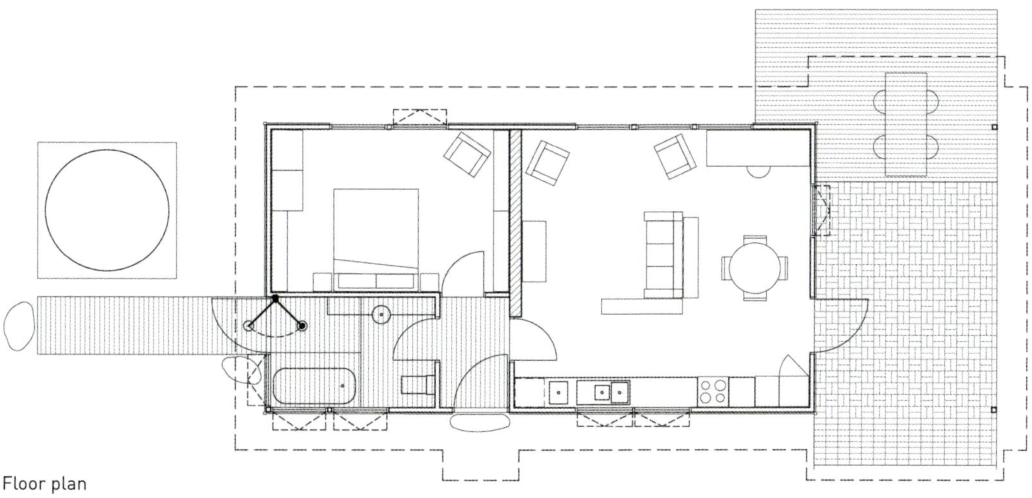

Floor plan

ALTAMAREA ARQUITECTURA

Altamarea office was created in 2015 by architect Gonzalo Herreros and engineer Matías Quinlan. It has been characterized mainly by the integral development of housing projects and investments for the coastal zone of Chile. We developed an architecture according to the place, recognizing the climatic conditions and their variables throughout the year. We build projects with simple materials of local origin, with great constructive and architectural results.
Based on our experience of life on the beach we create for our customers life experiences focused on energy efficiency the use of light and durability over time, key concepts in the development of our project. Today Altamarea concentrates in residential and commercial projects. We have worked in recent years also in the development of hotels and other kind of commercial projects, seeking through our proposal to give an architectural image to our environment.

Le bureau Altamarea a été créé en 2015 par l'architecte Gonzalo Herreros et l'ingénieur Matías Quinlan. Il se caractérise principalement par le développement intégral de projets de logements et d'investissements pour la zone côtière du Chili. Nous avons développé une architecture en fonction du lieu, reconnaissant les conditions climatiques et leurs variables tout au long de l'année. Nous construisons des projets avec des matériaux simples d'origine locale, avec de grands résultats constructifs et architecturaux.
Sur la base de notre expérience de la vie sur la plage, nous créons pour nos clients des expériences de vie axées sur l'efficacité énergétique, l'utilisation de la lumière et la durabilité dans le temps, concepts clés dans le développement de notre projet. Aujourd'hui Altamarea s'est développé dans le secteur résidentiel et commercial. Nous avons travaillé ces dernières années dans le développement de projets hôteliers et commerciaux cherchant par notre proposition à donner une image architecturale à notre environnement.

Das Büro Altamarea wurde 2015 vom Architekten Gonzalo Herreros und dem Ingenieur Matías Quinlan gegründet. Es tut sich vor allem durch die integrale Entwicklung von Wohnprojekten und Investitionen für die chilenische Küstenregion hervor. Wir haben eine Architektur nach dem Ort entwickelt, die die klimatischen Bedingungen und ihre Variablen das ganze Jahr über berücksichtigt. Wir bauen Projekte mit einfachen Materialien lokaler Herkunft, mit großen konstruktiven und architektonischen Ergebnissen.
Basierend auf unserer Erfahrung mit dem Leben am Strand schaffen wir für unsere Kunden Lebenserfahrungen, die sich auf Energieeffizienz, den Einsatz von Licht und Langlebigkeit im Laufe der Zeit konzentrieren – Schlüsselkonzepte bei der Entwicklung unseres Projekts. Heute wird Altamarea in den Bereichen Wohnen und Gewerbe entwickelt, in denen wir in den letzten Jahren an der Entwicklung von Hotel- und Gewerbeprojekten gearbeitet haben, die nach unserem Vorschlag ein architektonisches Bild unserer Umwelt vermitteln sollen.

La oficina Altamarea fue creada el año 2015 por el arquitecto Gonzalo Herreros y el ingeniero Matías Quinlan. Se ha caracterizado principalmente por el desarrollo integral de proyectos de vivienda e inversiones para la zona costera de Chile. Desarrollamos una arquitectura acorde al lugar reconociendo las condiciones climáticas y sus variables a lo largo del año. Construimos proyectos con materiales sencillos de origen local, con grandes resultados constructivos y arquitectónicos.
En base a nuestra experiencia de vida en la playa creamos para nuestros clientes experiencias de vida enfocados en la eficiencia energética el aprovechamiento de la luz y la perdurabilidad en el tiempo, conceptos claves en el desarrollo de nuestro proyecto. Hoy en día Altamarea se desarrolla en el ámbito habitacional y comercial hemos trabajado los últimos años en el desarrollo de proyectos de hotelería y comercio buscando mediante nuestra propuesta dar una imagen arquitectónica a nuestro entorno.

CASAS MQ

CASA RIOS

CASA WB

CASAS MQ

The project comprises two houses of equal height and similar architectural style, which are located on the plot so that the views are not interrupted. The main house rests on the highest hill of the plot, while the second is raised on a concrete plinth for parking, which allows to equalize the levels of the floors of both houses. The floor structure is developed in modules of 3 to 4m in order to optimize the materials, mainly wood.
The images of both houses are joined through materials and textures, considering similar details in both constructions. Structures and exposed beams are privileged together with materials such as wood, metal and exposed concrete. The finishes are worked in a rough way, seeking not to hide the nobility of the materials, leaving their elements to be shown as such.

Das Projekt umfasst zwei gleich hohe und ähnliche Häuser, die sich auf dem Grundstück befinden, so dass die Aussicht nicht unterbrochen wird. Das Haupthaus befindet sich auf dem höchsten Hügel des Grundstücks, während das zweite auf einem Betonsockel für den Parkplatz steht, der es ermöglicht, die Niveaus der Böden beider Häuser auszugleichen. Die Bodenstruktur wird in Modulen von 3 bis 4 m entwickelt, um die Materialien, hauptsächlich Holz, zu optimieren.
Die Bilder beider Häuser werden durch Materialien und Texturen verbunden, wobei ähnliche Details in beiden Konstruktionen berücksichtigt werden. Tragende Konstruktion und Sichtbalken werden mit Materialien wie Holz, Metall und Sichtbeton bevorzugt. Die Oberflächen sind grob bearbeitet, wobei versucht wird, die Noblesse der Materialien nicht zu verbergen, so dass ihre Elemente als solche gezeigt werden können.

Le projet comprend deux maisons de hauteur égale et de style architectural similaire, qui sont situées sur le terrain afin que les vues ne soient pas interrompues. La maison principale repose sur la plus haute colline de la parcelle, tandis que la seconde est surélevée sur un socle de béton pour le stationnement, ce qui permet d'égaliser les niveaux des étages des deux maisons. La structure du plancher est développée en modules de 3 à 4 m afin d'optimiser les matériaux, principalement le bois.
Les images des deux maisons sont reliées par des matériaux et des textures, en tenant compte de détails similaires dans les deux constructions. Les structures et les poutres apparentes sont privilégiées avec des matériaux tels que le bois, le métal et le béton apparent. Les finitions sont travaillées de manière grossière, en cherchant à ne pas masquer la noblesse des matériaux, en laissant leurs éléments se manifester en tant que tels.

El proyecto comprende dos casas de igual altura y de similar estilo arquitectónico, que se sitúan en la parcela de forma que no se interrumpan las vistas. La casa principal se posa sobre la loma más alta del solar, mientras que la segunda se alza sobre un zócalo de hormigón destinado a estacionamiento, hecho que permite igualar los niveles de las plantas de ambas casas. La estructura de piso se desarrolla en módulos de 3 a 4 m para de optimizar los materiales, principalmente madera.
Las imágenes de ambas casas se unen a través de materiales y texturas, considerando detalles similares en ambas construcciones. Se privilegia las estructuras y envigados a la vista conjuntamente con materiales como la madera, el metal y hormigón visto. Los acabados se trabajan de forma tosca, buscando no esconder la nobleza de los materiales, dejando que sus elementos se muestren como tal.

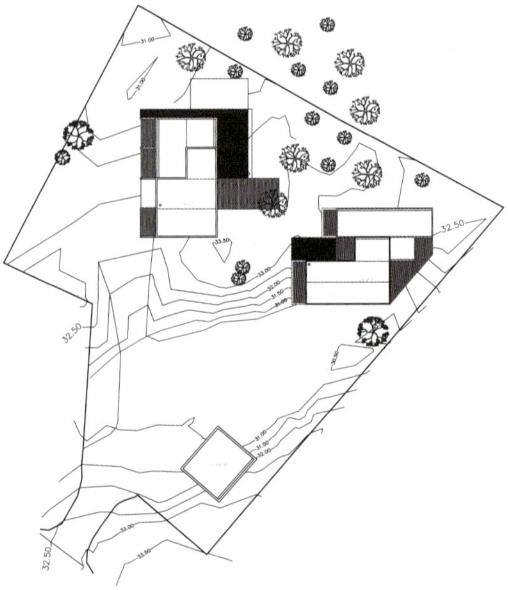

Site plan

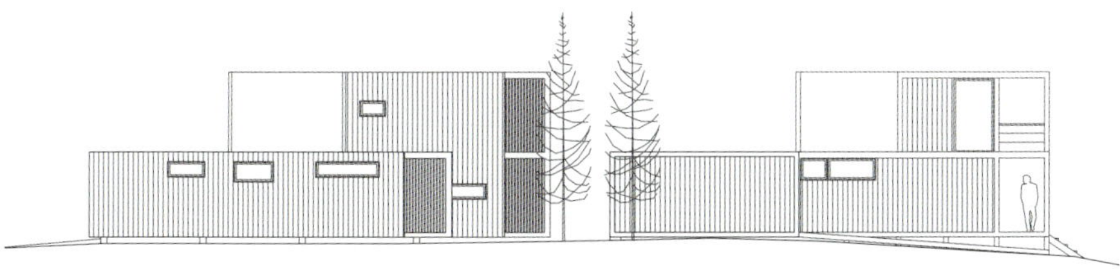

North elevation MQ houses

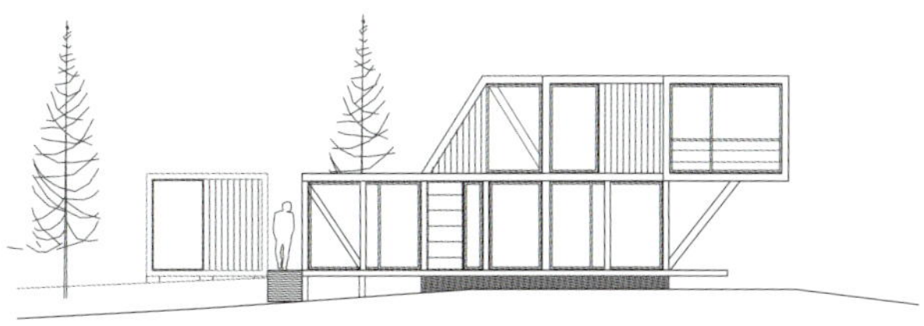

West elevation MQ house

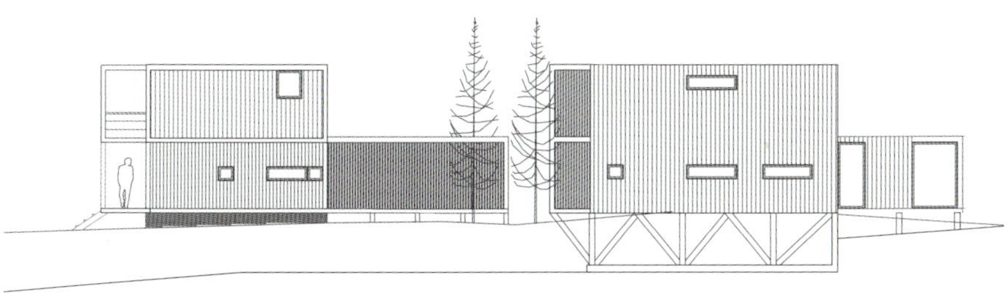

South elevation MQ houses

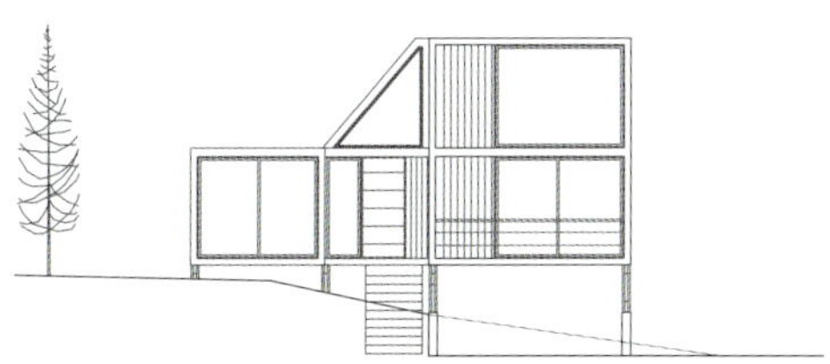

West elevation MQ2 house

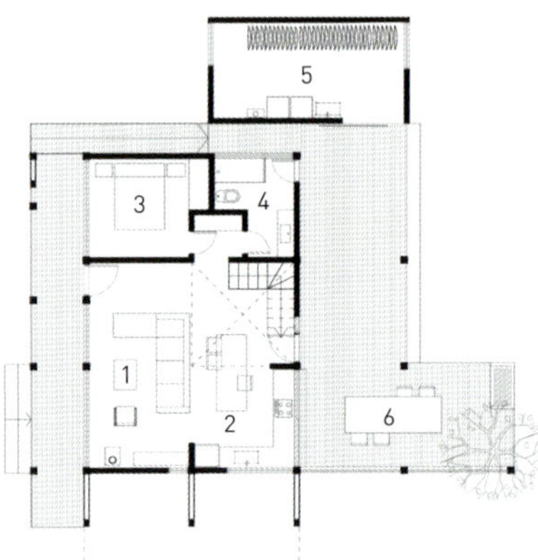

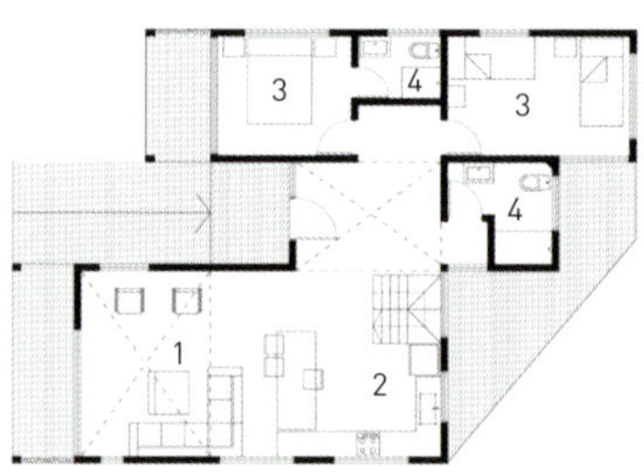

First level plan MQ houses

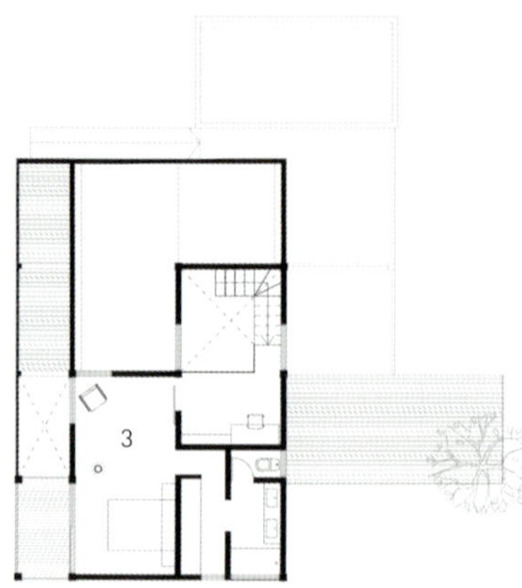

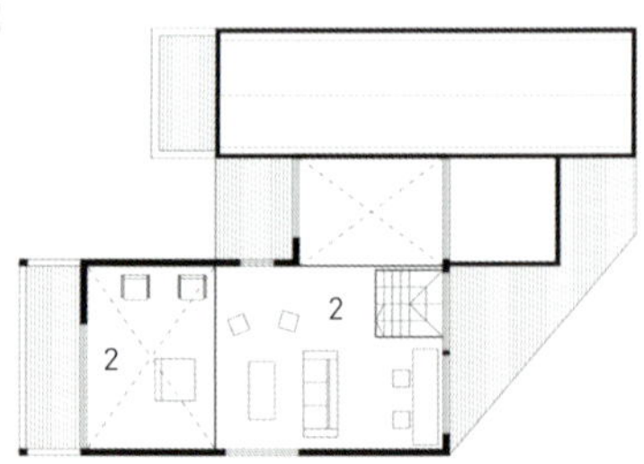

Second level plan MQ houses

1. Living room
2. Kitchen
3. Bedroom
4. Bathroom
5. Cellar
6. Deck

CASA RIOS

The project rests on a hill with spectacular views of the Pacific Ocean, about 200m from the sea. The house was designed in such a way that all the main spaces took advantage of the views. The first level is developed on a concrete skirting board for parking that moors the house to the sandy terrain.
The main spaces are worked from the privacy and luminosity. The enclosures are decorated with eaves and lattices that are incorporated into the façade of the house. Sliding doors made of local material are added helping this the interior solar control. The whole house is built with wood from local sawmills. External circulations are generated around the house in order to incorporate the external spaces to the interior social events frequent in this type of beach houses.

Das Projekt liegt auf einem Hügel mit spektakulärem Blick auf den Pazifik, etwa 200 m vom Meer entfernt. Das Haus wurde so konzipiert, dass alle Hauptträume die Aussicht nutzen. Die erste Ebene ist auf einer Betonscheuerleiste für Parkplätze entwickelt, die das Haus mit dem sandigen Gelände verbindet.
Die Hauptträume sind von Privatsphäre und Helligkeit geprägt. Die Schränke sind mit Traufen und Gittern verziert, die in die Fassade des Hauses integriert sind. Poniente Folien werden in Material eingearbeitet, das vor Ort bezogen wird und auf diese Weise zum inneren Sonnenschutz beiträgt. Das ganze Haus ist aus Holz von lokalen Sägewerken gebaut. Externe Zirkulationen werden um das ganze Haus herum erzeugt, um die Außenräume in die inneren sozialen Ereignisse einzubinden, die in dieser Art von Strandhäusern häufig vorkommen.

Le projet repose sur une colline avec une vue spectaculaire sur l'océan Pacifique, à environ 200 m de la mer. La maison a été conçue de manière à ce que tous les espaces principaux profitent de la vue. Le premier niveau est aménagé sur une plinthe en béton pour le stationnement qui amarre la maison sur le terrain sablonneux.
Les espaces principaux sont travaillés à partir de l'intimité et de la luminosité. Les enceintes sont décorées d'avant-toits et de treillis qui sont intégrés à la façade de la maison. Des diapositives de Poniente sont ajoutées dans le matériel provenant de l'endroit, aidant ainsi au contrôle solaire intérieur. Toute la maison est construite avec du bois provenant de scieries locales. Des circulations externes sont générées autour de toute la maison afin d'incorporer les espaces externes aux événements sociaux intérieurs fréquents dans ce type de maisons de plage.

El proyecto se posa sobre una loma con espectaculares vistas al Océano Pacifico, a unos 200 m del mar. La casa se proyectó de tal forma que todos los espacios principales aprovecharan las vistas. El primer nivel se desarrolla sobre un zócalo de hormigón destinado a estacionamiento que nos amarra la casa al terreno arenoso.
Los espacios principales se trabajan desde la privacidad y la luminosidad. Los recintos se ambientan por medio de aleros y celosías que se incorporan a las fachada de la casa. Se agregan correderas ponientes en material proveniente del lugar ayudando así al control solar interior. Toda la casa se construye en base a madera proveniente de aserraderos locales. Se generan circulaciones exteriores alrededor de toda la casa con el fin de incorporar los espacios exteriores a los acontecimientos sociales interiores frecuentes en este tipo de casas de playa.

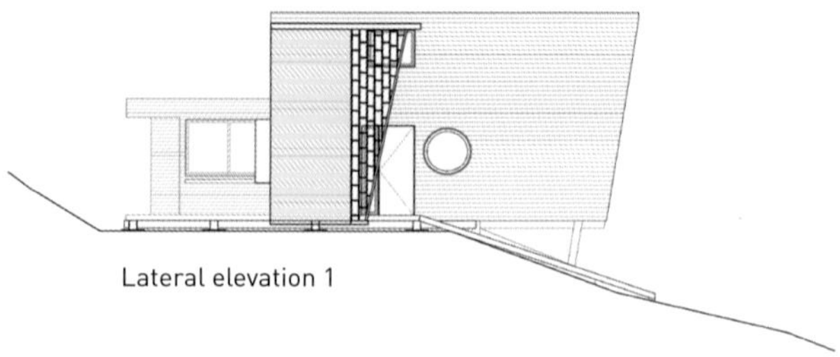
Lateral elevation 1

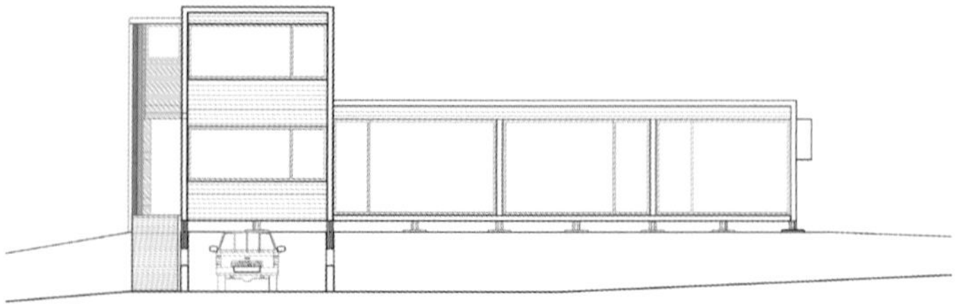
Front elevation

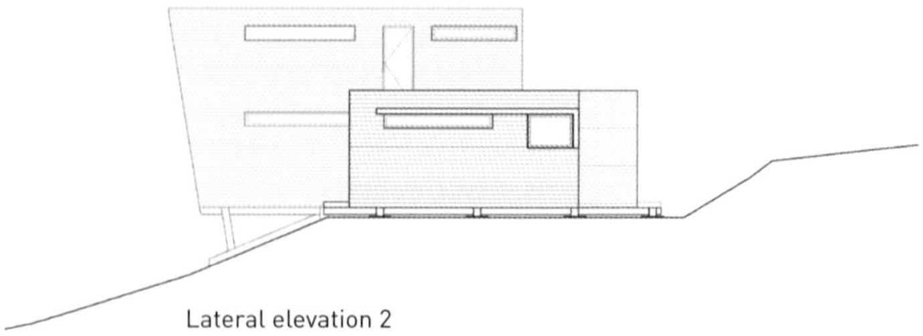
Lateral elevation 2

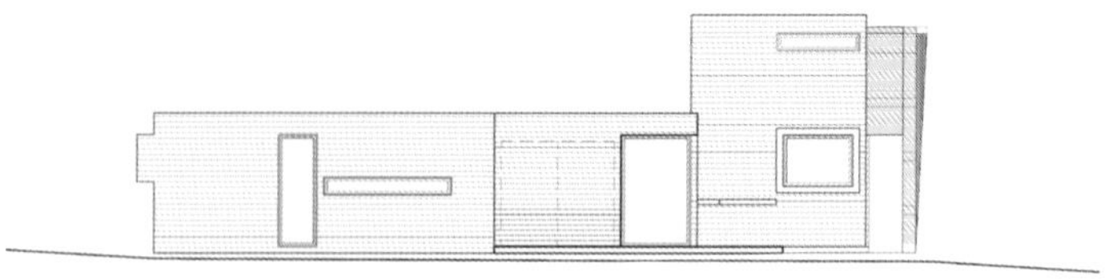
Rear elevation

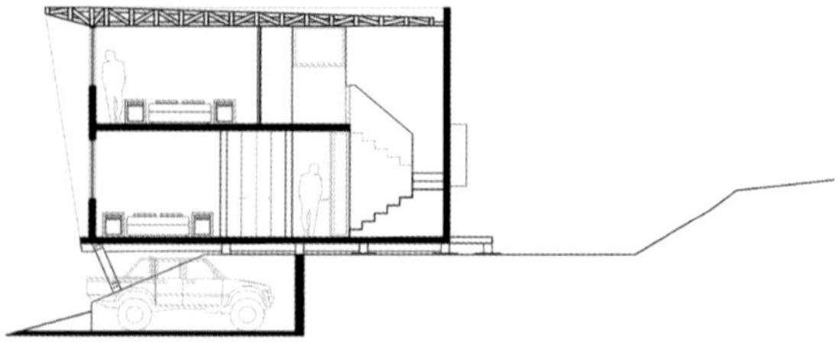
A-A' section

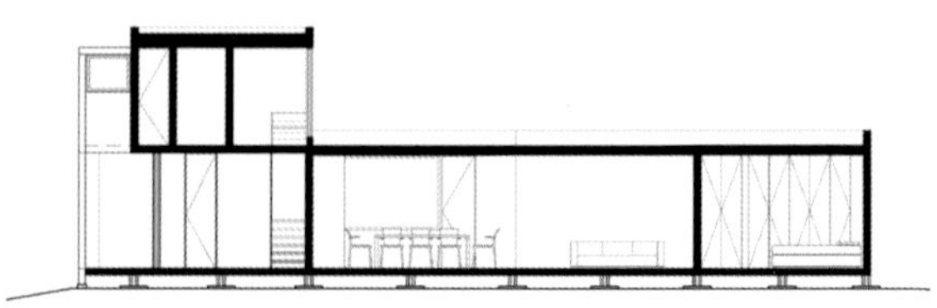
B-B' section

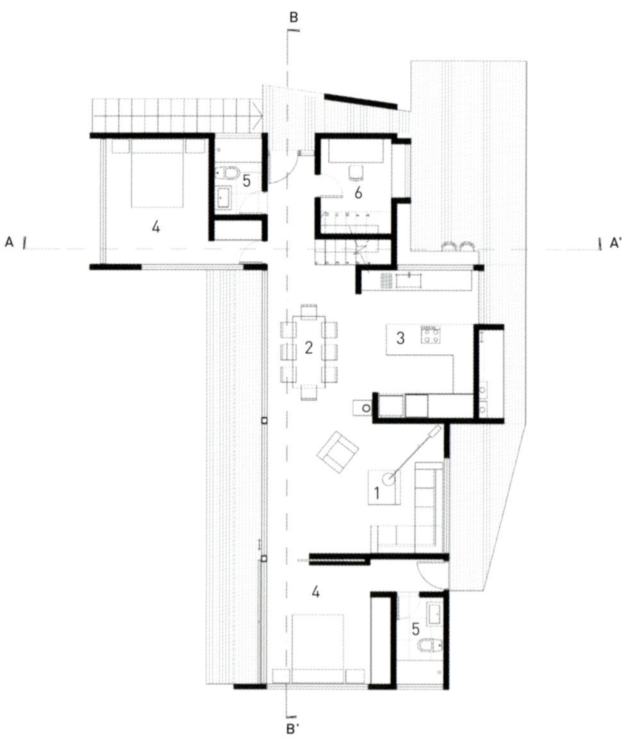

Ground floor plan

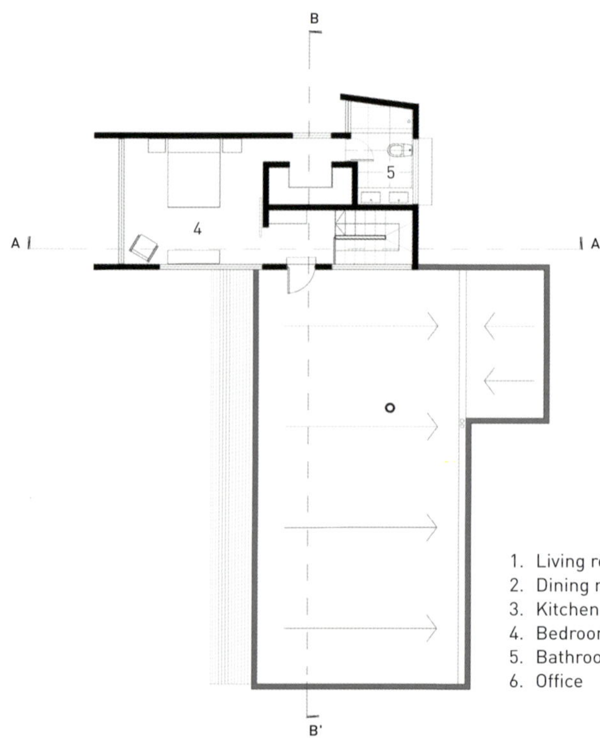

First floor plan

1. Living room
2. Dining room
3. Kitchen
4. Bedroom
5. Bathroom
6. Office

CASA WB

House WB is a progressive growth project that starts from a container used as a construction warehouse. The house sits on it looking for views towards the sea and is projected in height thinking of building later underneath. The house has a simple form, with spaces of great interior height finished in wood that allow to implement an attic destined to guests and a wine cellar. To keep costs under control, the house was built 100% in local wood and its ventilated façades were lined in corrugated metal sheet painted black. In addition, only recycled doors and windows were used on the main façade, giving an antique touch to a modern project. Once the construction was finished, the container was fitted out as a separate guest bedroom, setting the tone for the future expansion on the first floor.

Casa WB ist ein progressives Wachstumsprojekt, das von einem Container ausgeht, der als Baustellenlager genutzt wird. Das Haus liegt darauf, sucht den Blick auf das Meer und ist in die Höhe gehoben, um später darunter bauen zu können. Das Haus hat eine einfache Form, mit Räumen von großer Innenhöhe aus Holz, die es ermöglichen, ein Dachgeschoss für die Gäste und einen Weinkeller einzurichten. Um die Kosten unter Kontrolle zu halten, wurde das Haus zu 100% aus heimischem Holz gebaut und seine hinterlüfteten Fassaden mit schwarz lackiertem Wellblech verkleidet. Darüber hinaus wurden an der Hauptfassade nur recycelte Türen und Fenster verwendet, was einem aktuellen Projekt einen antiken Touch verleiht. Nach Abschluss des Baus wurde der Container als separates Gästezimmer eingerichtet und setzte damit den Akzent für die zukünftige Erweiterung im ersten Stock.

Casa WB est un projet de croissance progressive qui part d'un conteneur utilisé comme entrepôt de construction. La maison est posée dessus, cherchant une vue vers la mer, et est projetée en hauteur avec la pensée de construire plus tard en dessous. La maison a une forme simple, avec des espaces de grande hauteur intérieure finis en bois qui permettent d'aménager un grenier destiné aux hôtes et une cave à vin. Pour maîtriser les coûts, la maison a été construite à 100 % en bois local et ses façades ventilées ont été revêtues d'une tôle ondulée peinte en noir. De plus, seules des portes et fenêtres recyclées ont été utilisées sur la façade principale, ce qui donne une touche antique à un projet en cours. Une fois la construction terminée, le conteneur a été aménagé en chambre d'amis séparée, donnant ainsi le ton à l'agrandissement futur du premier étage.

Casa WB es un proyecto de crecimiento progresivo que parte de un contenedor utilizado como bodega de construcción. La casa se asienta sobre él buscando las vistas hacia el mar y se proyecta en altura pensando en construir posteriormente debajo. La vivienda tiene una forma sencilla, con espacios de gran altura interior acabados en madera que permiten implementar un altillo destinado a invitados y una bodega. Para mantener los costos controlados, la casa se construyó 100% en madera local y sus fachadas ventiladas se forraron en plancha ondulada metálica pintada de negro. Además, en la fachada principal se utilizaron solo puertas y ventanas recicladas, que otorgan un toque antiguo a un proyecto actual. Terminada la construcción, se habilitó el contenedor como dormitorio de invitados independiente, marcando la pauta para la futura ampliación en el primer piso.

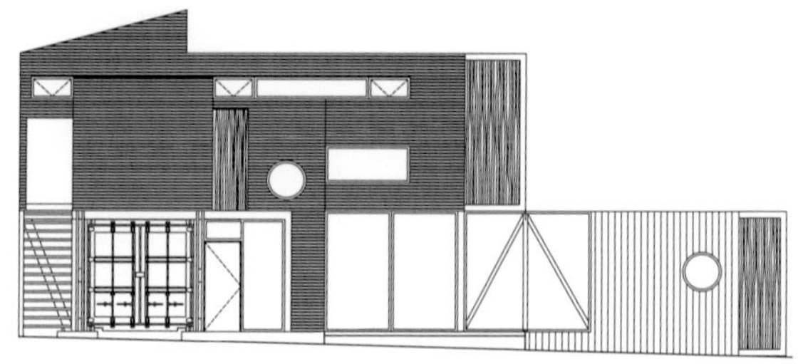
North elevation

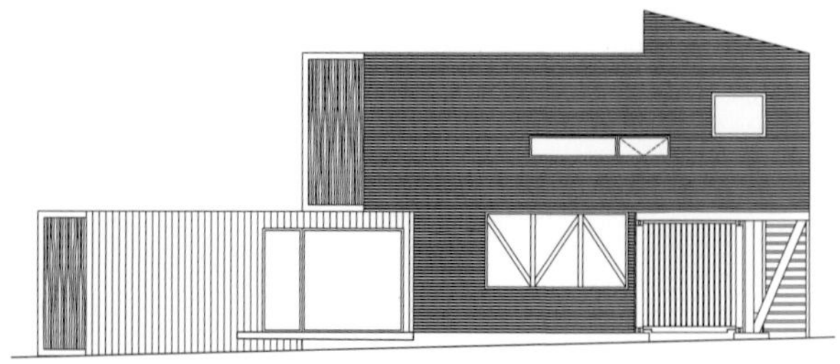
South elevation

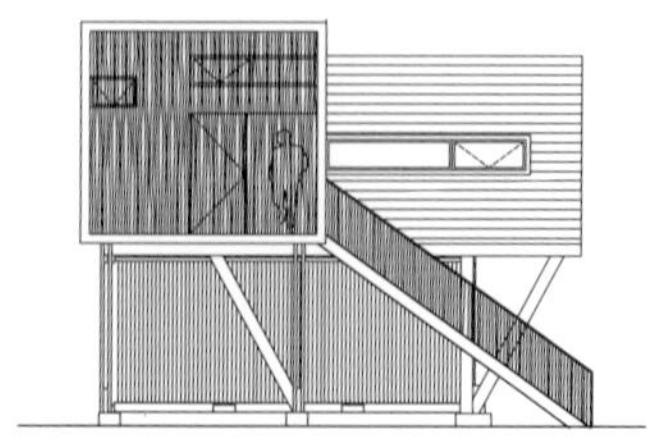
East elevation

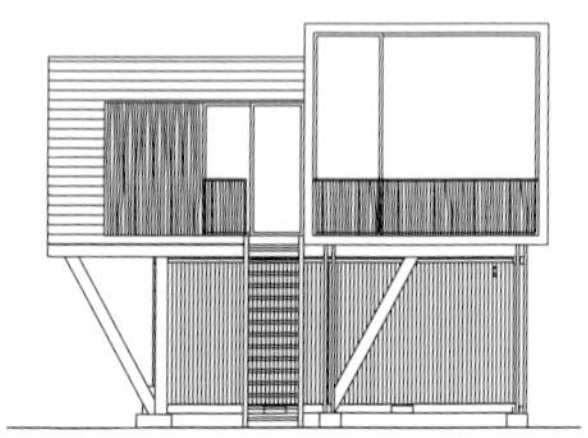
West elevation

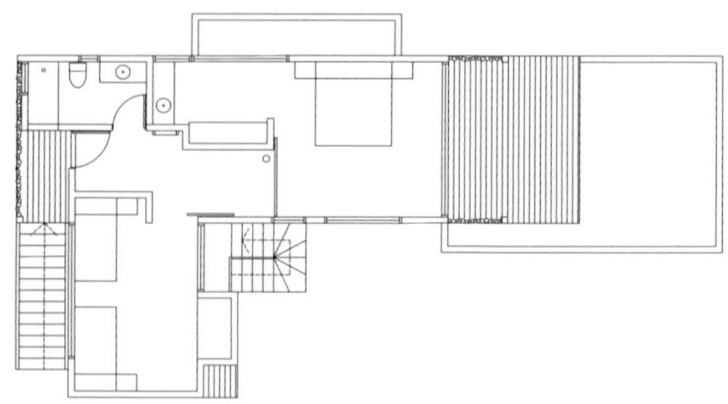
First floor plan

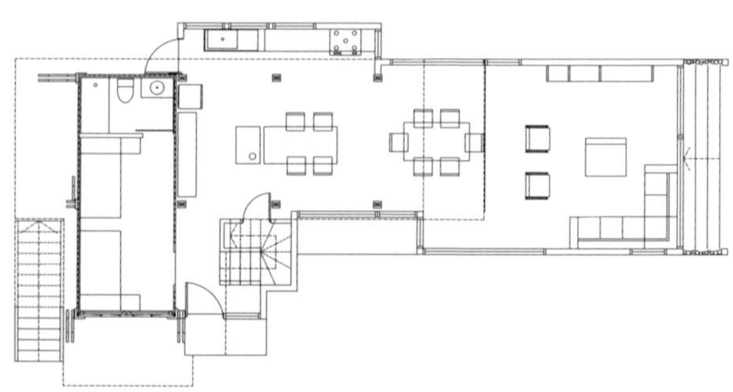
Ground floor plan

ARCHITECTS UNCHARTED

Architects Uncharted try to discovery the essential of architecture space based on the respect to the land and lives. By our design process, we intend to find the connection between nature and human beings. When seasons changes , people awaking body senses would enjoy their life in the nature. Nowadays, the issue of climate changes has been focused around the world, we explore the technology of passive design in Taiwan, which using plant or farming to shade and isolate in the building. Furthermore, We are more committed to the advancement and promotion of carbon-fixed wood construction, which was doubted by Taiwanese people. Đe devote to use wood construction to replace the reinforced concrete construction, which was wasting high-energy and high-pollution technology. In order to achieve the goal of residents' physical and mental health, and sustainable global environment.

Architectes Sans Cartes tente de découvrir l'essentiel de l'espace architectural basé sur le respect de la terre et de la vie. Par notre processus de conception, nous voulons trouver le lien entre la nature et les êtres humains. Quand les saisons changent, les gens réveillent les sens de leur corps et profitent de leur vie dans la nature. Aujourd'hui, la question du changement climatique a été axée sur le monde entier, nous explorons la technologie de la conception passive à Taiwan, qui en utilisant la plante ou l'agriculture pour ombrager et isoler dans le bâtiment. De plus, nous sommes plus engagés dans l'avancement et la promotion de la construction en bois fixé au carbone, ce dont doutait la population taïwanaise. Nous nous consacrons à l'utilisation de la construction en bois pour remplacer la construction en béton armé, qui gaspillait beaucoup d'énergie et de technologie très polluante, afin d'atteindre l'objectif de la santé physique et mentale des résidents et d'un environnement mondial durable.

Architects Uncharted versuchen, das Wesentliche des Architekturraums zu entdecken, der auf dem Respekt vor dem Land und dem Leben basiert. Mit unserem Gestaltungsprozess wollen wir die Verbindung zwischen Natur und Mensch herstellen. Wenn die Jahreszeiten wechseln, sollten Menschen zur Weckung ihrer Körperwahrnehmung das Leben in der Natur genießen. Heute, da sich das Problem des Klimawandels auf der ganzen Welt zeigt, erforschen wir die Technologie des passiven Designs in Taiwan, um mit Hilfe von Pflanzen oder Gartenanlagen Gebäude zu beschatten und zu isolieren. Darüber hinaus engagieren wir uns mehr für die Förderung des kohlenstoffbindenden Holzbaues, der von der taiwanesischen Bevölkerung skeptisch gesehen wird. Wir widmen uns der Holzbauweise als Ersatz für Stahlbetonkonstruktionen, die energieaufwändige und schadstoffreiche Techniken verwendet – im Dienste der körperlichen und geistigen Gesundheit der Bewohner und einer nachhaltigen globalen Umwelt.

Architects Uncharted intenta descubrir lo esencial del espacio arquitectónico basado en el respeto a la tierra y a la vida. A través de nuestro proceso de diseño, pretendemos encontrar la conexión entre la naturaleza y los seres humanos. Cuando cambian las estaciones, las personas que despiertan los sentidos del cuerpo disfrutan de su vida en la naturaleza. Hoy en día, la cuestión de los cambios climáticos se ha centrado en todo el mundo, exploramos la tecnología de diseño pasivo en Taiwán, que utiliza las plantas o la agricultura para dar sombra y aislar el edificio. Además, estamos más comprometidos con el avance y la promoción de la construcción en madera con fijación de carbono, lo cual fue puesto en duda por el pueblo taiwanés. Nos dedicamos a utilizar la construcción de madera para sustituir a la construcción de hormigón armado, que estaba desperdiciando tecnología de alta energía y alta contaminación, con el fin de lograr el objetivo de la salud física y mental de los residentes y el medio ambiente global sostenible.

CHIEN HOUSE

THE WHEEL

CHIEN HOUSE

This house, for the architect and his retired parents, is a return to the countryside to live a self-sufficient, healthy and environmentally friendly lifestyle, as well as a claim to the carbon reduction offered by traditional wood architecture in the face of the proliferation of reinforced concrete buildings in Taiwan. The project also acts as a place to promote healthy eating, through a home garden that also encourages agriculture as a form of exercise for the elderly.
The two-storey building, facing south to gain sunlight and protect itself from the wind, expands horizontally to minimize its impact on the landscape. Its façades use colours common in rural Taiwan and the open design of its rooms invites occupants to blend in with nature.

Dieses Haus ist für den Architekten und seine pensionierten Eltern eine Rückkehr aufs Land, um einen autarken, gesunden und umweltfreundlichen Lebensstil zu pflegen, sowie ein Anspruch auf die CO_2-Reduktion, die die traditionelle Holzarchitektur angesichts der zunehmenden Verbreitung von Stahlbetonbauten in Taiwan bietet. Das Projekt dient auch als Ort zur Förderung einer gesunden Ernährung durch einen Hausgarten, der auch die Landwirtschaft als eine Form der Bewegung für ältere Menschen fördert.
Das zweistöckige Gebäude, das nach Süden ausgerichtet ist, um Sonnenlicht zu gewinnen und sich vor dem Wind zu schützen, dehnt sich horizontal aus, um seine Auswirkungen auf die Landschaft zu minimieren. Die Fassaden sind in den im ländlichen Taiwan üblichen Farben gehalten, und die offene Gestaltung der Räume lädt dazu ein, sich in die Natur einzufügen.

Cette maison, pour l'architecte et ses parents retraités, est un retour à la campagne pour vivre une vie autonome, saine et respectueuse de l'environnement, ainsi qu'une revendication à la réduction de carbone offerte par l'architecture traditionnelle en bois face à la prolifération des bâtiments en béton armé à Taiwan. Le projet agit également comme un lieu de promotion d'une alimentation saine, par le biais d'un jardin familial qui encourage également l'agriculture comme forme d'exercice pour les personnes âgées.
Le bâtiment de deux étages, orienté vers le sud pour profiter de la lumière du soleil et se protéger du vent, s'étend horizontalement pour minimiser son impact sur le paysage. Ses façades utilisent des couleurs courantes dans les campagnes taïwanaises et le design ouvert de ses pièces invite les occupants à se fondre dans la nature.

Esta casa, para el arquitecto y sus padres jubilados, constituye un regreso al campo para vivir según un estilo de vida autosuficiente, saludable y respetuoso con el medio ambiente, así como una reivindicación de la reducción de carbono que ofrece la arquitectura de madera tradicional frente a la proliferación de edificios de hormigón armado en Taiwán. El proyecto actúa también como lugar de promoción de la alimentación saludable, a través de un huerto casero que también fomenta la agricultura como forma de ejercicio para los ancianos.
El edificio, de dos plantas de altura y orientado hacia el sur para ganar luz solar y protegerse del viento, se expande de forma horizontal para minimizar su impacto en el paisaje. Sus fachadas utilizan colores comunes en las zonas rurales de Taiwán y el diseño abierto de sus estancias invita a los ocupantes a mezclarse con la naturaleza.

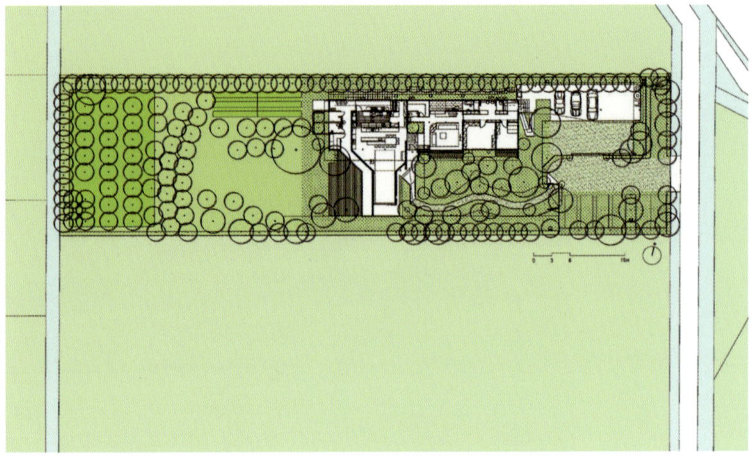

Site plan

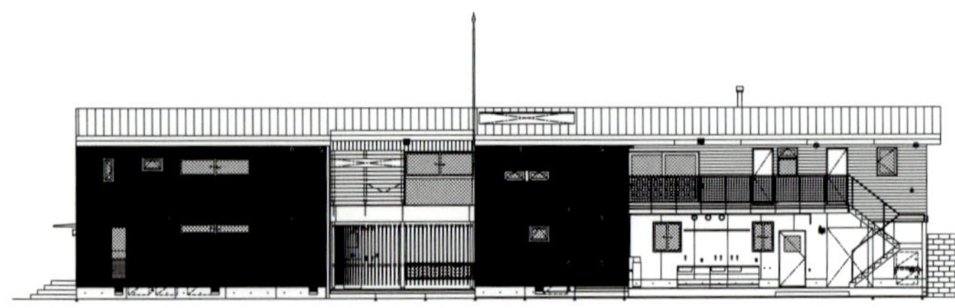

North elevation

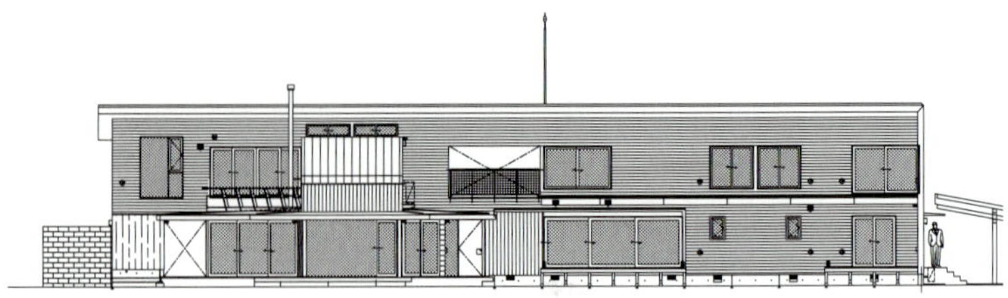

South elevation

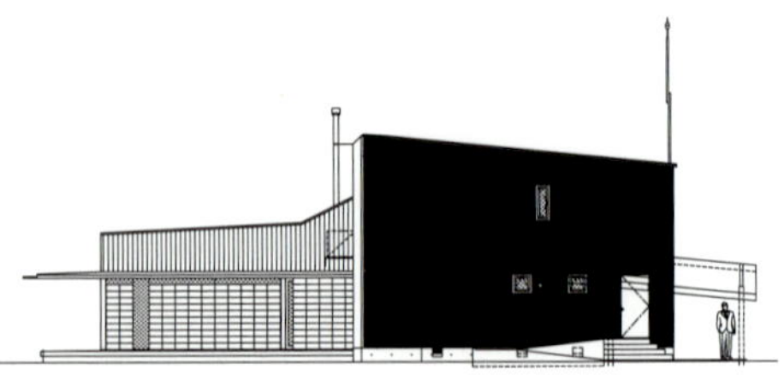

East elevation

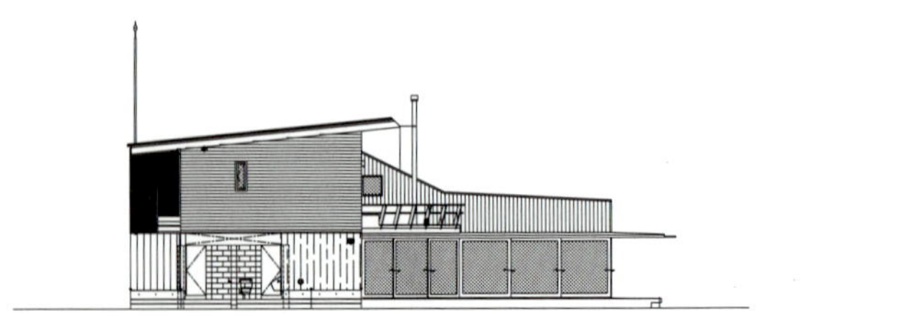

West elevation

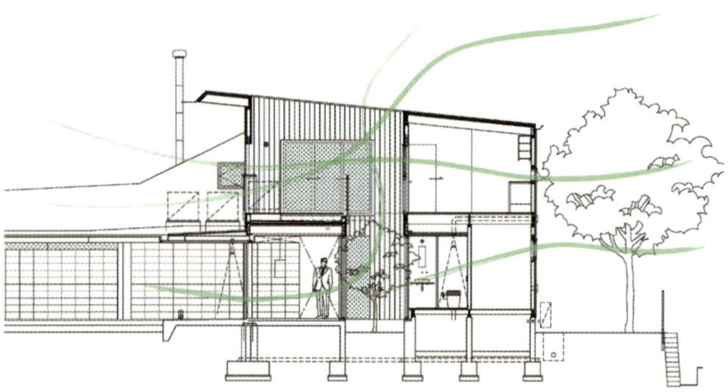

Section. Light courtyard

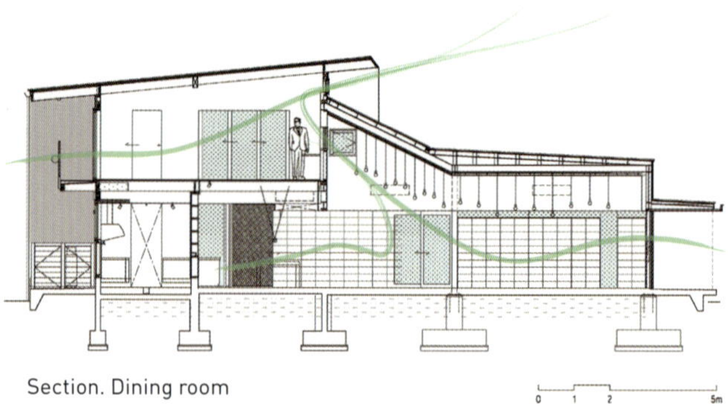

Section. Dining room

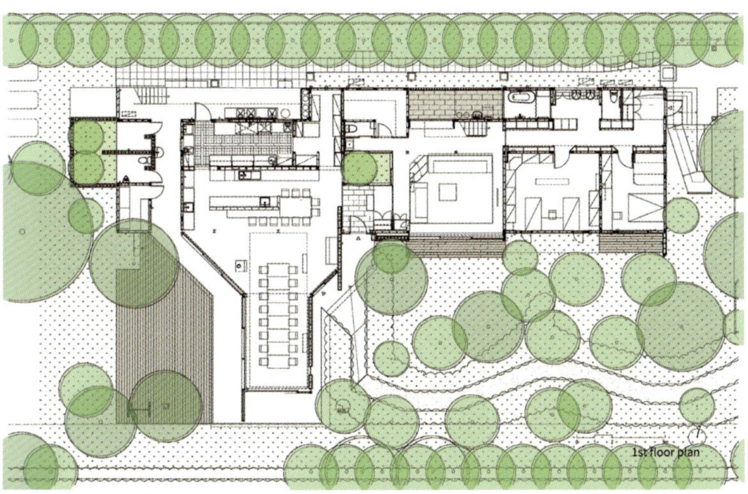

Ground floor plan

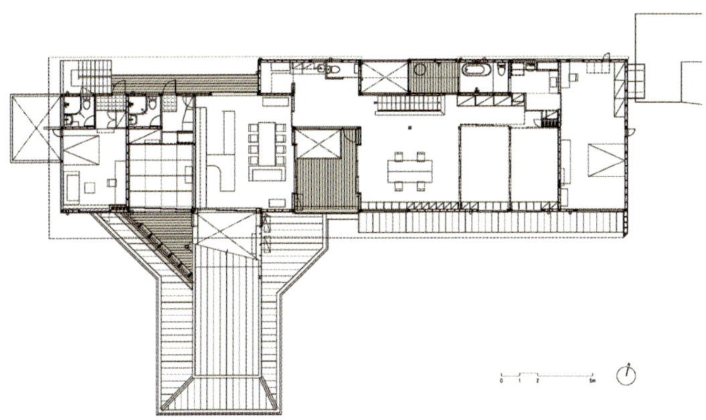

First floor plan

THE WHEEL

Built as part of the Taichung Flora World Expo in 2018 as a sustainable home showcase, the design of this four-person house proposes a lifestyle that reconnects people with nature.
Its circular shape, open to the south, places nature in the central nucleus of the dwelling to relate it to all the inhabitable areas, which in turn are surrounded by a forest. The rooms are arranged around the centre in volumes of different heights whose roofs extend into eaves that overlap and protect from the sun and rain.
The project incorporates passive design principles and seeks to achieve zero net CO_2 emissions. Natural materials were used in its construction, such as the all-wood structure, with an extremely low carbon footprint, recyclable and generating a minimum amount of waste.

Das im Rahmen der Taichung Flora World Expo 2018 als nachhaltige Wohnvitrine errichtete Vier-Personen-Haus bietet mit seinem Design einen Lebensstil, der den Menschen mit der Natur verbindet.
Seine kreisförmige, nach Süden offene Form stellt die Natur ins Zentrum der Wohnung und verbindet sie mit allen bewohnbaren Gebieten, die wiederum von einem Wald umgeben sind. Die Räume sind in unterschiedlich hohen Volumen um den Kern herum angeordnet, deren Dächer sich in überlappende Traufen erstrecken und vor Sonne und Regen schützen.
Das Projekt basiert auf passiven Konstruktionsprinzipien und zielt darauf ab, den CO_2-Ausstoß auf null zu senken. Bei der Konstruktion wurden natürliche Materialien wie die Vollholzstruktur verwendet, die extrem CO2-arm, recycelbar und abfallarm ist.

Construite dans le cadre de l'Exposition universelle de Taichung Flora en 2018 comme vitrine de la maison durable, la conception de cette maison de quatre personnes propose un style de vie qui reconnecte les gens avec la nature.
Sa forme circulaire, ouverte vers le sud, place la nature dans le noyau central de l'habitation pour la relier à toutes les zones habitables, qui à leur tour sont entourées par une forêt. Les pièces sont disposées autour du noyau en volumes de différentes hauteurs dont les toits s'étendent en avant-toits qui se chevauchent et protègent du soleil et de la pluie.
Le projet intègre des principes de conception passive et vise à atteindre l'objectif de zéro émission nette de CO_2. Des matériaux naturels ont été utilisés dans sa construction, tels que la structure tout bois, avec une empreinte carbone extrêmement faible, recyclable et générant un minimum de déchets.

Construida en el marco de la Exposición Mundial de Flora de Taichung en 2018 como muestra de hogar sostenible, el diseño de esta casa para cuatro personas propone un estilo de vida que vuelva a conectar a las personas con la naturaleza.
Su forma circular abierta hacia el sur sitúa la naturaleza en el núcleo central de la vivienda para relacionarla con todas las zonas habitables, a su vez rodeadas por un bosque. Las estancias se disponen alrededor del núcleo en volúmenes de diferentes alturas cuyas cubiertas se extienden en aleros que se solapan y protegen del sol y la lluvia.
El proyecto incorpora principios de diseño pasivo y busca conseguir unas emisiones netas cero de CO_2. En su construcción se utilizaron materiales naturales, como la estructura totalmente de madera, con huella de carbono extremadamente baja, reciclables y generadores de una cantidad mínima de residuos.

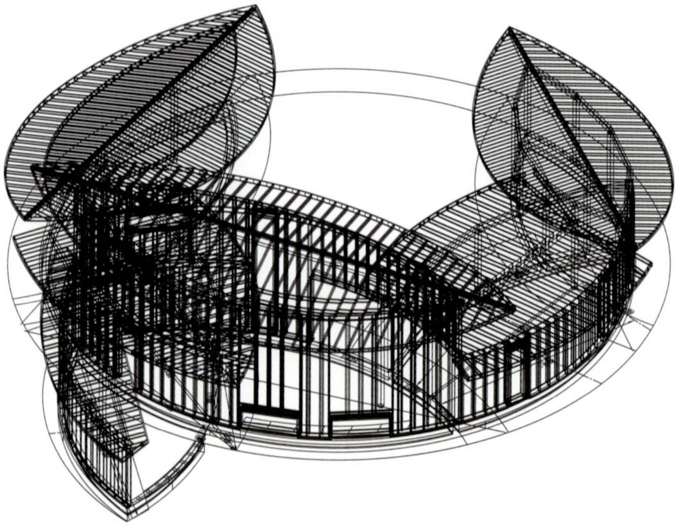

Structure diagram

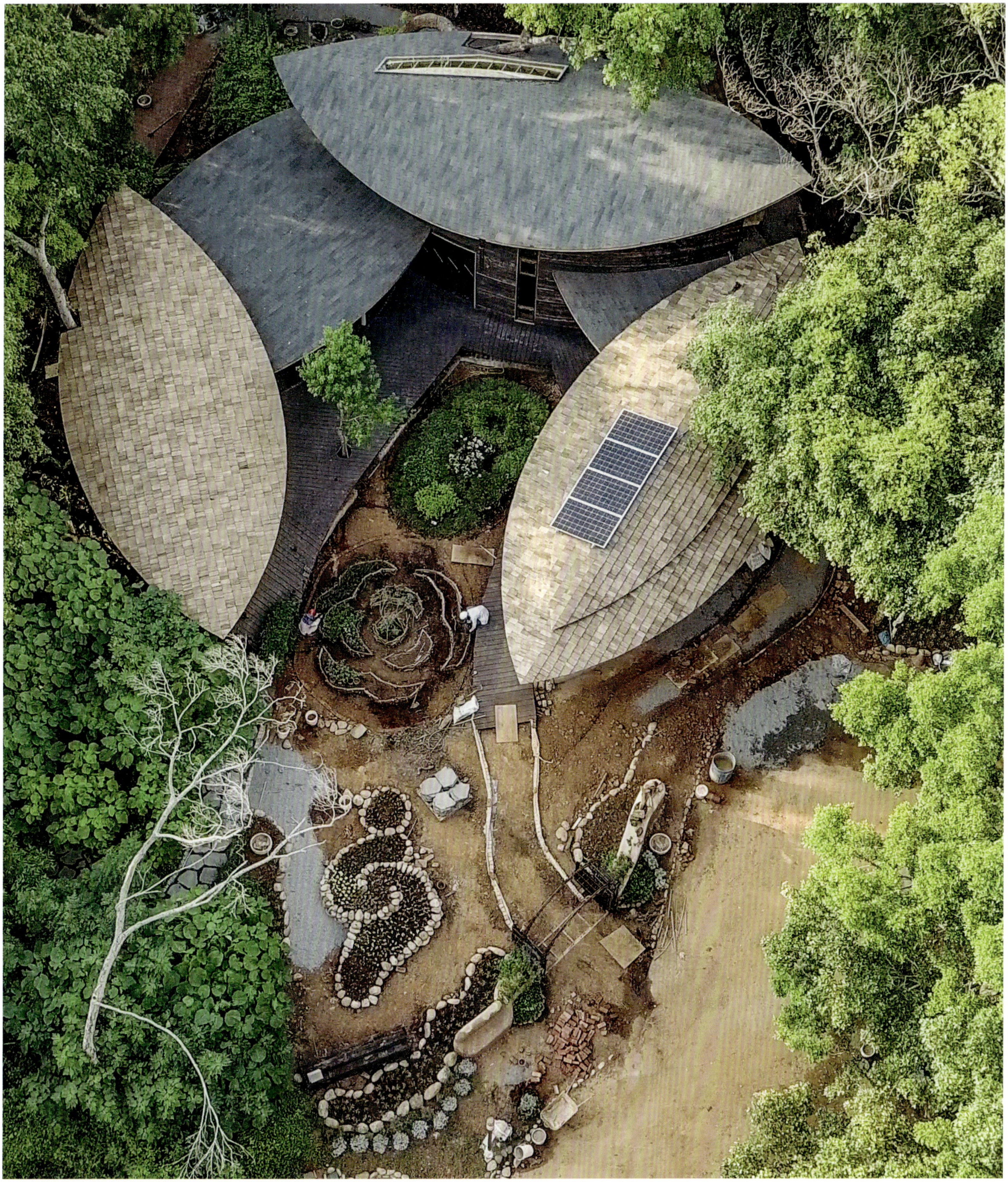

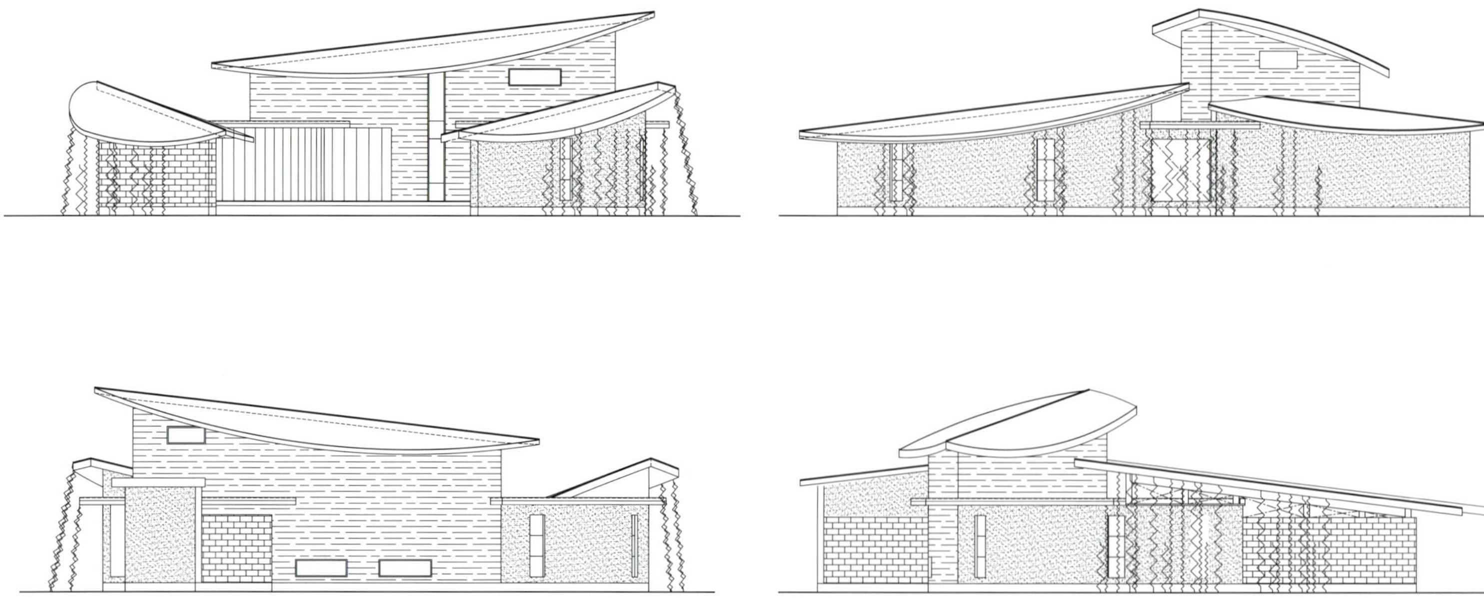

Elevations

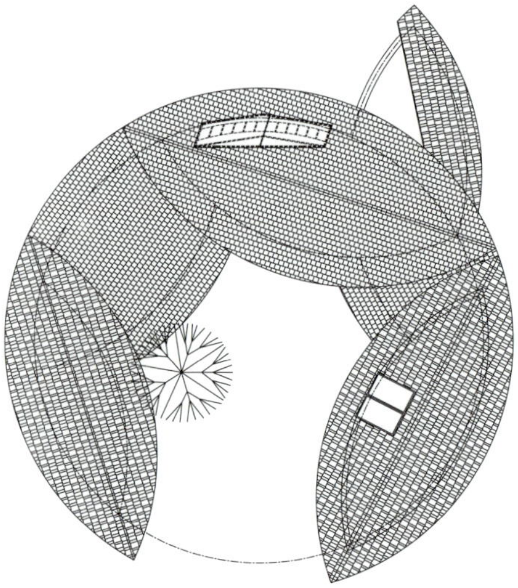

Roof plan

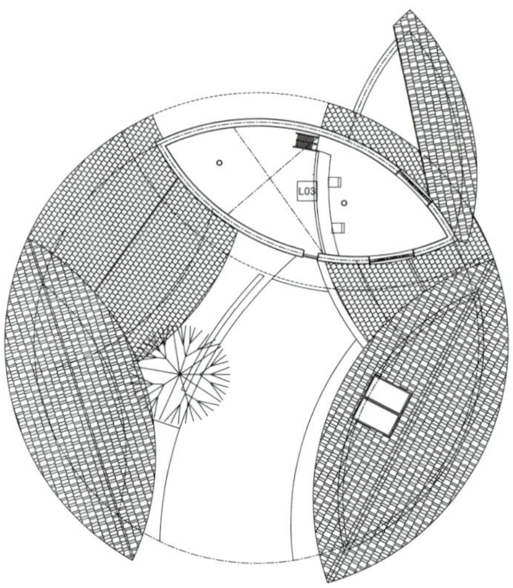

First floor plan

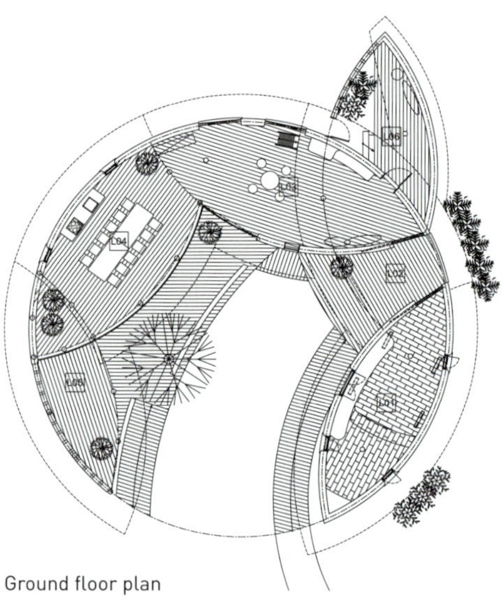

Ground floor plan

ATELIER RISTING

atelierRISTING is an architectural design studio located in Indianapolis, Indiana led by Steven Risting, AIA, LEED AP providing design leadership and Carol Risting providing firm management. With over thirty-five years of experience, Steve has been recognized for providing design excellence on a variety of project types, from detailed residential to complex commercial, civic and institutional buildings. atelierRISTING provides architectural, interior design and master planning services. Their design approach focuses on the relationship of the human experience, connecting the interior functions with the exterior circumstances to create sustainable designs.

atelierRISTING est un studio de design architectural situé à Indianapolis, dans l'Indiana, dirigé par Steven Risting, AIA, LEED AP et Carol Risting. Avec plus de trente-cinq ans d'expérience, Steve est reconnu pour l'excellence de sa conception sur une variété de types de projets, du bâtiment résidentiel détaillé au bâtiment complexe commercial, civique et institutionnel. atelierRISTING offre des services d'architecture, de design intérieur et de planification générale. Son approche du design se concentre sur la relation de l'expérience humaine, reliant les fonctions intérieures avec les circonstances extérieures pour créer des designs durables.

atelierRISTING ist ein Architekturbüro mit Sitz in Indianapolis, Indiana, unter der Leitung von Steven Risting, AIA, LEED AP, das die Designführung übernimmt, und Carol Risting, zuständig für das Firmenmanagement. Mit über 35 Jahren Erfahrung wurde Steve für seine hervorragende Designleistung bei einer Vielzahl von Projekttypen ausgezeichnet, von detaillierten Wohn- bis hin zu komplexen Gewerbe-, Bürger- und Institutionengebäuden. atelierRISTING bietet Architektur-, Innenarchitektur- und Masterplanungsleistungen. Sein Designansatz konzentriert sich auf das Verhältnis zur menschlichen Erfahrung und verbindet die inneren Funktionen mit den äußeren Gegebenheiten, um nachhaltige Designs zu schaffen.

atelierRISTING es un estudio de diseño arquitectónico ubicado en Indianápolis, Indiana, dirigido por Steven Risting, AIA, encargado del diseño, y Carol Risting como directora. Con más de treinta y cinco años de experiencia, Steve ha sido reconocido por proporcionar excelencia en el diseño en una variedad de tipos de proyectos, desde residenciales hasta edificios comerciales, cívicos e institucionales.
atelierRISTING proporciona servicios de arquitectura, diseño de interiores y planificación. Su enfoque de diseño se centra en la relación de la experiencia humana, conectando las funciones interiores con las circunstancias exteriores, con la intención principal de crear diseños de carácter sostenible.

GLASS CABIN

The GLASS CABIN provides an off-grid family retreat, designed and built by the architect. Reclaimed glass, regenerated prairie and land entrusted to the grandkids were the genesis of the design, located in northeastern Iowa. Nestled in a clearing of the woods near the Wapsipinicon River, the structure is raised on columns above the flood plain providing great views of the native Midwestern prairie. Designed for occasional use, the extension of the front columns creates a manmade edge to the clearing and allows sliding barn doors to close when not in use. Western Red Cedar is used for the exposed structure, decking and siding.

Die GLASKABINE bietet einen netzfernen Familienurlaub, der vom Architekten entworfen und gebaut wurde. Wiederverwendetes Glas, restaurierte Prärie und Land, das den Enkeln anvertraut wurde, waren die Geburtsstunde des Entwurfs, der sich im Nordosten von Iowa befindet. Die Struktur befindet sich in einer Waldlichtung in der Nähe des Wapsipinicon Rivers und ist auf Säulen über der Überschwemmungsebene aufgebaut, die einen großartigen Blick auf die ursprüngliche Prärie des Mittleren Westens bieten. Die Verlängerung der vorderen Säulen ist für den gelegentlichen Einsatz konzipiert und schafft eine künstliche Kante zur Lichtung und ermöglicht das Schließen von Schiebetoren bei Nichtgebrauch. Westliche Rotzeder wird für die freiliegende Struktur, die Terrassen und die Verkleidung verwendet.

La CABINE DE VITRE offre un refuge familial hors réseau, conçu et construit par l'architecte. Le verre réutilisé, la prairie restaurée et les terres confiées aux petits-enfants ont été à l'origine de cette conception, située au nord-est de l'Iowa. Niché dans une clairière près de la rivière Wapsipinicon, l'ouvrage est surélevé sur des colonnes au-dessus de la plaine inondable et offre une vue magnifique sur la prairie indigène du Midwest. Conçu pour un usage occasionnel, le prolongement des colonnes avant crée un bord artificiel à la clairière et permet aux portes de grange coulissantes de se fermer lorsqu'elles ne sont pas utilisées. Le cèdre rouge de l'Ouest est utilisé pour la structure exposée, les terrasses et le revêtement extérieur.

Esta cabaña, diseñada y construida por el arquitecto, ofrece un retiro familiar autosuficiente. Un terreno confiado a los nietos, y la voluntad de utilizar vidrio reciclado fueron la génesis del diseño de este proyecto, ubicado en el noreste de Iowa. Enclavada en un claro de los bosques cerca del río Wapsipinicon, la estructura se eleva sobre columnas encima de la planicie, lo que proporciona grandes vistas de las extensiones típicas del medio oeste americano. Diseñado para uso ocasional, la extensión de las columnas delanteras crea un voladizo hacia el claro y permite que las puertas corredizas del establo se cierren cuando no están en uso. El cedro rojo occidental se ha utilizado para la estructura exterior, el entarimado y el revestimiento.

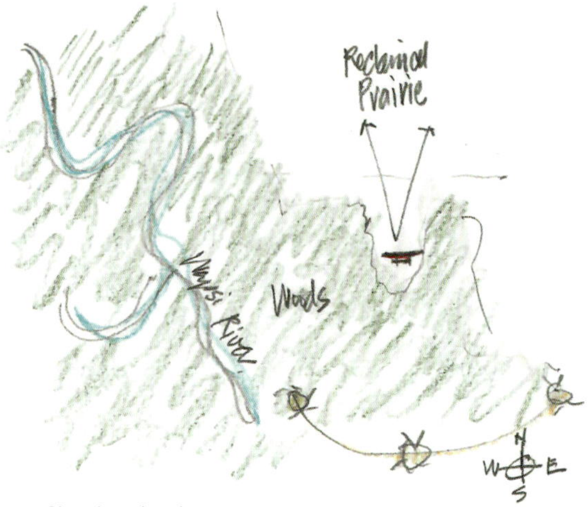

Site plan sketch

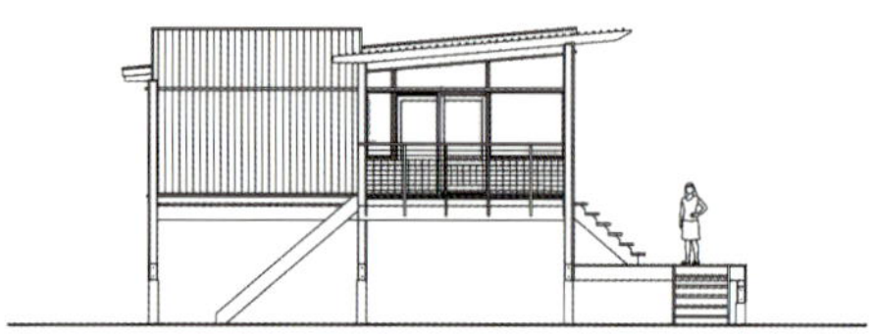

West elevation

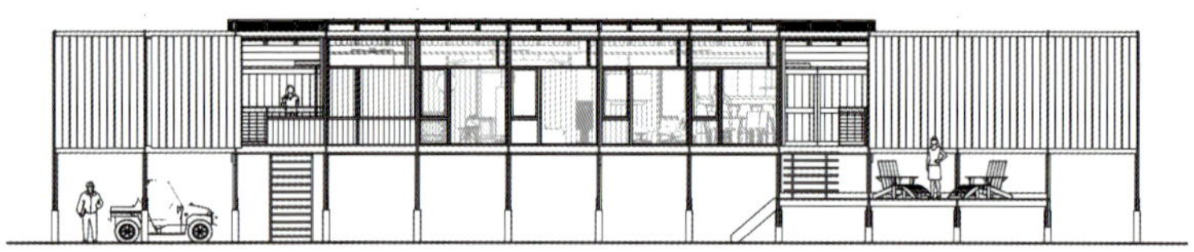

North elevation

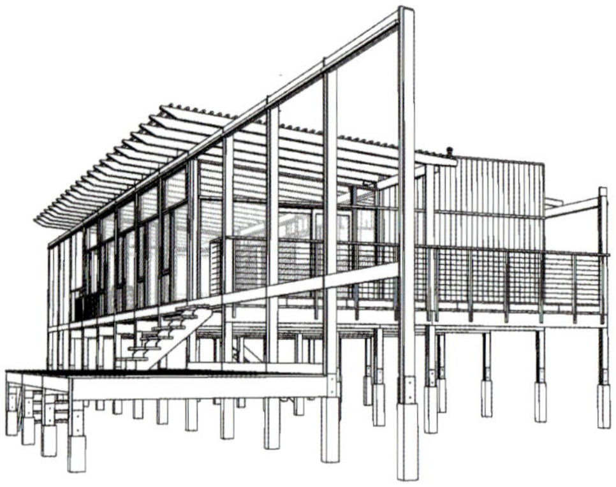

Axonometry

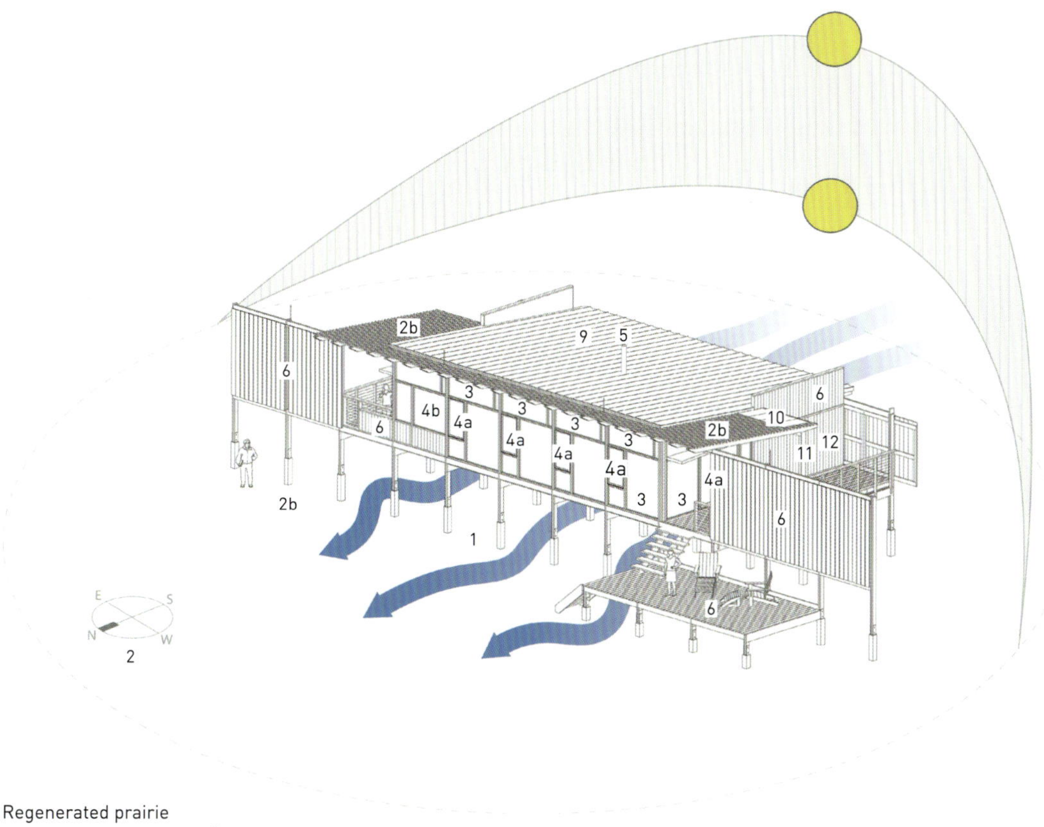

Regenerated prairie
Environmentally friendly / Sustainable design

The Glass Cabin is off-grid, and thus Net-Zero with the following passive features:

1. **Raised structure**
   Allows flood water to flow freely below.
   Minimum disturbance of the grasslands.
2. **North- south orientation**
   2a. Northern window wall
   2b. Trellis for east & west shading
3. **Reclaimed 1" low-E insulated glass**
   Provides daylighting and views
   From a commercial office building expansion
4. **Natural ventilation**
   4a. Operable windows and patio doors
   4b. Screened-in porch
   4c. Ceiling fans.
5. **Wood burning efficient stove**
   warmth and light
6. **Western red cedar structure,** siding and decking
   Natural finish
   Water, fire and insect resistant
7. **Minimum construction waste**
   Standard lumber sizes.
8. Insulated floor, roof and walls.
   R-30 floor, R-22 roof and R-15 walls
   Mineral wool and rigid insulation
   +2x6 wood floor and roof decking
9. **White metal roof**
   Minimize heat gain
10. **Solar panels and battery power**
    LED lighting
    DC motor ceiling fans
11. **Compost toilet**
12. **Gray water filtration**

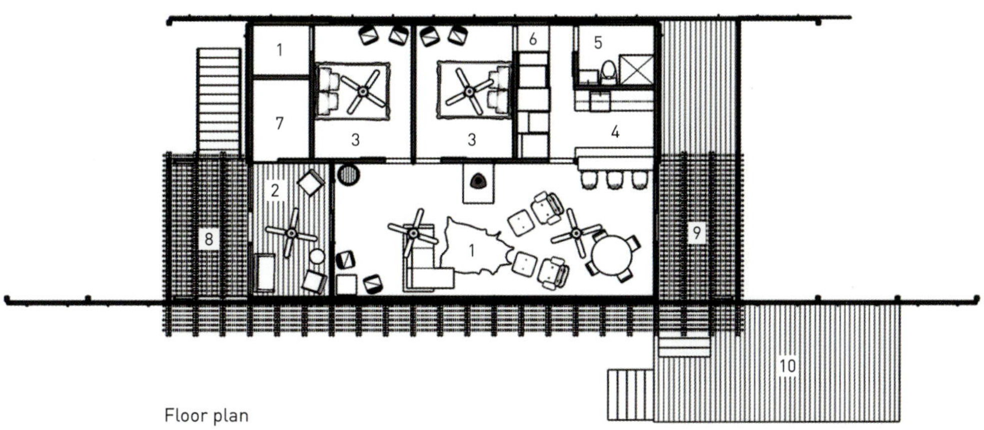

Floor plan

1. Great room
2. Screened in porch
3. Bedroom
4. Kitchenette
5. Bathroom
6. Passageway
7. Storage
8. East terrace
9. West terrace
10. Lower terrace

BIO ARCHITECTS

BIO Architects is an office founded by the Russian architect Ivan Ovchinnikov, whose main activities, project and construction of architectural and design objects, range from stools to cities. A 2003 graduate of the Moscow Architectural Institute, Ivan has been nominated for the Golden Section Award, winner of the ARCHIWOOD Prize and has participated in numerous international competitions.
In 2013, Ivan Ovchinnikov develops the modular frame house DublDom with the mission of creating an affordable and massive architecture, and creates the company of the same name that produces it. Over the past 6 years, DublDom has manufactured and installed over 600 houses in and outside of Russia.
We continue to move forward and DublinDom is constantly expanding. New models and accessories are being launched and we are working on the necessary structures to provide a full range of construction, maintenance and modernisation services for DublinDom. If we don't evolve, we degrade.

BIO Architects est un bureau fondé par l'architecte russe Ivan Ovchinnikov, dont les activités principales, le projet et la construction d'objets architecturaux et de design, vont des tabourets aux villes. Diplômé en 2003 de l'Institut d'architecture de Moscou, Ivan a été nominé pour le Prix de la Section d'Or, lauréat du Prix ARCHIWOOD et a participé à de nombreux concours internationaux.
En 2013, Ivan Ovchinnikov développe la maison à ossature modulaire DublDom avec la mission de créer une architecture massive et abordable, et crée la société du même nom qui la produit. Au cours des 6 dernières années, DublDom a fabriqué et installé plus de 600 maisons en Russie et à l'étranger.
Nous continuons à aller de l'avant et DublinDom est en constante expansion. De nouveaux modèles et accessoires sont lancés et nous travaillons sur les structures nécessaires pour fournir une gamme complète de services de construction, de maintenance et de modernisation pour DublinDom. Si nous n'évoluons pas, nous nous dégradons.

BIO Architects ist ein von dem russischen Architekten Ivan Ovchinnikov gegründetes Büro, dessen Haupttätigkeiten, Projektierung und Bau von Architektur- und Designobjekten, vom Hocker bis zur Stadt reichen. Ivan, Absolvent des Moskauer Architekturinstituts, wurde 2003 für den Golden Section Award nominiert, erhielt den ARCHIWOOD-Preis und nahm an zahlreichen internationalen Wettbewerben teil.
Im Jahr 2013 entwickelt Ivan Ovchinnikov das modulare Rahmenhaus DublDom mit der Mission, eine erschwingliche und massive Architektur zu schaffen, und gründete das gleichnamige Unternehmen, das es produziert. In den letzten 6 Jahren hat DublDom über 600 Häuser in und außerhalb Russlands hergestellt und installiert.
Wir schreiten weiter voran und DublDom expandiert ständig. Neue Modelle und Zubehörteile werden auf den Markt gebracht, und wir arbeiten an den notwendigen Strukturen, um ein umfassendes Angebot an Bau-, Wartungs- und Modernisierungsleistungen für DublDom zu erbringen. Wenn wir uns nicht weiterentwickeln, werden wir degradiert.

BIO Architects es una oficina fundada por el arquitecto ruso Ivan Ovchinnikov, cuyas actividades principales, proyecto y construcción de objetos arquitectónicos y de diseño, abarcan desde taburetes hasta ciudades. Graduado en 2003 en el Moscow Architectural Institute, Iván ha sido nominado al Golden Section Award, ganador del Premio ARCHIWOOD y ha participado en numerosos concursos internacionales.
En 2013, Ivan Ovchinnikov desarrolla la casa de armazón modular DublDom con la misión de crear una arquitectura asequible y masiva, y funda la empresa del mismo nombre que la produce. Durante los últimos 6 años, DublDom ha fabricado e instalado más de 600 casas dentro y fuera de Rusia.
Seguimos avanzando y DublDom se está expandiendo constantemente. Nuevos modelos y accesorios están siendo lanzados y trabajamos en las estructuras necesarias para proporcionar una gama completa de servicios de construcción, mantenimiento y modernización para DublDom. Si no evolucionamos, nos degradamos.

DD77

BRIDGE HOUSE

DD77

DD77 is a recent prototype of the DublinDom prefabricated house series, which continues research to develop an accessible, mass-produced modular architecture.
The project implements many architectural principles within a standard modular product: an ergonomic interior space, a simple exterior volume that allows adaptation to any environment, a multifunctional central space, interaction with the natural environment, application of passive house principles, maximum use of natural light and the possibility of easily extending the house.
Simple and ecological materials are used for the finishes: solid pine on the inside and a combination of glass, metal and painted and burned wood on the outside. The interior, designed in collaboration with the company Archpole, continues with the idea of brevity and simplicity in design.

DD77 ist ein aktueller Prototyp der DublinDom Fertighausserie, die die Forschung zur Entwicklung einer zugänglichen, massenproduzierten modularen Architektur fortsetzt.
Das Projekt setzt viele architektonische Prinzipien in einem modularen Standardprodukt um: einen ergonomischen Innenraum, ein einfaches Außenvolumen, das die Anpassung an jede Umgebung ermöglicht, einen multifunktionalen Zentralraum, Interaktion mit der natürlichen Umgebung, Anwendung von Passivhausprinzipien, maximale Nutzung des natürlichen Lichts und die Möglichkeit, das Haus leicht zu erweitern.
Für die Veredelung werden einfache und ökologische Materialien verwendet: innen massives Kiefernholz und außen eine Kombination aus Glas, Metall und lackiertem und karbonisiertem Holz. Das Interieur, das in Zusammenarbeit mit der Firma Archpole entworfen wurde, setzt die Idee der Kürze und Einfachheit des Designs fort.

DD77 est un prototype récent de la série de maisons préfabriquées DublinDom, qui poursuit ses recherches pour développer une architecture modulaire accessible et produite en série.
Le projet met en œuvre de nombreux principes architecturaux au sein d'un produit modulaire standard : un espace intérieur ergonomique, un volume extérieur simple qui permet de s'adapter à tout environnement, un espace central multifonctionnel, l'interaction avec l'environnement naturel, l'application des principes de la maison passive, l'utilisation maximale de la lumière naturelle et la possibilité d'extension facile.
Des matériaux simples et écologiques sont utilisés pour les finitions : du pin massif à l'intérieur et une combinaison de verre, métal et bois peint et brûlé à l'extérieur. L'intérieur, conçu en collaboration avec la société Archpole, continue avec l'idée de brièveté et de simplicité du design.

DD77 es un reciente prototipo de la serie de casas prefabricadas DublDom, que continúa la investigación para desarrollar una arquitectura modular accesible y con una producción masiva.
El proyecto implementa muchos principios arquitectónicos dentro de un producto modular estándar: un espacio interior ergonómico, un volumen exterior simple que permite la adaptación a cualquier entorno, un espacio central multifuncional, la interacción con el entorno natural, la aplicación de los principios de casa pasiva, el máximo uso de luz natural y la posibilidad de ampliar fácilmente la casa.
Para los acabados se utilizan materiales simples y ecológicos: pino macizo en el interior y una combinación de vidrio, metal y madera pintada y quemada en el exterior. El interior, proyectado en colaboración con la empresa Archpole, continúa con la idea de brevedad y simplicidad en el diseño.

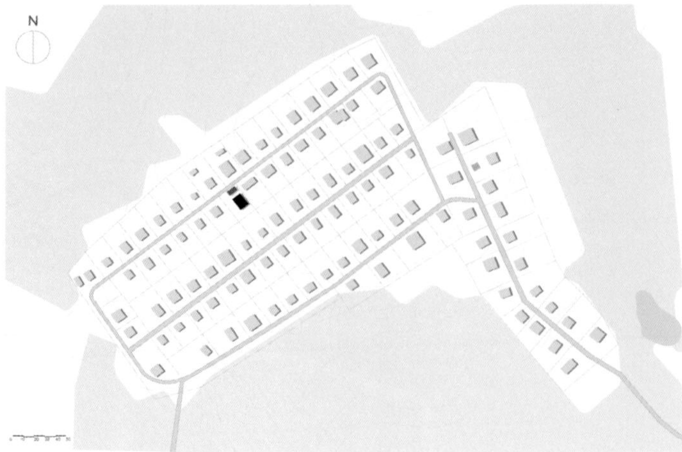

Site plan

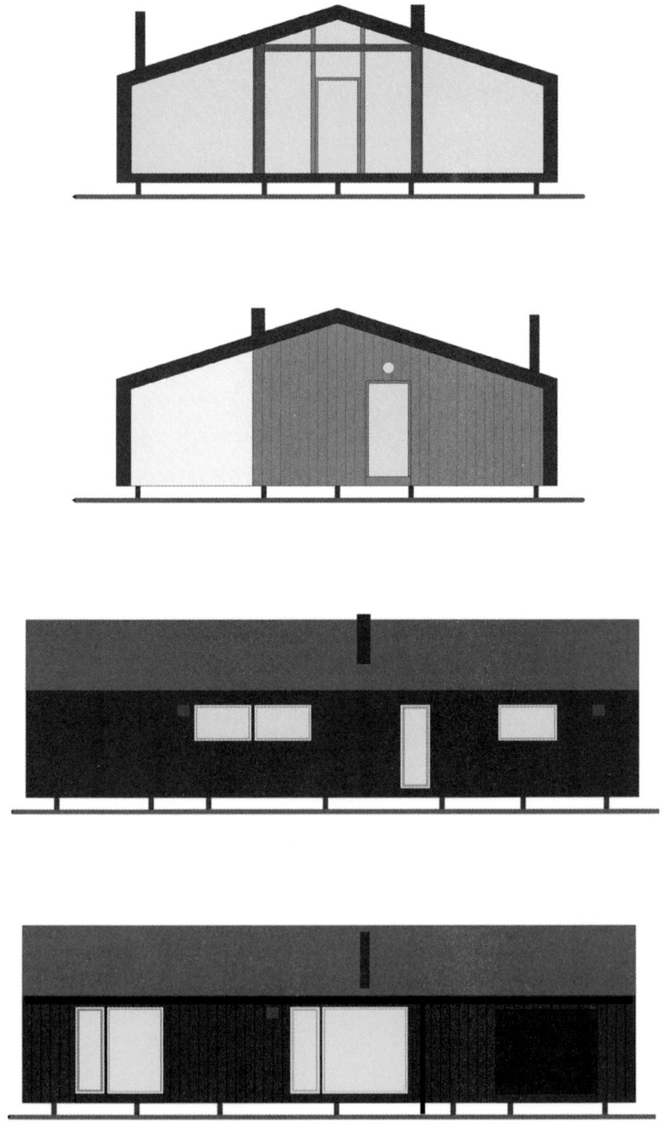

Elevations

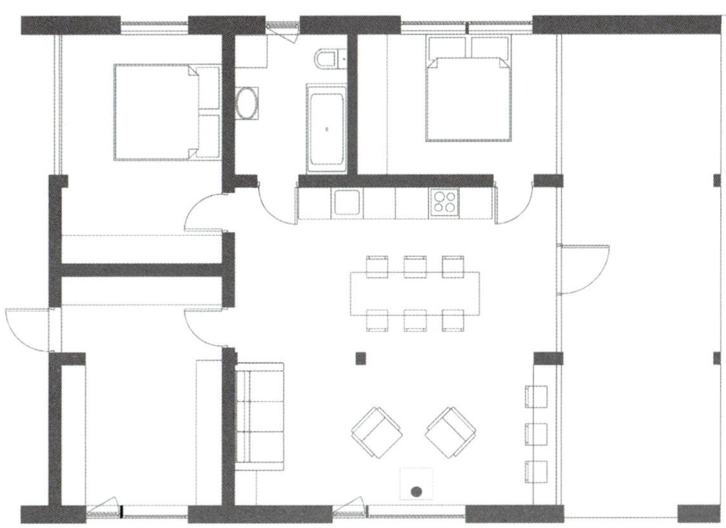

Floor plan

#ARCHPOLE

#ARCHPOLE

BRIDGE HOUSE

Out of comfort zone.
You always need to go beyond your limits in order to be succussfull in business, art or any other field. We are going in the mountains, swimming in the oceans, falling in love, discovering new places in order to feel something new.
This project has become a challenge for us and an unexpectable decision for a client. The idea of the second house on site was transformed into a game of the wooden structure between two banches.
The internal space that was formed by the structure has become the wide open place for creative work. All the loadcarrying structure is made of wood. There is a living room with the kitchen, two sleeping rooms with the bathrooms and sleeping spaces on the second floor of the living room.
"People are lonely because they build walls instead of bridges" (Joseph Fort Newton).

Außerhalb der Komfortzone.
Du musst immer über deine Grenzen hinausgehen, um im Geschäft, in der Kunst oder in jedem anderen Bereich erfolgreich zu sein. Wir gehen in die Berge, schwimmen in den Ozeanen, verlieben uns, entdecken neue Orte, um etwas Neues zu spüren.
Dieses Projekt ist für uns zu einer Herausforderung und einer unerwarteten Entscheidung für einen Kunden geworden. Die Idee des zweiten Hauses vor Ort wurde in ein Spiel der Holzstruktur zwischen zwei Bänken verwandelt.
Der durch die Struktur gebildete Innenraum ist zum weitläufigen Ort für kreative Arbeit geworden. Die gesamte Tragkonstruktion ist aus Holz gefertigt. Es gibt ein Wohnzimmer mit Küche, zwei Schlafzimmer mit Badezimmern und Schlafplätze im zweiten Stock des Wohnzimmers.
„Die Menschen sind einsam, weil sie Mauern statt Brücken bauen" (Joseph Fort Newton).

Hors de la zone de confort.
Il faut toujours dépasser ses limites pour réussir en affaires, en art ou dans tout autre domaine. Nous allons dans les montagnes, nager dans les océans, tomber amoureux, découvrir de nouveaux endroits afin de ressentir quelque chose de nouveau.
Ce projet est devenu un défi pour nous et une décision inexplicable pour un client. L'idée de la deuxième maison sur le site a été transformée en un jeu de la structure en bois entre deux bancs.
L'espace intérieur formé par la structure est devenu le grand espace ouvert au travail créatif. Toute la structure portante est en bois. Il y a un salon avec la cuisine, deux chambres à coucher avec les salles de bains et des chambres à coucher au deuxième étage de la salle de séjour.
« Les gens se sentent seuls parce qu'ils construisent des murs au lieu de ponts » (Joseph Fort Newton).

Fuera de la zona de confort.
Siempre tienes que ir más allá de tus límites para tener éxito en los negocios, el arte o cualquier otro campo. Vamos a las montañas, nadamos en los océanos, nos enamoramos, descubrimos nuevos lugares para sentir algo nuevo.
Este proyecto se ha convertido en un reto para nosotros y en una decisión inexplicable para un cliente. La idea inicial de una segunda casa se transformó en un juego de la estructura de madera entre dos bancos.
El espacio interior formado por la estructura se ha convertido en el espacio abierto para el trabajo creativo. Toda la estructura portante es de madera. Hay una sala de estar con la cocina, dos dormitorios con los baños y espacios para dormir en el segundo piso de la sala de estar.
«La gente se siente sola porque construye muros en lugar de puentes» (Joseph Fort Newton).

Conceptual rendering

Elevation

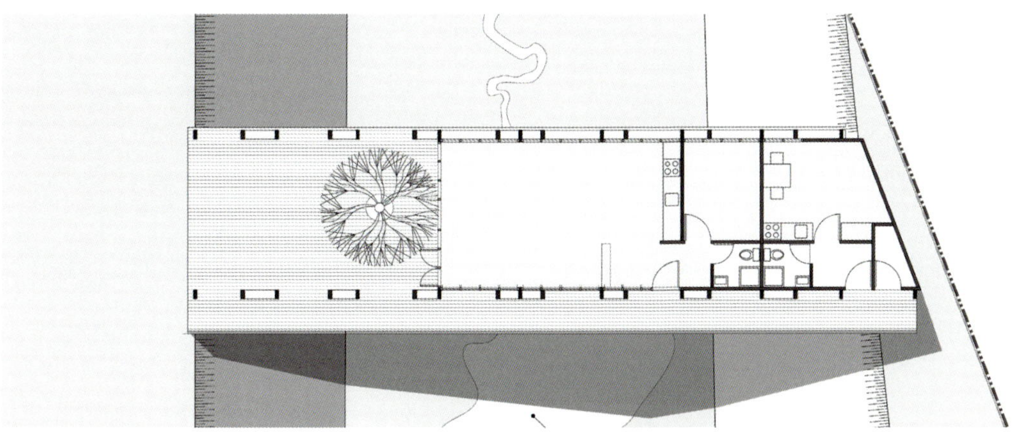

Ground floor plan

BROISSIN
M. Arch. Gerardo Broissin

Gerardo Broissin, founder and CEO of BROISSIN, is known for his creative design approach, problem-solving skills and customer service. He is influenced by the experience of many cities, the type of spaces that generate them and the iconic buildings that contribute to innovation and the pleasure of everyday life. Its objective is to achieve a multidisciplinary work; from its architectural beauty, context, economy and functionality.
BROISSIN is a company of professional experts who work together with clients and specialists to develop and implement innovative solutions for the projects in which they participate. With 20 years of experience, the firm works throughout Mexico with offices located in Mexico City, San Luis Potosi and Tijuana, developing projects that generate trust, inspire security and forge lasting relationships organized around the relationship with the customer.

Gerardo Broissin, fondateur et PDG de BROISSIN, est reconnu pour son approche créative du design, ses compétences en résolution de problèmes et son service client. Il est influencé par l'expérience de nombreuses villes, le type d'espaces qui les génèrent et les bâtiments emblématiques qui contribuent à l'innovation et au plaisir de la vie quotidienne. Son objectif est de réaliser une œuvre multidisciplinaire ; de par sa beauté architecturale, son contexte, son économie et sa fonctionnalité.
BROISSIN est une entreprise d'experts professionnels qui travaillent avec des clients et des spécialistes pour développer et mettre en œuvre des solutions innovantes pour les projets auxquels ils participent. Avec 20 ans d'expérience, il travaille dans tout le Mexique avec des bureaux situés à Mexico, San Luis Potosi et Tijuana, développant des projets qui génèrent la confiance, inspirent la sécurité et forgent des relations durables, organisées autour de la relation avec le client.

Gerardo Broissin, Gründer und CEO von BROISSIN, ist bekannt für seinen kreativen Designansatz, seine Problemlösungskompetenz und seinen Kundenservice. Er ist geprägt von der Erfahrung vieler Städte, der Art der Räume, die sie generieren, und den ikonischen Gebäuden, die zu Innovationen und der Freude am Alltag beitragen. Sein Ziel ist es, ein multidisziplinäres Werk zu schaffen, das sich durch seine architektonische Schönheit, seinen Kontext, seine Wirtschaftlichkeit und seine Funktionalität auszeichnet.
BROISSIN ist ein Unternehmen aus professionellen Experten, die gemeinsam mit Kunden und Spezialisten innovative Lösungen für die Projekte entwickeln und umsetzen, an denen sie teilnehmen. Mit 20 Jahren Erfahrung arbeitet sie in ganz Mexiko mit Büros in Mexiko-Stadt, San Luis Potosi und Tijuana und entwickelt Projekte, die Vertrauen schaffen, Sicherheit bieten und dauerhafte Beziehungen zum Kunden aufbauen.

Gerardo Broissin, fundador y Director Ejecutivo de BROISSIN, es conocido por su enfoque de diseño creativo, capacidad de resolución de problemas y servicio al cliente. Está influenciado por la vivencia de muchas ciudades, el tipo de espacios que las generan y los edificios icónicos que contribuyen a la innovación y el placer de la vida cotidiana. Su objetivo es lograr un trabajo multidisciplinario; desde su belleza arquitectónica, contexto, economía y funcionalidad.
BROISSIN es una empresa de expertos profesionales que trabajan junto con clientes y especialistas para desarrollar e implementar soluciones innovadoras para los proyectos en los que participan. Con 20 años de experiencia, trabaja en toda la República Mexicana con oficinas ubicadas en Ciudad de México, San Luis Potosí y Tijuana, elaborando proyectos que generan confianza, inspiran seguridad y forjan relaciones duraderas, organizados en torno a la relación con el cliente.

IREKUA ANATANI

Situated in a spot of colourful trees and sloping topography, the house adapts its shape and programme to the site to enjoy and preserve it. Its name, "family house under the trees" in the language of the Tarascan Indians, describes the starting concept of the project.

The building is oriented to adapt to the temperate and semi-humid climate of the area. The linear and opaque south-east façade is characterised by a curtain of wooden slats that sifts solar radiation. In contrast, the southwest façade, mainly made of glass, captures the afternoon sun. The open layout of the north façade, oriented towards a lake, reinforces the intention to live holistically with the environment. The fifth façade is 100% green, which maintains a uniform temperature in the ceilings throughout the year and camouflages the residence in its context, the original goal of the design.

Das Haus liegt in einem Ort mit bunten Bäumen und schräger Topographie und passt seine Form und sein Programm an den Ort an, um ihn zu genießen und zu erhalten. Der Name „Familienhaus unter den Bäumen" beschreibt das Ausgangskonzept des Projekts in der Sprache der Tarascan-Indianer.

Das Gebäude ist so ausgerichtet, dass es sich an das gemäßigte und unbeständige Klima der Region anpasst. Die lineare und opake Südostfassade zeichnet sich durch einen Vorhang aus Holzlamellen aus, den die Sonneneinstrahlung durchdringt. Die Südwestfassade, die überwiegend aus Glas besteht, fängt dagegen die Nachmittagssonne ein. Die offene, auf einen See ausgerichtete Nordfassade verstärkt die Absicht, ganzheitlich mit der Umwelt zu leben. Die fünfte Fassade ist zu 100% grün, was eine gleichmäßige Temperatur in den Decken das ganze Jahr über gewährleistet und die Wohnung optisch in der Umgebung verschmelzen lässt, das ursprüngliche Ziel der Planung.

Située dans un écrin d'arbres colorés et de topographie en pente, la maison adapte sa forme et son programme au site pour en profiter et le préserver. Son nom, « maison familiale sous les arbres » dans la langue des Indiens Tarascans, décrit le concept de départ du projet.

Le bâtiment est orienté pour s'adapter au climat tempéré et semi-humide de la région. La façade sud-est, linéaire et opaque, est caractérisée par un rideau de lattes de bois qui tamise le rayonnement solaire. En revanche, la façade sud-ouest, principalement en verre, capte le soleil de l'après-midi. La disposition ouverte de la façade nord, orientée vers un lac, renforce l'intention de vivre de manière holistique avec l'environnement. La cinquième façade est 10 0% verte, ce qui maintient une température uniforme dans les plafonds tout au long de l'année et camoufle la résidence dans son contexte, l'objectif initial du projet.

Situada en un paraje de vistosos árboles y topografía en pendiente, la casa adapta su forma y programa al emplazamiento para disfrutar de él y preservarlo. Su nombre, «casa familiar bajo los árboles» en lengua de los indígenas tarascos, describe el concepto de partida del proyecto.

El edificio se orienta para adecuarse al clima templado y semihúmedo de la zona. La fachada sureste, lineal y opaca, se caracteriza por una cortina de lamas de madera que tamiza la radiación solar. En contraste, la fachada suroeste, principalmente de vidrio, captura el sol de la tarde. La disposición abierta de la fachada norte, orientada hacia un lago, refuerza la intención de vivir de manera holística con el entorno. La quinta fachada es 100% verde, lo que mantiene una temperatura uniforme en los techos durante todo el año y camufla la residencia en su contexto, objetivo original del diseño.

Cross section

Front elevation

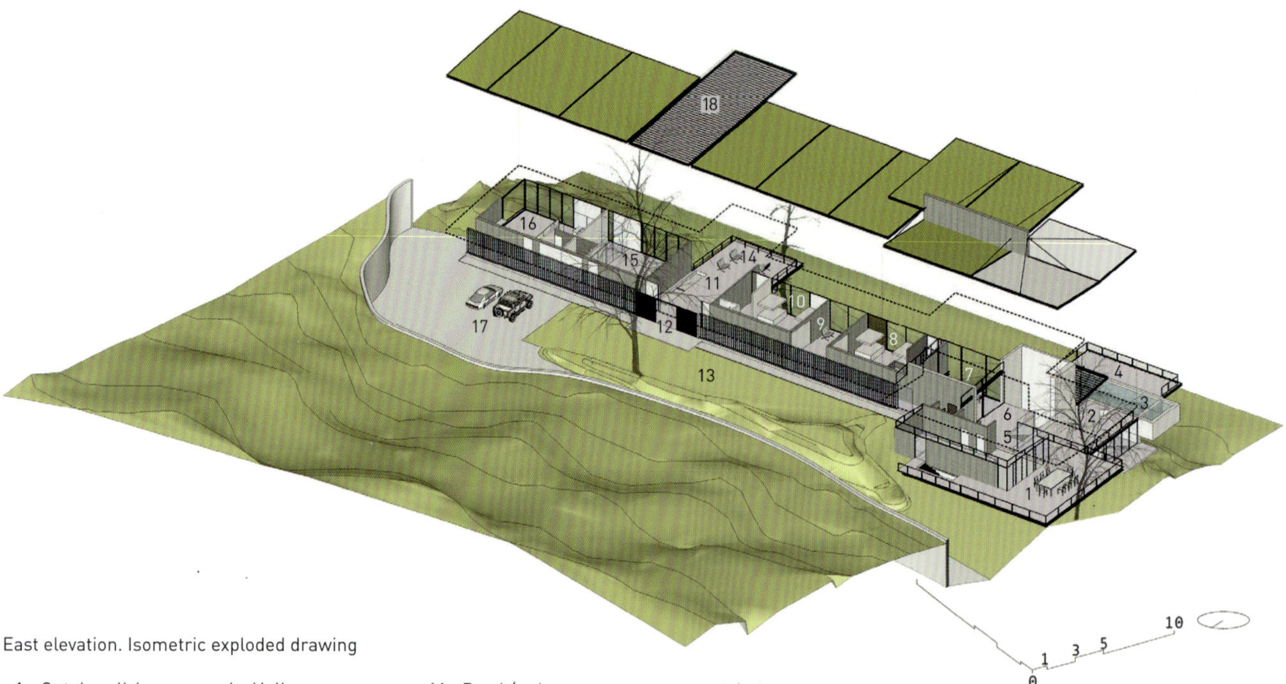

East elevation. Isometric exploded drawing

1. Out door living
2. Fire pit
3. Swimming pool
4. Sundeck
5. Kitchen
6. Hall
7. Family room
8. Boy's room
9. Kids playroom
10. Girl's room
11. Read / relax outside living
12. Foyer
13. Garden
14. Viewpoint / mountain terrace
15. Master bedroom W
16. Master bedroom Z
17. Garage
18. Green roof

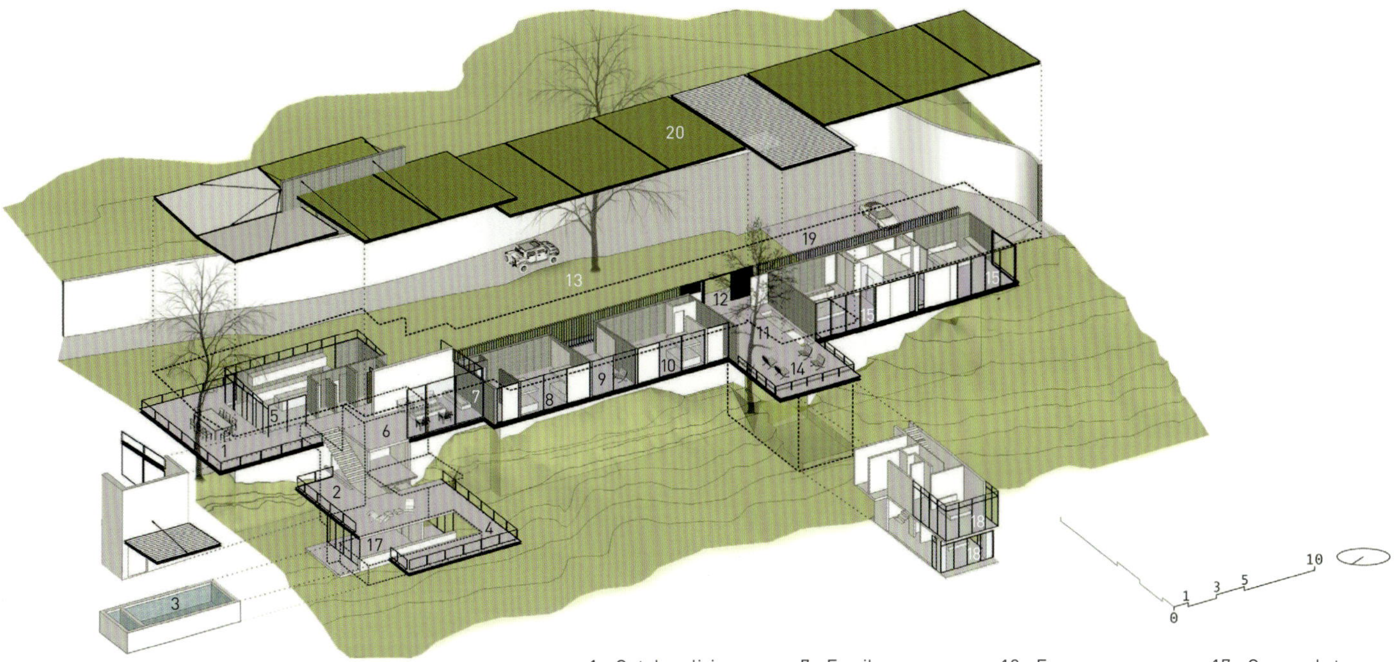

West elevation. Isometric exploded drawing

1. Out door living
2. Fire pit
3. Swimming pool
4. Sundeck
5. Kitchen
6. Hall
7. Family room
8. Boy's room
9. Kids playroom
10. Girl's room
11. Read / relax outside living
12. Foyer
13. Garden
14. Viewpoint / mountain terrace
15. Master bedroom W
16. Master bedroom Z
17. Gym and steam room
18. Guest rooms
19. Garage
20. Green roof

1. Outdoor dining
2. Terrace
3. Fire pit
4. Swimming pool
5. Jacuzzi
6. Sundeck
7. Dining
8. Pantry
9. Kitchen
10. Public area access
11. Hall
12. Family room
13. Boy's room
14. Kids playroom
15. Girl's room
16. Read / relax outside living
17. Foyer
18. Garden
19. Viewpoint / mountain terrace
20. Master bedroom W
21. Master bedroom Z
22. Wardrobe
23. Garage
24. Bathroom

Floor plan

DELIN ARKITEKTKONTOR

Delin Arkitektkontor is an office based in Stockholm and founded in 2002 by the architect Buster Delin.
I think of myself as a craftsman or a tailor. A tailor because a house should be like a suit that fits the client perfectly. A craftsman because the hand should put its imprint on the building, revealing the building process, because minimalism without human presence feels dead and industrial.
I experience the site, find the best spots and design the house from the inside perspective, framing the best views and create a landscape in which one can move freely in and out. The building is an extension of this landscape as the landscape is an extension of the building. The exterior and interior are in close dialogue with each other through the glass, preventing it from becoming a barrier between man and nature.
The detailed design takes place simultaneously with the overall design. From every different level of detail in the project you learn something that is applicable in other aspects.

Delin Arkitektkontor ist ein Büro mit Sitz in Stockholm und wurde 2002 vom Architekten Buster Delin gegründet.
Ich betrachte mich selbst als Handwerker oder Schneider. Ein Schneider, weil ein Haus wie ein Anzug sein sollte, der perfekt zum Kunden passt. Ein Handwerker, weil die Hand ihren Abdruck auf das Gebäude legen sollte, der den Bauprozess offenbart, denn Minimalismus ohne menschliche Anwesenheit fühlt sich tot und industriell an.
Ich erlebe den Ort, finde die besten Plätze und gestalte das Haus aus der Innenperspektive, rahme die besten Aussichten ein und schaffe eine Landschaft, in der man sich frei ein- und ausfahren kann. Das Gebäude ist eine Erweiterung dieser Landschaft, da die Landschaft eine Erweiterung des Gebäudes ist. Außen und Innen stehen durch das Glas in engem Dialog miteinander und verhindern, dass es zu einer Barriere zwischen Mensch und Natur wird.
Die Detailplanung erfolgt zeitgleich mit der Gesamtplanung. Aus jeder Detailstufe des Projekts lernt man etwas, das auch in anderen Aspekten anwendbar ist.

Delin Arkitektkontor est un bureau basé à Stockholm et fondé en 2002 par l'architecte Buster Delin.
Je me considère comme un artisan ou un tailleur. Un tailleur parce qu'une maison doit être comme un costume qui convient parfaitement au client. Un artisan parce que la main doit laisser son empreinte sur le bâtiment, révélant le processus de construction, parce que le minimalisme sans présence humaine est mort et industriel.
J'expérimente le site, je trouve les meilleurs endroits et je conçois la maison du point de vue intérieur, en encadrant les meilleures vues et en créant un paysage où l'on peut entrer et sortir librement. Le bâtiment est une extension de ce paysage comme le paysage est une extension du bâtiment. L'extérieur et l'intérieur sont en dialogue étroit l'un avec l'autre à travers le verre, évitant ainsi qu'il ne devienne une barrière entre l'homme et la nature.
La conception détaillée a lieu en même temps que la conception globale. A chaque niveau de détail du projet, vous apprenez quelque chose qui est applicable à d'autres aspects.

Delin Arkitektkontor es una oficina con sede en Estocolmo fundada en 2002 por el arquitecto Buster Delin.
Me considero un artesano o un sastre. Un sastre porque una casa debe ser como un traje que se ajuste perfectamente al cliente. Un artesano porque la mano debe poner su huella en el edificio, revelando el proceso de construcción, porque el minimalismo sin presencia humana se percibe muerto e industrial.
Experimento el lugar, encuentra las mejores localizaciones y diseño la casa desde dentro, enmarcando las mejores vistas y creando un paisaje en el que se puede entrar y salir libremente. El edificio es una extensión de este paisaje, ya que el paisaje es una extensión del edificio. El exterior y el interior están en estrecho diálogo a través del cristal, evitando que se convierta en una barrera entre el hombre y la naturaleza.
El diseño detallado se lleva a cabo simultáneamente con el diseño general. De cada nivel de detalle del proyecto se aprende algo que es aplicable en otros aspectos.

LUNDNÄS HOUSE

VILLA RAKU

LUNDNÄS HOUSE

This house, which is the architect's summer residence, was built on the foundations of an old ceramic stove factory. The building was erected over seven years in which design and construction evolved simultaneously and in which several experimental ideas were used, including a floor heated with air from the chimney, passive solar heating and a new type of wooden roof.
The location and views over the landscape led to the creation of three glass facades that enclose the large common areas of the house and can be regulated by locally produced linen curtains. The bathroom and bedrooms are located in the back, between walls of recovered bricks. The project imbued the house with a poetic dimension as a place of direct connection with the surrounding nature.

Das Haus, das die Sommerresidenz des Architekten ist, wurde auf den Fundamenten einer alten Keramikofenfabrik errichtet. Das Gebäude wurde in sieben Jahren errichtet, in denen sich Design und Konstruktion gleichzeitig entwickelten und in denen mehrere experimentelle Ideen umgesetzt wurden, darunter ein mit Kaminluft beheizter Boden, passive Solarheizung und ein neuartiges Holzdach.
Die Lage und der Blick über die Landschaft führten zur Schaffung von drei Glasfassaden, die die großen Gemeinschaftsflächen des Hauses umschließen und durch lokal hergestellte Leinenvorhänge reguliert werden können. Das Badezimmer und die Schlafzimmer befinden sich im hinteren Teil, zwischen den Wänden aus Ziegelsteinen, die von diesem Ort geborgen wurden. Das Projekt verlieh dem Haus eine poetische Dimension als Ort der direkten Verbindung mit der umgebenden Natur.

Cette maison, qui est la résidence d'été de l'architecte, a été construite sur les fondations d'une ancienne fabrique de poêles en céramique. Le bâtiment a été construit sur une période de sept ans au cours de laquelle la conception et la construction ont évolué simultanément et où plusieurs idées expérimentales ont été utilisées, notamment un plancher chauffé par l'air de la cheminée, un chauffage solaire passif et un nouveau type de toit en bois.
L'emplacement et les vues sur le paysage ont conduit à la création de trois façades vitrées qui entourent les grandes parties communes de la maison et qui peuvent être régulées par des rideaux de lin produits localement. La salle de bains et les chambres sont situées à l'arrière, entre les murs de briques récupérées sur place. Le projet a imprégné la maison d'une dimension poétique en tant que lieu de connexion directe avec la nature environnante.

Esta casa, que constituye la residencia de verano del arquitecto, fue construida sobre los cimientos de una antigua fábrica de estufas de cerámica. El edificio se levantó durante siete años en los que el diseño y la construcción evolucionaron simultáneamente y en los que se utilizaron varias ideas experimentales, que incluyen un suelo calentado con aire procedente de la chimenea, calefacción solar pasiva y un nuevo tipo de cubierta de madera.
La ubicación y las vistas sobre el paisaje condujeron a crear tres fachadas de vidrio que encierran las amplias zonas comunes de la casa y que pueden regularse mediante cortinas de lino de producción local. El baño y los dormitorios se ubican en la parte trasera, entre paredes de ladrillos recuperados del lugar. El proyecto imbuyó a la casa de una dimensión poética como lugar de conexión directa con la naturaleza circundante.

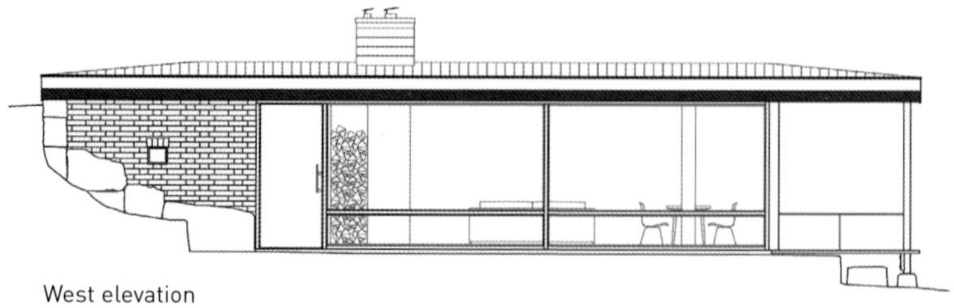

West elevation

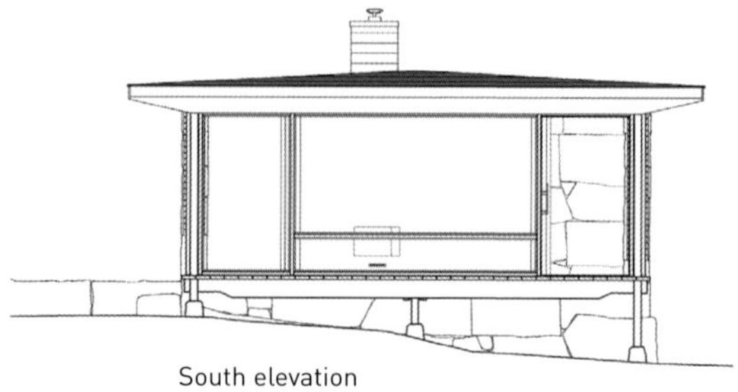

South elevation

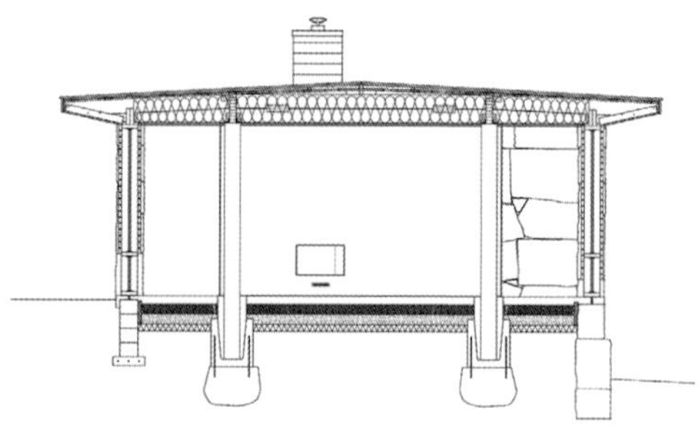

Section

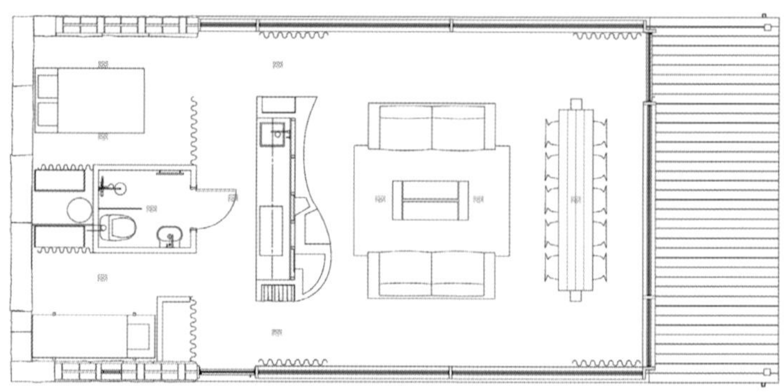

Floor plan

SOMMAR
BOKEN

VILLA RAKU

Located on top of a lush hill, this two-story home also houses workspaces for its two owners, a potter and a garden designer. An important factor in the design of the house was the use of the heat generated by the pottery ovens located on the lower floor, which accumulates in the intermediate concrete slab and is released on the upper floor, providing a comfortable and uniform temperature. The house was built on a grid of wooden pillars 2.35 m apart, which gives character and a clear rhythm to the design, forming a system in which interior and exterior walls as well as windows and doors are inserted.
Villa Raku is a house that is well integrated into its surroundings. It minimises its ecological footprint and in which two people can live and work with a creative lifestyle.

Auf einem üppigen Hügel gelegen, beherbergt dieses zweistöckige Haus auch Arbeitsplätze für seine beiden Besitzer, einen Töpfer und einen Gartenarchitekten. Ein wichtiger Faktor bei der Gestaltung des Hauses war die Nutzung der Wärme, die von den im Untergeschoss befindlichen Keramiköfen erzeugt wird, die sich in der Betonzwischendecke ansammelt und im Obergeschoss freigesetzt wird und für eine angenehme und gleichmäßige Temperatur sorgt. Das Haus wurde auf einem Raster von Holzpfeilern im Abstand von 2,35 m errichtet, das dem Design Charakter und einen klaren Rhythmus verleiht und ein System bildet, in das Innen- und Außenwände sowie Fenster und Türen eingesetzt werden.
Villa Raku ist ein gut in die Umgebung integriertes Haus, das seinen ökologischen Fußabdruck minimiert und in dem zwei Menschen mit einem auf Kreativität ausgerichteten Lebensstil leben und arbeiten können.

Située au sommet d'une colline luxuriante, cette maison de deux étages abrite également des espaces de travail pour ses deux propriétaires, un potier et un jardinier. Un facteur important dans la conception de la maison a été l'utilisation de la chaleur générée par les fours de poterie situés à l'étage inférieur, qui s'accumule dans la dalle de béton intermédiaire et est libérée à l'étage supérieur, assurant une température confortable et uniforme. La maison a été construite sur une grille de piliers en bois espacés de 2,35 m, ce qui donne du caractère et un rythme clair à la conception, et forme un système dans lequel les murs intérieurs et extérieurs ainsi que les fenêtres et portes sont insérés.
Villa Raku est une maison bien intégrée dans son environnement, qui minimise son empreinte écologique et dans laquelle deux personnes peuvent vivre et travailler avec un style de vie axé sur la créativité.

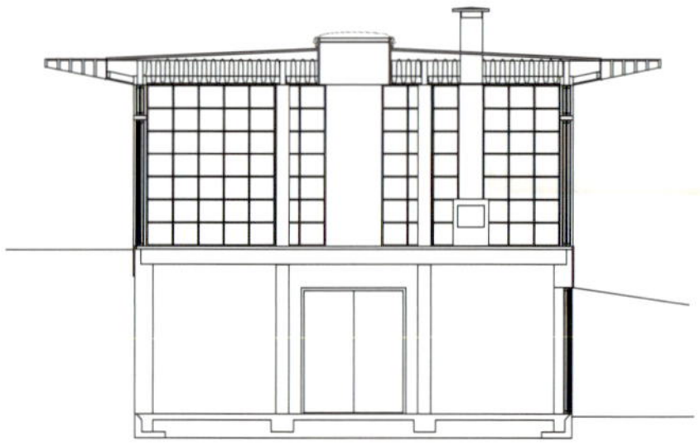

Ubicada en lo alto de una frondosa colina, esta vivienda de dos plantas alberga también espacios de trabajo para sus dos propietarios, un alfarero y un diseñador de jardines. Un factor importante del diseño de la casa fue el aprovechamiento del calor generado por los hornos de alfarería situados en la planta inferior, que se acumula en el forjado intermedio de hormigón y es liberado en el piso superior, proporcionando una temperatura confortable y uniforme. La casa se construyó sobre una retícula de pilares de madera de 2,35 m de separación, que da carácter y un ritmo claro al diseño, y que forma un sistema en el que se insertan muros interiores y exteriores así como ventanas y puertas.
Villa Raku es una casa bien integrada en su entorno, que minimiza su huella ecológica y en la que dos personas pueden vivir y trabajar con un estilo de vida centrado en la creatividad.

Sections

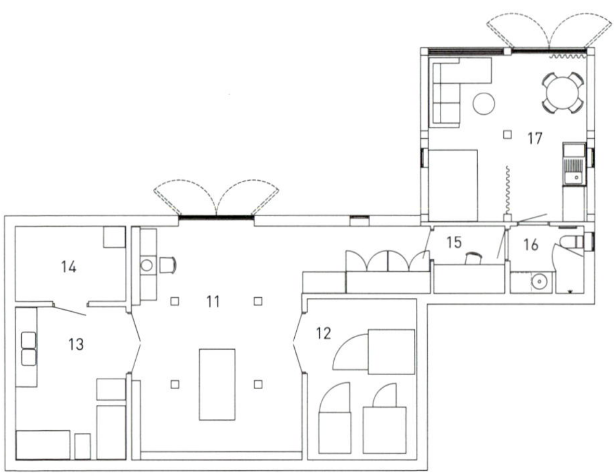

Basement plan

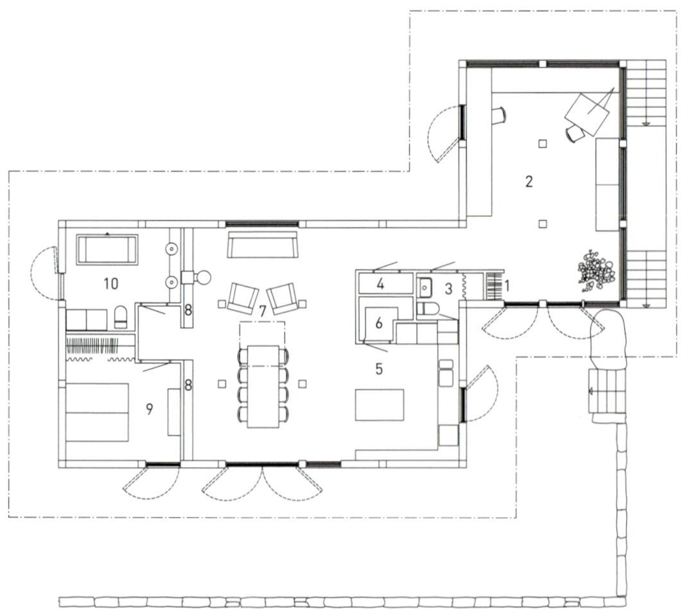

First floor plan

1. Main entrance
2. Studio
3. WC
4. Storing
5. Kitchen
6. Pantry
7. Dining / living area
8. Book shelves
9. Bedroom
10. Bathroom
11. Pottery
12. Oven room
13. Glazing room
14. Technical
15. Office
16. Guest room
17. Bathroom

EQUIPO DE ARQUITECTURA

Equipo de Arquitectura is a young studio based in Asunción, directed by architects Horacio Cherniavsky, Viviana Pozzoli and Roque Fanego. Our vision of architecture is primitive for its conceptual relationship to the origin of architecture and essential to avoid the unnecessary. We work with materials, we transform them and we have them in different ways to create spaces. We treat light also as a material that intensifies and shapes space. We seek to integrate the existing natural environment with what is built, strengthening the preexistences that characterise it. We reconsider the use and re-use of certain materials and choose to work with those appropriate to each specific situation. We are attracted by material sincerity as project ethics, which we translate into a clear reading of the architectural elements. We are fascinated by the interdisciplinary nature of architecture and consider teaching to be fundamental as a productive exchange between practical and academic.

Equipo de Arquitectura est un jeune atelier basé à Asunción, dirigé par les architectes Horacio Cherniavsky, Viviana Pozzoli et Roque Fanego, dont la vision de l'architecture est primitive pour son rapport conceptuel à l'origine de l'architecture et essentielle pour éviter le superflu. Nous travaillons avec la matière, nous la transformons et nous l'utilisons de différentes manières pour créer des espaces. Nous traitons la lumière comme un matériau qui intensifie et façonne l'espace et les matériaux qui le créent. Nous cherchons à intégrer l'environnement naturel existant avec ce qui est construit, en renforçant les préexistences qui le caractérisent. Nous reconsidérons l'utilisation et la réutilisation de certains matériaux et choisissons de travailler avec ceux qui conviennent à chaque situation spécifique. Nous sommes attirés par la sincérité matérielle en tant qu'éthique de projet, que nous traduisons par une lecture claire des éléments architecturaux, nous sommes fascinés par la nature interdisciplinaire de l'architecture et considérons l'enseignement comme fondamental, comme un échange productif entre les professions pratiques et universitaires.

Equipo de Arquitectura ist ein junges Studio mit Sitz in Asunción unter der Leitung der Architekten Horacio Cherniavsky, Viviana Pozzoli und Roque Fanego, die eine sehr bodenständige Vision von Architektur pflegen, die konzeptionell in Beziehung zu ihrem Ursprung steht und als unerlässlich angesehen wird, um Unnötiges zu vermeiden. Wir arbeiten mit der Materie, wir transformieren sie und wir haben sie auf verschiedene Weise, um Räume zu schaffen. Wir behandeln Licht als ein Material, das den Raum und die Materialien, die ihn erschaffen, intensiviert und gestaltet. Wir streben danach, die bestehende natürliche Umwelt in das Bauwerk zu integrieren und die Präexistenzen, die sie kennzeichnen, zu stärken. Wir überdenken die Verwendung und Wiederverwendung bestimmter Materialien und entscheiden uns für die Arbeit mit denjenigen, die für jede spezifische Situation geeignet sind. Wir fühlen uns von der materiellen Aufrichtigkeit als Projektethik angezogen, die wir in eine klare Lesart der architektonischen Elemente übersetzen, sind fasziniert von der Interdisziplinarität der Architektur und betrachten die Lehre als grundlegend für einen produktiven Austausch zwischen Praxis und Wissenschaft.

Equipo de Arquitectura es un joven estudio con base en Asunción, dirigido por los arquitectos Horacio Cherniavsky, Viviana Pozzoli y Roque Fanego. Nuestra visión de la arquitectura es primitiva por su relación conceptual al origen de la arquitectura y esencial para evitar lo innecesario. Trabajamos con materia, la transformamos y la disponemos de distintas maneras para crear espacios. Tratamos a la luz como material que intensifica y da forma al espacio y a los materiales que lo crean. Buscamos integrar el entorno natural existente con lo construido, potenciando las preexistencias que lo caracterizan. Reconsideramos el uso y re-uso de ciertos materiales y optamos trabajar con aquellos adecuados a cada situación específica. Nos atrae la sinceridad material como ética proyectual, que plasmamos en una clara lectura de los elementos arquitectónicos Nos fascina la interdisciplinariedad de la arquitectura y consideramos fundamental la docencia como intercambio productivo entre la profesión práctica y la académica.

CAJA DE TIERRA

CASA PATIOS

CAJA DE TIERRA

The project for this small pavilion destined for the office starts with the experimental process of using and transforming available and recovered materials, such as recycled glass and wood, configuring them between two existing trees: the chivato, and the guavirá, which is located in the middle of the space. The 30 cm tapial walls of concrete floor support the weight of the slab, which rests on 20 cm of the wall, without any anchorage or mooring, taking advantage of the structural qualities of the material. The remaining 10cm are left outside, to hide the slab, delimiting the exterior only with the walls. All the furniture and doors are made of phenolic plates that were used in the slab formwork. Inside, the library is detached from the walls so that the light can continue its way.

Das Projekt für diesen kleinen Pavillon, der als Büro vorgesehen ist, beginnt mit dem experimentellen Prozess der Verwendung und Transformation von verfügbaren und zurückgewonnenen Materialien wie Erde, Recyclingglas und Schalungsholz, die zwischen zwei bestehenden Bäumen konfiguriert werden: dem Chivato, der außen liegt, aber gerahmt, und dem Guavirá, der sich in der Mitte des Raumes befindet. Die 30 cm langen Schrägwände aus Beton tragen das Gewicht der Platte, die auf 20 cm der Wand ruht, ohne jegliche Verankerung, und nutzen die strukturellen Eigenschaften des Materials. Die restlichen 10 cm bleiben draußen, um die Platte zu verstecken, und begrenzen das Äußere nur mit den Wänden. Alle Möbel und Türen sind aus Phenolharzplatten gefertigt, die in der Deckenschalung verwendet wurden. Im Inneren ist die Bibliothek von den Wänden getrennt, so dass das Licht seine Bahn fortsetzen kann.

Le projet de ce petit pavillon destiné au bureau commence par le processus expérimental d'utilisation et de transformation des matériaux disponibles et récupérés, tels que la terre, le verre recyclé et le bois de coffrage, en les configurant entre deux arbres existants : le chivato, qui est extérieur mais encadré, et le guavirá, qui est situé au milieu de l'espace. Les murs tapissés de 30 cm de sol en béton supportent le poids de la dalle, qui repose sur 20 cm du mur, sans ancrage ni amarrage, en profitant des qualités structurelles du matériau. Les 10 cm restants sont laissés à l'extérieur, pour cacher la dalle, délimitant l'extérieur seulement avec les murs. Tous les meubles et les portes sont faits de plaques phénoliques qui ont été utilisées dans le coffrage de dalle. A l'intérieur, la bibliothèque est détachée des murs pour que la lumière puisse poursuivre sa trajectoire.

El proyecto de este pequeño pabellón destinado a oficina arranca con el proceso experimental de aprovechamiento y transformación de materiales disponibles y recuperados, como lo son la tierra, vidrios reciclados y madera de encofrado, configurándolos entre dos árboles existentes: el chivato, que queda fuera pero enmarcado, y el guavirá que se ubica en el medio del espacio. Los muros tapiales de suelo cemento de 30 cm aguantan el peso de la losa, que descansa sobre 20 cm del muro, sin ningún anclaje ni amarre, aprovechando las cualidades estructurales del material. Los 10 cm restantes quedan por fuera, para esconder la losa, delimitando el exterior solamente con los muros. Todos los muebles y las puertas son de las placas fenólicas que se utilizaron en el encofrado de la losa. En el interior, la biblioteca se desprende de los muros para que la luz continúe su trayectoria.

A-A' Section

Floor plan

CASA PATIOS

Starting from a structural scheme defined by beams with large spans, the dwelling develops on one level and extends over a sequence of spaces and courtyards that allows cross ventilation of all the rooms and is articulated by means of a circulation axis that becomes the backbone of the building. The roofs also function as patios, thus understanding the terrain as a succession of spaces at different heights. The creation of large openings creates a spatial continuity that links the natural with the artificial environment. The ceramic vaults provide the interior with a spatial quality appropriate for the region's climate. The use of the bioclimatic strategies adopted, green roofs, crossed ventilation, rainwater collection and solar protection, responds to the needs derived from the climatic conditions of Asunción.

Ausgehend von einem durch Balken mit großen Spannweiten definierten Tragwerk entwickelt sich die Wohnung auf einer Ebene und erstreckt sich über eine Abfolge von Räumen und Höfen, die eine Querbelüftung aller Räume ermöglicht und über eine Verkehrsachse gegliedert ist, die das Rückgrat des Gebäudes bildet. Die Dächer fungieren auch als Terrassen, so dass das Gelände als eine Folge von Terrassen in verschiedenen Höhen verstanden wird. Die Schaffung großer Lichter generiert eine räumliche Kontinuität, die die natürliche Umgebung mit der künstlichen verbindet. Die Keramikgewölbe verleihen dem Innenraum eine dem Klima der Region angemessene Raumqualität. Die Nutzung der bioklimatischen Strategien – Gründächer, gekreuzte Belüftung, Regenwassersammlung und Sonnenschutz – entspricht den Bedürfnissen, die sich aus den klimatischen Bedingungen von Asunción ergeben.

Partant d'un schéma structurel défini par des poutres à grandes portées, l'habitation se développe sur un niveau et s'étend sur une séquence d'espaces et de cours qui permet la ventilation croisée de toutes les pièces et s'articule au moyen d'un axe de circulation qui devient l'ossature du bâtiment. Les toits fonctionnent également comme des patios, ce qui permet de comprendre le terrain comme une succession de patios à différentes hauteurs. La création de grandes lumières crée une continuité spatiale qui entrelace l'environnement naturel avec l'environnement artificiel. Les voûtes en céramique confèrent à l'intérieur une qualité spatiale adaptée au climat de la région. L'utilisation des stratégies bioclimatiques adoptées : toits verts, ventilation croisée, collecte des eaux de pluie et protection solaire, répond aux besoins dérivés des conditions climatiques d'Asunción.

Partiendo de un esquema estructural definido por vigas de grandes luces, la vivienda se desarrolla en un nivel y se extiende en una secuencia de espacios y patios que permite la ventilación cruzada de todos los ambientes y que se articula mediante un eje de circulación que se convierte en la espina dorsal del edificio. Las cubiertas funcionan también como patios, entendiendo así al terreno como una sucesión de patios a distintas alturas. La creación de grandes luces crea una continuidad espacial que entrelaza el entorno natural con el artificial. Las bóvedas cerámicas dotan al interior de una calidad espacial apropiada para el clima de la región. El uso de las estrategias bioclimáticas adoptadas: cubiertas verdes, ventilación cruzada, recolección de aguas pluviales y protección solar, responde a las necesidades derivadas de las condiciones climáticas de Asunción.

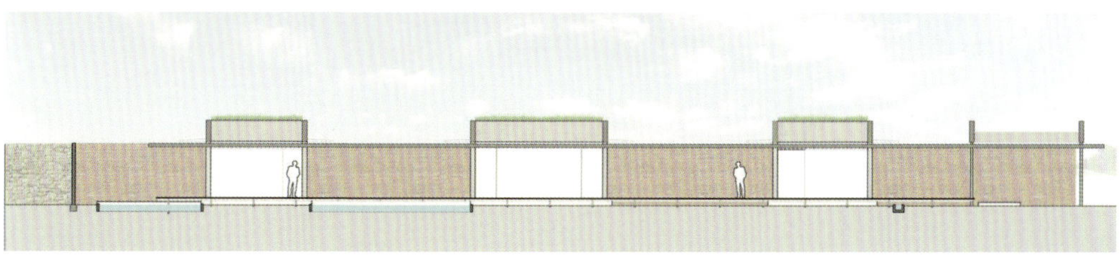

A-A section

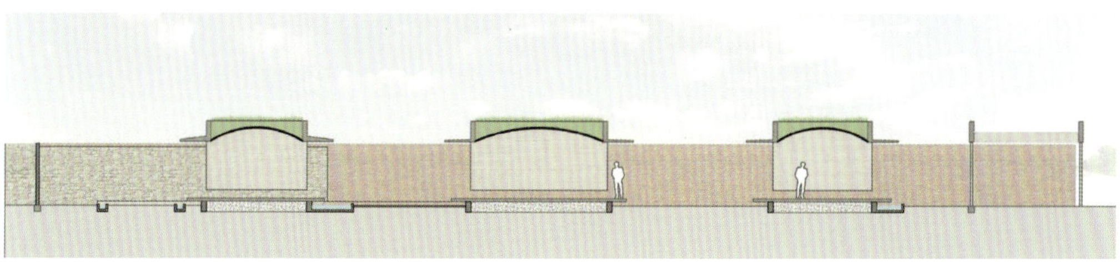

B-B section

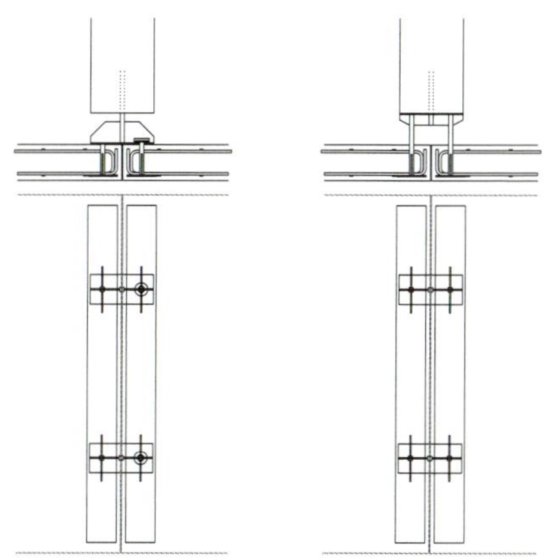

Tensioner joint detail

Floor plan

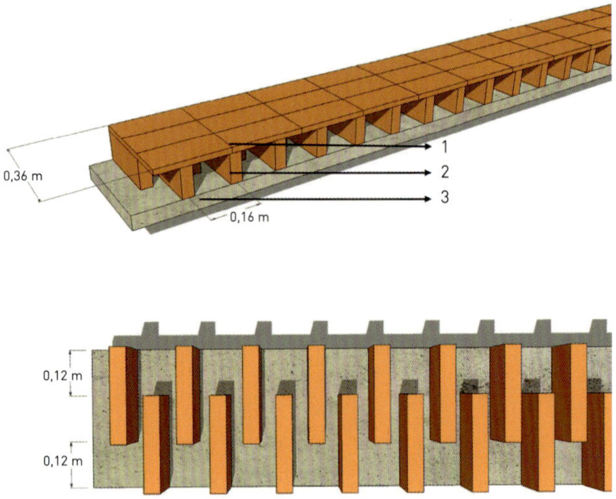

1. Tejuelita
2. Semi-pressed brick
3. Prestressed concrete base

Lattice construction details

ESTUDIO VALDÉS

Our Architectural Studio was born in 2003 as a modern response to the needs of the new times. This office, as group of Young architects, has proposed to improve the quality in the building process, incorporating greater precision in the solutions and a greater commitment with the art and the aesthetics.
This challenge was assumed by the office with a group of professionals who share common values and a structure that allows architects to assume an active role in each project, being partners in each of them.
Our firm has concentrated its energies on the development of projects of various scales, with a strong emphasis on urban design, always incorporating new proposals of programs, uses and typologies, complementing the passionate work in the search for different architectural expressions, with original and expressive materials.

Notre studio d'architecture est né en 2003 comme une réponse moderne aux besoins des temps nouveaux. Ce bureau en tant que groupe d'architectes a proposé d'améliorer la qualité dans le développement des Projets d'Architecture, en améliorant la rapidité devant les exigences, en incorporant plus de précision et de rigueur dans les solutions et un plus grand engagement avec l'art et l'esthétique.
Ce défi a été relevé par le bureau avec un groupe de professionnels qui partagent des valeurs communes et une structure qui permet aux architectes d'assumer un rôle actif dans chaque projet, en étant partenaires dans chacun d'eux.
Notre cabinet a concentré ses énergies sur le développement de projets de différentes échelles, avec un fort accent sur le design urbain, en incorporant toujours de nouvelles propositions de programmes, d'usages et de typologies, complétant le travail passionné dans la recherche de différentes expressions architecturales, avec des matériaux originaux et expressifs.

Unser Architekturstudio wurde 2003 als moderne Antwort auf die Bedürfnisse der neuen Zeit geboren. Dieses Büro als eine Gruppe von Architekten hat vorgeschlagen, die Qualität in der Entwicklung architektonischer Projekte zu verbessern, die Geschwindigkeit vor den Anforderungen zu erhöhen, mehr Präzision und Strenge in die Lösungen einzubeziehen und ein größeres Engagement für die Kunst und die Ästhetik umzusetzen.
Diese Herausforderung wurde vom Büro mit einer Gruppe von Fachleuten angenommen, die gemeinsame Werte teilen, und einer Struktur, die es Architekten ermöglicht, eine aktive Rolle in jedem Projekt zu übernehmen und Partner in jedem von ihnen zu sein.
Unsere Firma hat ihre Energien auf die Entwicklung von Projekten verschiedener Größenordnungen konzentriert, mit einem starken Schwerpunkt auf dem Städtebau, wobei sie immer wieder neue Vorschläge von Programmen, Nutzungen und Typologien einbezieht und die leidenschaftliche Arbeit auf der Suche nach verschiedenen architektonischen Ausdrucksformen mit originellen und expressiven Materialien ergänzt.

Nuestro Estudio de Arquitectura nace en el año 2003 como una respuesta moderna a las necesidades que plantean los nuevos tiempos. Esta oficina como grupo de arquitectos se ha propuesto mejorar la calidad en el desarrollo de los Proyectos de Arquitectura, mejorando la velocidad ante los requerimientos, incorporando mayor precisión y rigor en las soluciones y un mayor compromiso con el arte y la estética.
Este desafío fue asumido por la oficina con un grupo de profesionales que comparten valores en común y una estructura que permite que los arquitectos asuman un rol activo en cada proyecto, siendo socios en cada uno de ellos.
Nuestro Estudio ha concentrado sus energías en el desarrollo de proyectos; de diversas escalas, con un fuerte énfasis en el diseño urbano, siempre incorporando nuevas propuestas de programas, usos y tipologías, complementariamente al trabajo apasionado en la búsqueda de expresiones arquitectónicas diferentes, con materialidades originales y expresivas.

GALPÓN RANCO

This summer house is one of the three projects born as a proposal to recycle an old shed located in the Aculeo Lagoon that was damaged after the earthquake of February 2010. The project reuses wood elements in the interiors and combines them with wood from the area for pillars and exterior cladding. The house is composed of a rectangular volume, simple and clean, characterized by a succession of recycled trusses supported on a sequence of perimeter pillars. The programme is thus developed in a diaphanous space, in which the terrace, living room and dining room are located in the main space and the bedrooms, bathrooms, kitchen and service area are grouped in one of the corners. The transparent image of the building blurs the boundaries between interior and exterior and converts it into a large light box at night.

Dieses Sommerhaus ist eines der drei Projekte, die als Vorschlag für das Recycling eines alten Schuppens in der Lagune von Aculeo geboren wurden, der beim Erdbeben vom Februar 2010 beschädigt wurde. Im Rahmen des Projekts werden Pappelholzelemente in Traversen und Innenverkleidungen wiederverwendet und mit Holz aus dem Bereich Säulen und Außenverkleidungen kombiniert.
Das Haus besteht aus einem rechteckigen Volumen, einfach und sauber, gekennzeichnet durch eine Reihe von recycelten Traversen, die auf einer Reihe von Umfangssäulen getragen werden. So entsteht das Programm in einem durchsichtigen Raum, in dem sich Terrasse, Wohn- und Esszimmer im Hauptschiff befinden und die Schlafzimmer, Bäder, Küche und Servicebereich in einer der Ecken gruppiert sind. Das transparente Bild des Gebäudes verwischt die Grenzen zwischen Innen und Außen und verwandelt es nachts in einen großen Leuchtkasten.

Cette maison d'été est l'un des trois projets nés d'une proposition de recyclage d'un ancien hangar situé dans la lagune d'Aculeo qui a été endommagé après le séisme de février 2010. Le projet réutilise les éléments en bois de peuplier dans les fermes et les revêtements intérieurs et les combine avec le bois de la région pour les piliers et les revêtements extérieurs.
La maison est composée d'un volume rectangulaire, simple et propre, caractérisé par une succession de fermes recyclées soutenues par une séquence de piliers périmétriques. Le programme se développe ainsi dans un espace diaphane, où la terrasse, le salon et la salle à manger sont situés dans la nef principale et où les chambres, les salles de bains, la cuisine et la zone de service sont regroupées dans un des angles. L'image transparente du bâtiment brouille les frontières entre l'intérieur et l'extérieur et le transforme en un grand caisson lumineux la nuit.

Esta casa de veraneo es uno de los tres proyectos nacidos como propuesta de reciclaje de un antiguo galpón situado en la Laguna de Aculeo que quedó dañado tras el terremoto de febrero del 2010. El proyecto reutiliza elementos de madera de álamo en cerchas y revestimientos interiores y los combina con madera de la zona para pilares y revestimientos exteriores.
La casa se compone de un volumen rectangular, simple y limpio, caracterizado por una sucesión de cerchas recicladas apoyadas sobre una secuencia de pilares perimetrales. El programa se desarrolla así en un espacio diáfano, en el que terraza, sala de estar y comedor se ubican en la nave principal y los dormitorios, baños, cocina y área de servicio se agrupan en una de las esquinas. La imagen de transparencia del edificio difumina los límites entre interior y exterior y la convierte por la noche en una gran caja de luz.

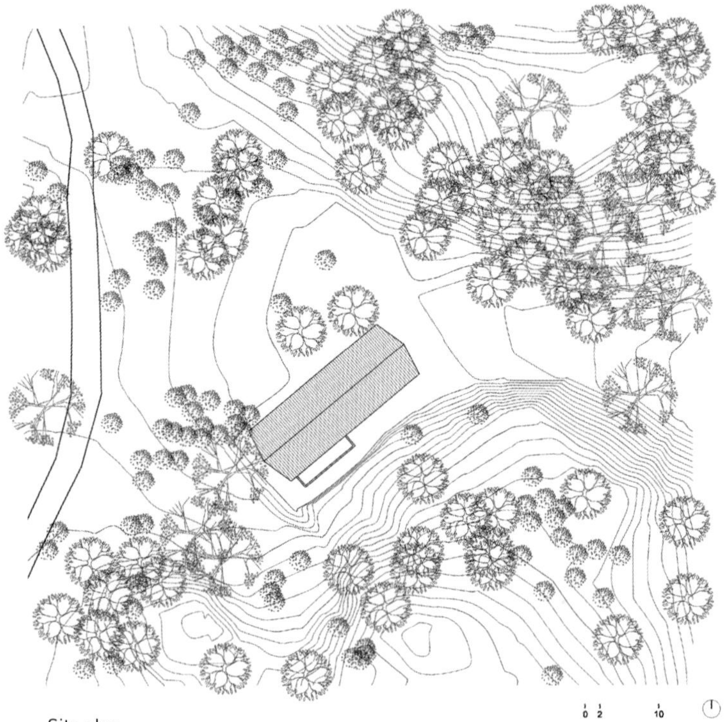

Site plan

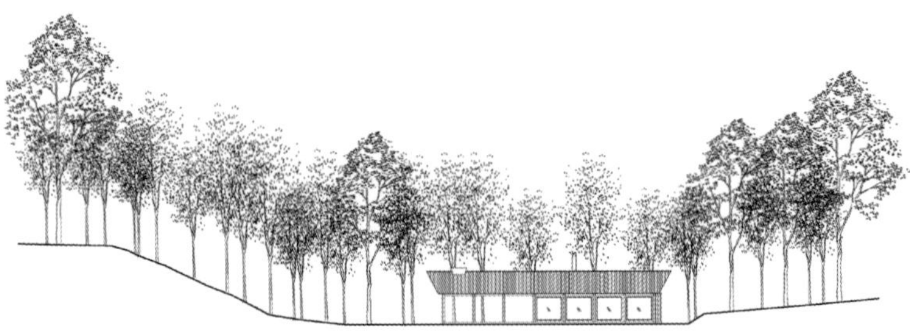
Longitudinal elevation

Front elevation

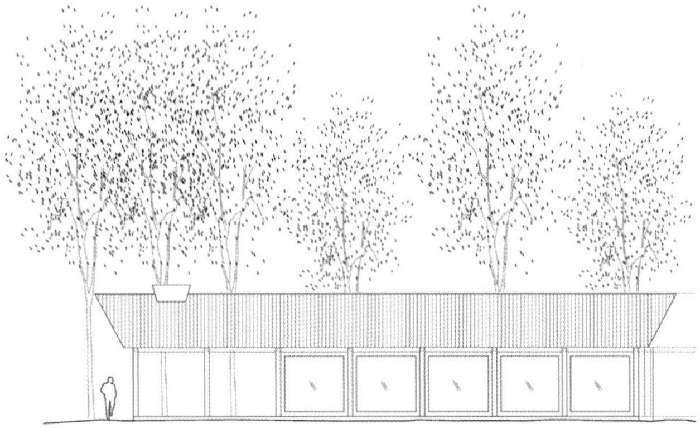

North elevation

South elevation

East elevation

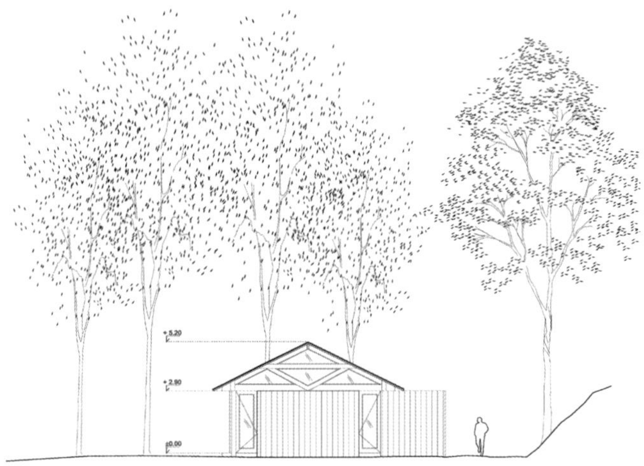

West elevation

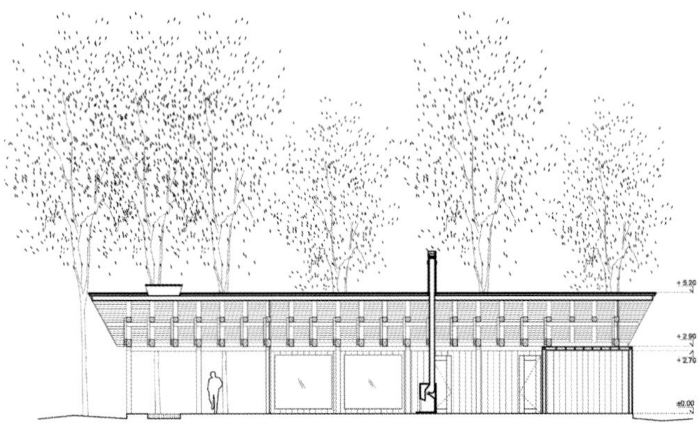

A-A section

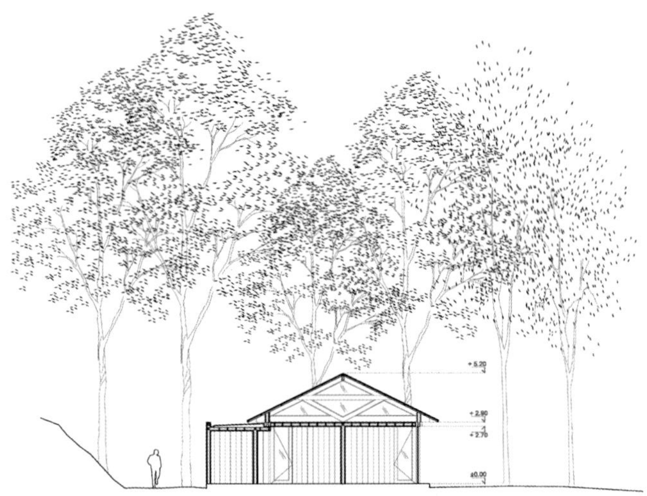

B-B section

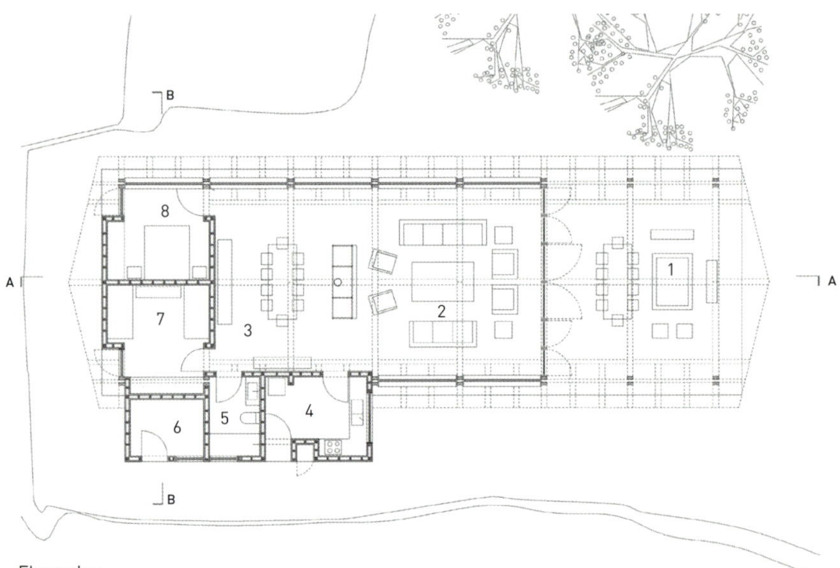

Floor plan

1. Terrace
2. Living
3. Dining
4. Kitchen
5. Bathroom
6. Bodega
7. Bedroom 1
8. Bedroom 2

FINNE ARCHITECTS

Nils Finne, AIA, is principal of the award-winning FINNE Architects in Seattle. His residential work has been widely published locally and nationally in over 100 books and magazines. FINNE has been recognized as one of the best Seattle design firms by local and national media. In addition to architecture, Nils has been involved in the design and fabrication of more than 80 pieces of furniture, lighting and hardware. Prior to founding FINNE Architects in 1991, Nils was a Senior Associate at Richard Meier and Partners, and served as Project Architect for the $350 million Getty Museum, approximately one-third of the $1 billion Getty Center complex in Los Angeles. Following undergraduate training at Brown University and Rhode Island School of Design, Nils received a Masters degree in Architecture from Harvard University in 1980. Nils has been practicing sustainable design for over 25 years, and is a member of the U.S. Green Building Council.

Nils Finne, AIA, est le directeur du cabinet FINNE Architects à Seattle. Son travail résidentiel a été largement publié localement et nationalement dans plus de 100 livres et magazines. FINNE a été reconnue comme l'une des meilleures firmes de design de Seattle par les médias locaux et nationaux. En plus de l'architecture, Nils a participé à la conception et à la fabrication de plus de 80 meubles, luminaires et quincaillerie. Avant de fonder FINNE Architects en 1991, M. Nils était associé principal chez Richard Meier and Partners et a agi à titre d'architecte de projet pour le Getty Museum d'une valeur de 350 millions de dollars, soit environ un tiers du complexe Getty Center de Los Angeles d'une valeur de 1 milliard de dollars. Après une formation de premier cycle à l'Université Brown et à la Rhode Island School of Design, Nils a obtenu une maîtrise en architecture de l'Université Harvard en 1980. Nils pratique le design durable depuis plus de 25 ans et est membre du U.S. Green Building Council.

Nils Finne, AIA, ist Direktor der preisgekrönten FINNE Architects in Seattle. Seine Wohnarbeiten wurden lokal und national in über 100 Büchern und Zeitschriften veröffentlicht. FINNE wurde von den lokalen und nationalen Medien als eine der besten Designfirmen in Seattle ausgezeichnet. Neben der Architektur war Nils an der Entwicklung und Herstellung von mehr als 80 Möbelstücken, Leuchten und Beschlägen beteiligt. Vor der Gründung von FINNE Architects im Jahr 1991 war Nils Senior Associate bei Richard Meier und Partners und diente als Projektarchitekt für das 350 Millionen Dollar teure Getty Museum, etwa ein Drittel des 1 Milliarde Dollar teuren Getty-Center-Komplexes in Los Angeles. Nach einer Grundausbildung an der Brown University und der Rhode Island School of Design erhielt Nils 1980 einen Master-Abschluss in Architektur von der Harvard University. Nils praktiziert seit über 25 Jahren nachhaltiges Design und ist Mitglied des U.S. Green Building Council.

Nils Finne, AIA, es el director del galardonado FINNE Architects en Seattle. Su trabajo residencial ha sido ampliamente publicado a nivel local y nacional en más de 100 libros y revistas. FINNE ha sido reconocida como una de las mejores firmas de diseño de Seattle por los medios de comunicación locales y nacionales. Además de la arquitectura, Nils ha participado en el diseño y fabricación de más de 80 piezas de mobiliario, iluminación y ferretería. Antes de fundar FINNE Architects en 1991, Nils fue Asociado Senior en Richard Meier and Partners, y se desempeñó como Arquitecto de Proyectos para el Museo Getty de 350 millones de dólares, aproximadamente un tercio del complejo Getty Center de 1 billón de dólares en Los Ángeles. Después de estudiar en la Universidad de Brown y en la Escuela de Diseño de Rhode Island, Nils recibió una Master en Arquitectura de la Universidad de Harvard en 1980. Nils ha estado practicando el diseño sostenible durante más de 25 años y es miembro del Consejo de Edificios Ecológicos de los Estados Unidos.

MAZAMA HOUSE

PORT LUDLOW HOUSE

MAZAMA HOUSE

Situated next to some trees on the edge of a large meadow, the house consists of two volumes that reveal its internal organisation: the first sits on the land and houses the bedrooms; the second, which contains the common areas, seems to float on the meadow thanks to six steel pillars that raise it from the ground. The changes in the inclination of the roof, reflected in the wooden beams seen from the inside, reinforce the lightweight image of this pavilion. The project has been designed to be sustainable, with 40% higher insulation values than code requirements, radiant concrete slab heating, efficient natural ventilation, abundant natural lighting, water-conserving plumbing fixtures, and locally sourced materials. Inspired by the concept of "handcrafted modernism", the project includes several pieces of furniture and lighting specially designed for the house.

Das Haus liegt neben einigen Bäumen und am Rande einer großen Wiese und besteht aus zwei Teilen, die seine innere Organisation offenbaren: Der erste sitzt auf dem Land und beherbergt die Schlafzimmer; der zweite, der die Gemeinschaftsräume enthält, scheint dank sechs Stahlpfeilern, die es vom Boden erheben, über der Wiese zu schweben. Die Veränderungen in der Dachneigung, die sich in den von innen sichtbaren Holzbalken widerspiegeln, verstärken das leichte Bild dieses Pavillons. Das Projekt wurde so konzipiert, dass es nachhaltig ist, mit 40% höheren Dämmwerten als die Anforderungen der Vorschriften, strahlender Betonplattenheizung, effizienter natürlicher Belüftung, reichlich natürlicher Beleuchtung, wassersparenden Sanitärarmaturen und lokal bezogenen Materialien. Inspiriert vom Konzept der „handgefertigten Moderne" umfasst das Projekt mehrere Möbel und Leuchten, die speziell für das Haus entworfen wurden.

Située à côté de quelques arbres et au bord d'une grande prairie, la maison se compose de deux volumes qui révèlent son organisation interne : le premier est assis sur le terrain et abrite les chambres ; le second, qui contient les parties communes, semble flotter sur la prairie grâce aux six piliers en acier qui la soulèvent du sol. Les changements d'inclinaison de la toiture, qui se reflètent dans les poutres de bois vues de l'intérieur, renforcent l'image de légèreté de ce pavillon. Le projet a été conçu pour être durable, avec des valeurs d'isolation supérieures de 40 % aux exigences du code, un chauffage par dalle de béton radiant, une ventilation naturelle efficace, un éclairage naturel abondant, des appareils sanitaires économiseurs d'eau et des matériaux de source locale. Inspiré par le concept du « modernisme artisanal », le projet comprend plusieurs meubles et luminaires spécialement conçus pour la maison.

Situada junto a unos árboles y en el límite de un gran prado, la casa se compone de dos volúmenes que revelan su organización interna: el primero se asienta en el terreno y alberga los dormitorios; el segundo, que contiene las zonas comunes, parece flotar sobre el prado gracias a seis pilares de acero que lo elevan del suelo. Los cambios de inclinación de la cubierta, reflejados en las vigas de madera vistas del interior, refuerzan la imagen de ligereza de este pabellón. El proyecto ha sido diseñado para ser sostenible, con valores de aislamiento un 40% más altos que los requeridos por el código, calefacción por baldosas radiantes de hormigón, ventilación natural eficiente, abundante iluminación natural, instalaciones de fontanería que ahorran agua y materiales de origen local. Inspirándose en el concepto de «modernismo artesanal», el proyecto incluye diversas piezas de mobiliario e iluminación especialmente diseñadas para la casa.

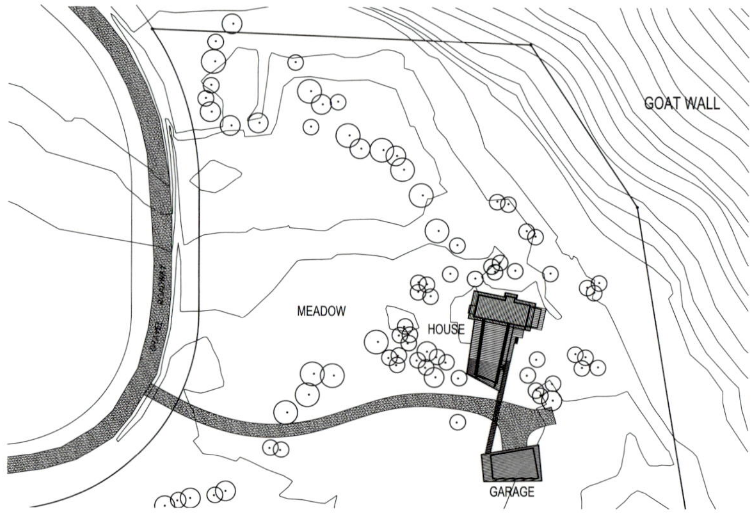

Site plan

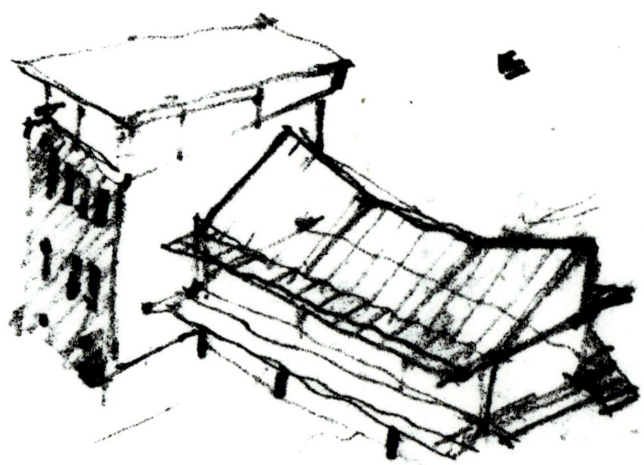

Sketch

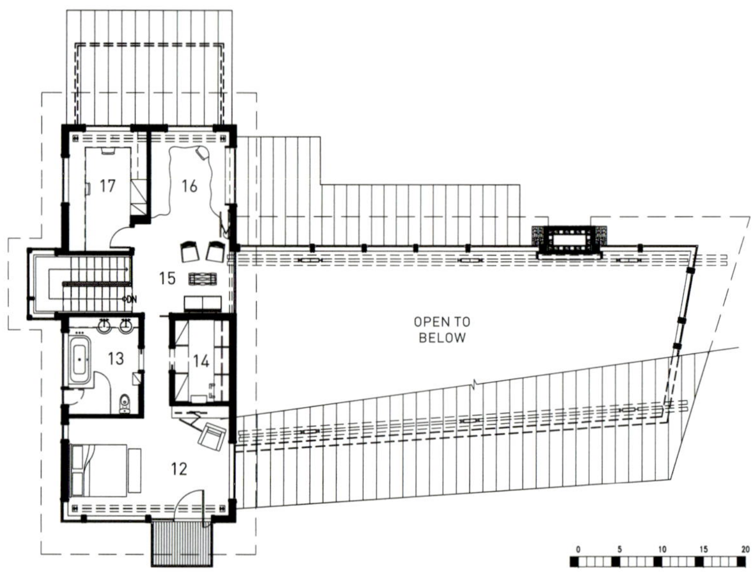

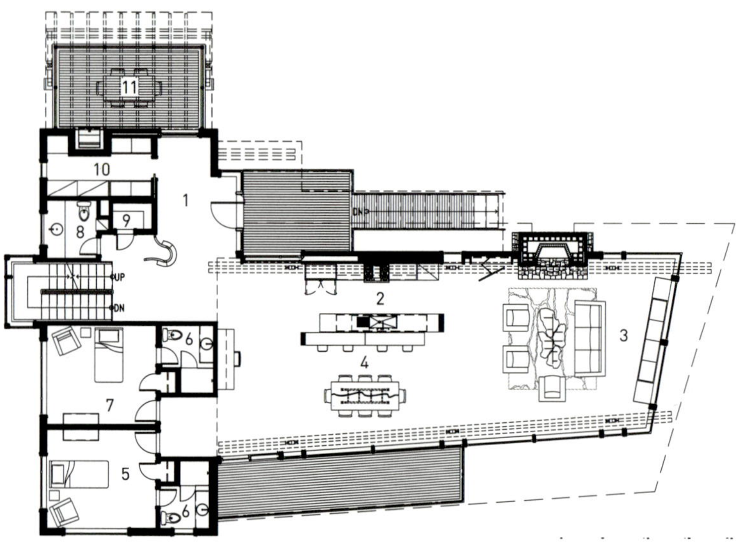

First floor plan

1. Entry
2. Kitchen
3. Living
4. Living
5. Bedroom
6. Bathroom
7. Bedroom
8. Powder room
9. Pantry
10. Mud room
11. Screen porch
12. Master bedroom
13 Master bathroom
14. Master closet
15. Sitting
16. Office
17. Craft room

PORT LUDLOW HOUSE

Located on a wooded plot in Washington State, this house is characterized by a large glazed space for common areas that opens onto a terrace overlooking Hood Canal. The sliding glass doors generate a continuity between interior and exterior that during the summer turns the living room into a porch. In the northern part of the building, a two-storey volume contains the bedrooms and workspaces. The interior finishes are ecological, simple and elegant. Maintenance-free materials are used for the exteriors, such as recycled steel metal cladding and aluminum windows. The house includes other sustainable features, such as exterior walls with 40% higher insulation value than code requirements, generous glass areas providing natural light and ventilation, and a highly energy efficient heat pump mechanical system.

Auf einem bewaldeten Grundstück im Bundesstaat Washington gelegen, zeichnet sich dieses Haus durch einen großen verglasten Raum für Gemeinschaftsräume aus, der sich auf eine Terrasse mit Blick auf den Hood Canal öffnet. Die Glasschiebetüren erzeugen eine Kontinuität zwischen innen und außen, die das Wohnzimmer im Sommer in eine Veranda verwandelt. Im nördlichen Teil des Gebäudes befinden sich in einem zweigeschossigen Volumen die Schlaf- und Arbeitsbereiche. Der Innenausbau ist ökologisch, einfach und elegant. Für den Außenbereich werden wartungsfreie Materialien wie recycelte Stahlblechverkleidungen und Aluminiumfenster verwendet. Das Haus verfügt über weitere nachhaltige Merkmale, wie Außenwände mit 40% höherem Dämmwert als vorgeschrieben, großzügige Glasflächen für natürliches Licht und Belüftung und eine hocheffiziente Wärmepumpenmechanik.

Située sur un terrain boisé de l'État de Washington, cette maison se caractérise par un grand espace vitré pour les parties communes qui donne sur une terrasse donnant sur le Hood Canal. Les portes vitrées coulissantes génèrent une continuité entre l'intérieur et l'extérieur qui, en été, transforme le salon en véranda. Dans la partie nord du bâtiment, un volume de deux étages contient les chambres et les espaces de travail. Les finitions intérieures sont écologiques, simples et élégantes. Des matériaux sans entretien sont utilisés pour l'extérieur, comme les revêtements métalliques en acier recyclé et les fenêtres en aluminium. La maison comprend d'autres caractéristiques durables, comme des murs extérieurs dont la valeur d'isolation est supérieure de 40 % à celle exigée par le code, des surfaces vitrées généreuses offrant une lumière et une ventilation naturelles et un système mécanique à pompe à chaleur très éconergétique.

Ubicada en una parcela boscosa en el Estado de Washington, esta casa se caracteriza por un gran espacio acristalado para áreas comunes que se abre en una terraza con vistas al Canal Hood. Las puertas correderas de vidrio generan una continuidad entre interior y exterior que durante el verano convierte la sala de estar en un porche. En la parte norte del edificio, un volumen de dos plantas contiene los dormitorios y espacios de trabajo. Los acabados interiores son ecológicos, simples y elegantes. Para los exteriores se emplean materiales sin mantenimiento, como revestimientos metálicos de acero reciclado y ventanas de aluminio. La casa integra otras características sostenibles, como un valor de aislamiento de sus muros un 40% superior al habitual, generosas superficies de vidrio que aportan luz y ventilación natural o una de bomba de calor de alta eficiencia energética.

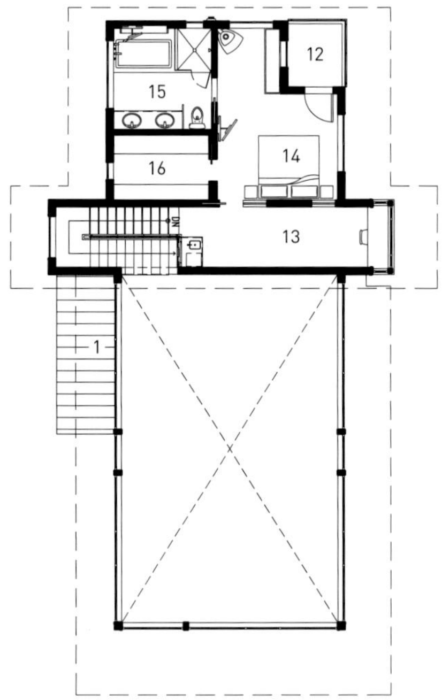

Second floor plan

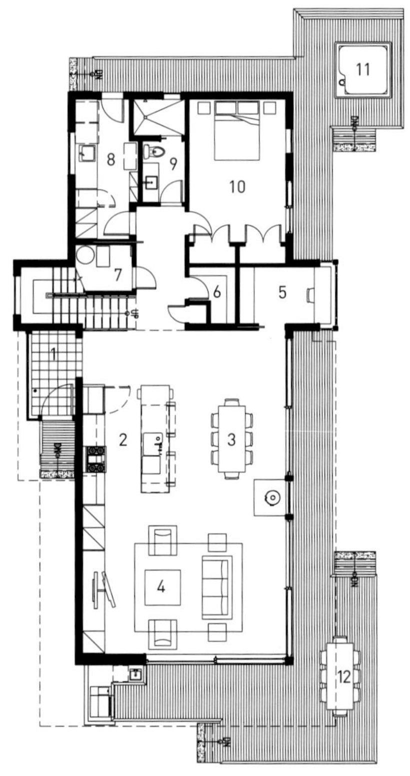

Main floor plan

1. Entry
2. Kitchen
3. Dining
4. Living
5. Office
6. Pantry
7. Mech.
8. Laundry
9. Bathroom
10. Guest room
11. Hot tub
12. Deck
13. Study
14. Master bedroom
15. Master bathroom
16. Master closet

SAFARI

GIORDANO HADAMIK ARCHITECTS

Giordano Hadamik Architects was first founded in Düsseldorf, Germany, in 2012 and later in Andora, Italy, in 2015 by the Italian Architect Daniele Giordano and his wife Dipl.-Ing. Nadine Hadamik working within an atelier-style structure. GHA has an artisan approach to design inspired by the morphology of the surrounding context and materials starting from the landscape leading to the actual design with an eye on the contemporary architectural debate but free from school of thought and any style dogma.
Their architecture responds to the exposition of its environment making the best of views, solar gains and sustainability. Design elements are based on a clear concept and motivated by their function and proportion. In 2015 GHA wins their first competition "Live Outside the Box" with the project Villa Nemes. From there, following varies publications and architectural awards, the company receives residential and commercial commissions in Italy, Germany, Greece, Cyprus, Croatia and Norway.

Giordano Hadamik Architects a d'abord été fondé à Düsseldorf, en Allemagne, en 2012, puis à Andora, en Italie, en 2015, par l'architecte italien Daniele Giordano et son épouse Nadine Hadamik, ingénieur diplômé, travaillant dans une structure en atelier. GHA a une approche artisanale du design inspirée par la morphologie du contexte environnant et des matériaux à partir du paysage jusqu'au design actuel, en tenant compte du débat architectural contemporain mais sans école de pensée et sans dogme de style.
Leur architecture répond à l'exposition de son environnement en tirant le meilleur parti des vues, des gains solaires et de la durabilité. Les éléments de design sont basés sur un concept clair et motivés par leurs fonctions et leurs proportions. En 2015, GHA remporte son premier concours « Live Outside the Box » avec le projet Villa Nemes. De là, à la suite de diverses publications et récompenses architecturales, la société reçoit des commandes résidentielles et commerciales en Italie, en Allemagne, en Grèce, à Chypre, en Croatie et en Norvège.

Giordano Hadamik Architects wurden erstmals 2012 in Düsseldorf, Deutschland, und später, im Jahr 2015, erneut in Andora, Italien, gegründet. Die Gründer sind der italienische Architekt Daniele Giordano und seine Frau Dipl.-Ing. Nadine Hadamik, die in einem atelierartigen Gebäude arbeiten. GHA hat einen handwerklichen Ansatz für Design, der von der Morphologie des umgebenden Kontextes und der Materialien inspiriert ist, beginnend mit der Landschaft, die zum eigentlichen Design führt, mit einem Blick auf die zeitgenössische Architekturdebatte, aber unabhängig von jeder Denkschule und frei jeden Stildogmas.
Ihre Architektur reagiert auf die Exposition ihrer Umgebung und nutzt die besten Aussichten, solaren Gewinn und Nachhaltigkeit. Gestaltungselemente basieren auf einem klaren Konzept und sind durch ihre Funktion und Proportion motiviert. Im Jahr 2015 gewannen GHA ihren ersten Wettbewerb "Live Outside the Box" mit dem Projekt Villa Nemes. In der Folge erhielt das Unternehmen nach unterschiedlichen Publikationen und Architekturpreisen Wohn- und Gewerbeaufträge in Italien, Deutschland, Griechenland, Zypern, Kroatien und Norwegen.

Giordano Hadamik Architects fue fundado en Düsseldorf, Alemania, en 2012 y más tarde en Andora, Italia, en 2015 por el arquitecto italiano Daniele Giordano y su esposa, la Ing. Nadine Hadamik, trabajando dentro de una estructura de estilo taller. GHA tiene un enfoque artesanal del diseño inspirado en la morfología del contexto y de los materiales que lo rodean, partiendo del paisaje hasta el diseño actual, con la mirada puesta en el debate arquitectónico contemporáneo, pero libre de la escuela de pensamiento y de cualquier dogma de estilo.
Su arquitectura responde a la exposición de su entorno aprovechando al máximo las vistas, los beneficios solares y la sostenibilidad. Los elementos de diseño se basan en un concepto claro y motivado por su función y proporción. En 2015 GHA gana su primer concurso «Live Outside the Box» con el proyecto Villa Nemes. A partir de ahí, tras varias publicaciones y premios de arquitectura, la empresa recibe encargos residenciales y comerciales en Italia, Alemania, Grecia, Chipre, Croacia y Noruega.

VILLA NEMES

Located in the hills overlooking the Gulf of Imperia, this villa integrates the landscape of terraces and dry stone walls of Liguria. It consists of two semi-buried volumes arranged on a single level, divided by the entrance cut, from which emerge the natural stone facade, realized with material retrieve during excavation. The elevation is carved by large openings which maximize the views and the entry of light. The retaining walls create a continuity between the building, the interior and the surroundings, and the green roof contributes to the harmonious insertion into the landscape, minimising the visual impact. The great insulation provided by the half-buried location of the building, the efficient control of sunlight and the use of renewable energies significantly reduce the energy consumption of the building and improve interior comfort, elevating the building to Passivhaus standards.

In den Hügeln über dem Golf von Imperia gelegen, integriert diese Villa die Landschaft der Terrassen und Trockenmauern von Ligurien. Es besteht aus zwei halbvergrabenen Volumen, die auf einer Ebene angeordnet sind, geteilt durch den Eingangsschnitt, aus dem die Natursteinfassade hervorgeht, die mit dem beim Aushub entnommenen Material realisiert wurde. Die Höhe wird von großen Öffnungen geschnitzt, die die Aussicht und den Lichteinfall maximieren. Die Stützmauern schaffen eine Kontinuität zwischen Gebäude, Innenraum und Umgebung, und das begrünte Dach trägt zur harmonischen Eingliederung in die Landschaft bei und minimiert die optische Wirkung des Gebäudes. Die gute Wärmedämmung durch die halbvergrabene Lage des Gebäudes, die effiziente Steuerung des Sonnenlichts und die Nutzung erneuerbarer Energien reduzieren den Energieverbrauch des Gebäudes deutlich, verbessern den Innenraumkomfort und heben das Gebäude auf Passivhausstandard.

Située dans les collines surplombant le golfe d'Imperia, cette villa intègre le paysage de terrasses et de murs en pierre sèche de la Ligurie. Il se compose de deux volumes semi-enterrés disposés sur un seul niveau, divisés par la tranchée d'entrée, d'où émerge la façade en pierre naturelle, réalisée avec récupération des matériaux lors des excavations. L'élévation est sculptée par de grandes ouvertures qui maximisent les vues et l'entrée de la lumière. Les murs de soutènement créent une continuité entre le bâtiment, l'intérieur et l'environnement, et le toit vert contribue à l'insertion harmonieuse dans le paysage, minimisant l'impact visuel du bâtiment. La grande isolation apportée par l'emplacement semi-enterré du bâtiment, le contrôle efficace de la lumière du soleil et l'utilisation d'énergies renouvelables réduisent considérablement la consommation d'énergie du bâtiment et améliorent le confort intérieur, élevant le bâtiment aux normes Passivhaus.

Situada en las colinas con vistas al Golfo de Imperia, esta villa se integra el paisaje de terrazas y muros de piedra seca de Liguria. Consta de dos volúmenes semienterrados dispuestos en un solo nivel, divididos por el corte de entrada, de donde emerge la fachada de piedra natural, realizada con material recuperado durante la excavación. La elevación está tallada por grandes aberturas que maximizan las vistas y la entrada de luz. Los muros de contención crean una continuidad entre edificio, interior y entorno, y la cubierta verde contribuye a la inserción armónica en el paisaje, minimizando el impacto visual del edificio. El gran aislamiento que proporciona la ubicación semienterrada del edificio, el control eficiente de la luz solar y el uso de energías renovables reducen significativamente el consumo de energía del edificio y mejoran el confort interior, elevando el edificio a los estándares Passivhaus.

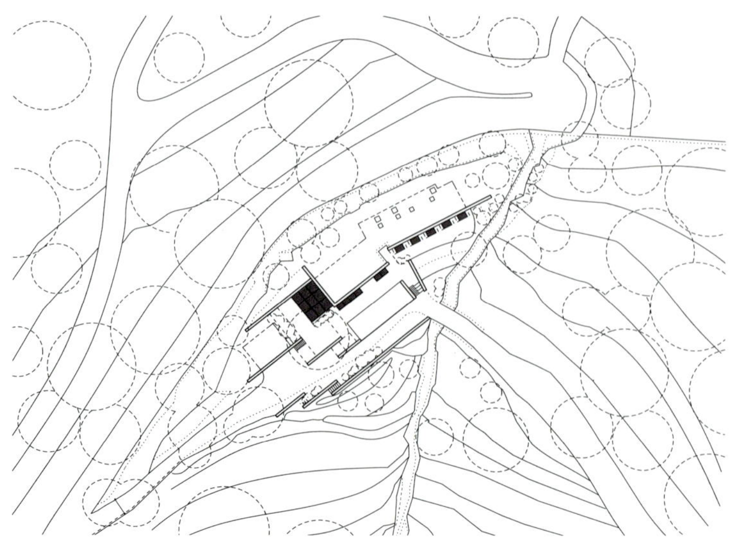

Site plan

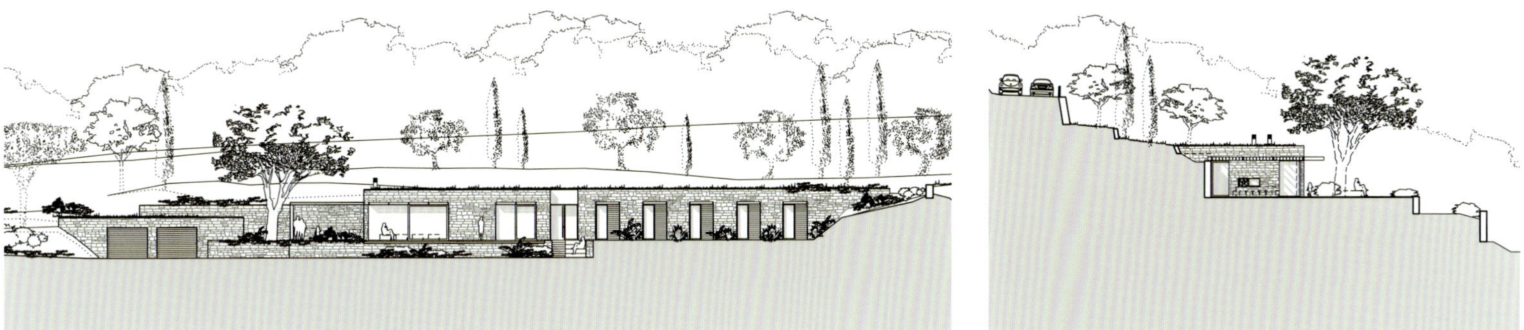

Elevations

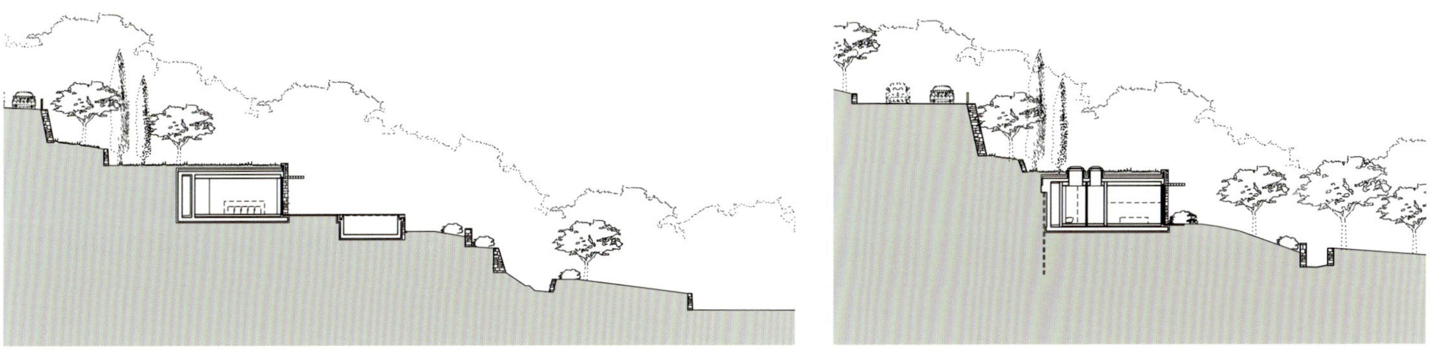

Sections

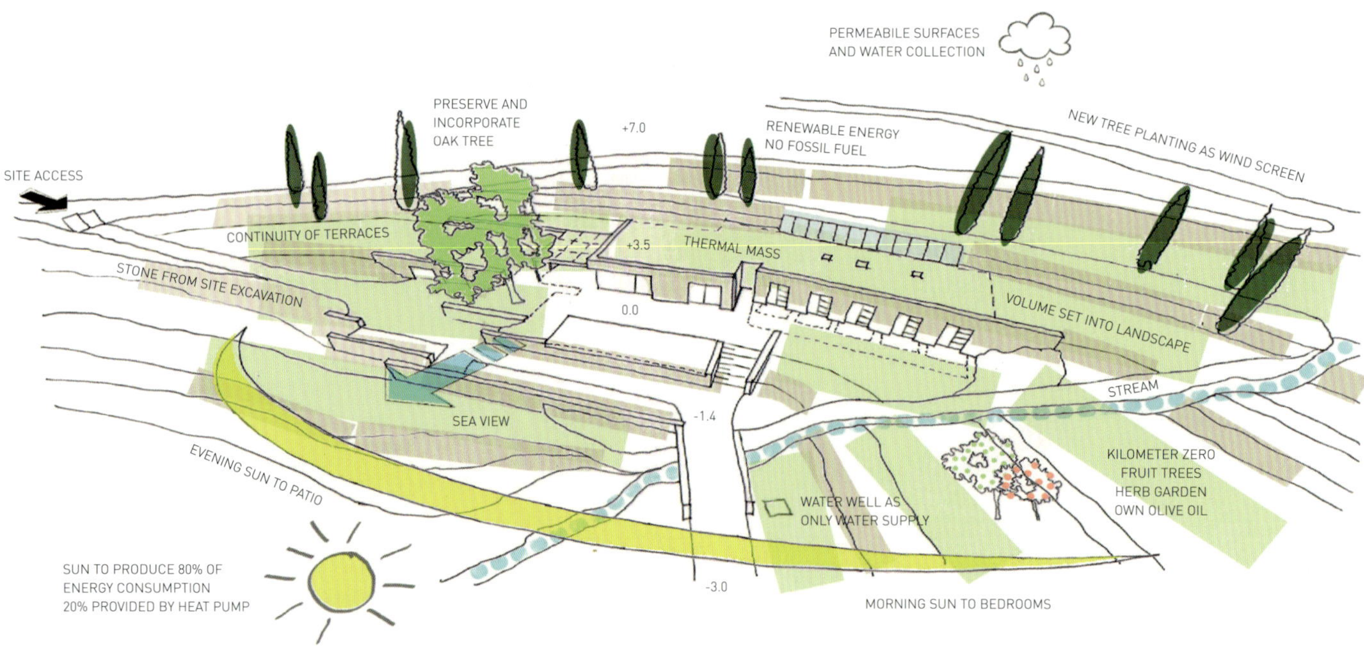

Design approach

- Respond and respect the surrounding environment
- Utilize given terrain maintaining character of the site
- Simple timeless design, spaces follow the existing morphology
- Building as a continuity of the ligurian terraces
- Use natural sources and materials from site, local craftsmanship

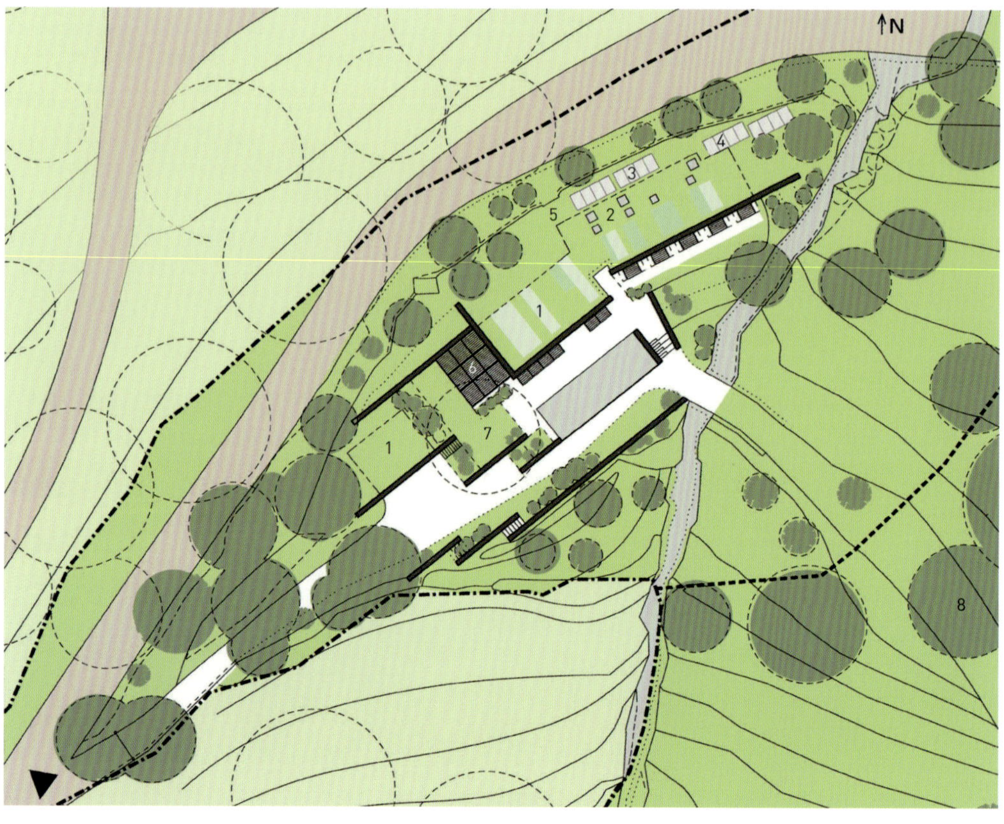

1. Green roof
2. Skylight
3. Solar panel
4. Photovoltaic
5. Heat pump
6. Patio
7. Oak tree
8. Olive groves and Orchard

Roof plan

Floor plan

1. Entrance
2. Living
3. Sleeping
4. Plant room
5. Pantry
6. Bathroom
7. Storage
8. Laundry
9. Garden patio
10. Timber sun deck
11. Infinity pool
12. Terrace
13. Garden
14. Oak tree
15. Herb garden
16. Garage
17. Gravel
18. Olive groves and Orchard

GRIEVE GILLETT ANDERSEN

Founded in 1982, Grieve Gillett Andersen's diverse portfolio of projects spans the sectors of residential, public, educational, commercial and heritage architecture in South Australia and across Australia.
Underpinned by an integrated approach to architecture, interior environments and landscape, the firm's design ethos results in sustainable, functional and high quality, well-crafted design solutions. With an eagerness to solve problems thoughtfully through genuine collaboration, their work is in the pursuit of conceptual and aesthetic clarity.
Grieve Gillett Andersen employs a well-balanced, practical approach to sustainable design, where the desire for sustainability is considered early in the design phase and is responsive to the local environment, context and purpose of each unique project.
The firm's excellence in design, innovation and sustainability has appeared in various publications and been recognised with multiple architecture and design awards.

Fondé en 1982, le portefeuille de projets de Grieve Gillett Andersen couvre les secteurs de l'architecture résidentielle, publique, éducative, commerciale et patrimoniale en Australie-Méridionale et partout en Australie.
S'appuyant sur une approche intégrée de l'architecture, de l'environnement intérieur et de l'aménagement paysager, la philosophie de conception du cabinet se traduit par des solutions de conception durables, fonctionnelles, de haute qualité et bien conçues. Désireux de résoudre les problèmes de manière réfléchie grâce à une véritable collaboration, son travail est axé sur la recherche de clarté conceptuelle et esthétique.
Grieve Gillett Andersen utilise une approche équilibrée et pratique de la conception durable, où le désir de durabilité est pris en compte dès le début de la phase de conception et tient compte de l'environnement local, du contexte et du but de chaque projet unique.
L'excellence du cabinet en matière de design, d'innovation et de durabilité a fait l'objet de nombreuses publications et a reçu de nombreux prix d'architecture et de design.

Grieve Gillett Andersen wurde 1982 gegründet und verfügt über ein vielfältiges Portfolio an Projekten, das die Bereiche Wohn-, öffentliche, Bildungs-, Handels- und Kulturerbearchitektur in Südaustralien und ganz Australien umfasst.
Gestützt auf einen integrierten Ansatz in Architektur, Innenarchitektur und Landschaft führt das Designethos des Unternehmens zu nachhaltigen, funktionalen und qualitativ hochwertigen gut durchdachten Designlösungen. Unter der Prämisse, Probleme durch echte Zusammenarbeit durchdacht zu lösen, streben sie nach konzeptioneller und ästhetischer Klarheit.
Grieve Gillett Andersen verfolgt einen ausgewogenen, praktischen Ansatz für nachhaltiges Design, bei dem der Wunsch nach Nachhaltigkeit bereits in der Designphase berücksichtigt wird und auf die lokale Umgebung, den Kontext und den Zweck jedes einzelnen Projekts eingeht.
Die Exzellenz des Unternehmens in Bezug auf Design, Innovation und Nachhaltigkeit wurde in verschiedenen Publikationen gepriesen und mit zahlreichen Architektur- und Designpreisen ausgezeichnet.

Fundada en 1982, la diversa cartera de proyectos de Grieve Gillett Andersen abarca los sectores de arquitectura residencial, pública, educativa, comercial y patrimonial en toda Australia.
Respaldado por un enfoque integrado de la arquitectura, los ambientes interiores y el paisaje, el espíritu de la firma da como resultado soluciones de diseño sostenibles, funcionales y de alta calidad. Con el afán de resolver los problemas a través de una colaboración genuina, su trabajo está en la búsqueda de la claridad conceptual y estética.
Grieve Gillett Andersen emplea un enfoque práctico y bien equilibrado del diseño sostenible, en el que el deseo de sostenibilidad se tiene en cuenta al principio de la fase de diseño y responde al entorno local, al contexto y al propósito de cada proyecto único.
La excelencia en diseño, innovación y sostenibilidad de la firma ha aparecido en diversas publicaciones y ha sido reconocida con múltiples premios de arquitectura y diseño.

CRAYON HOUSE

GOOLWA BEACH HOUSE

CRAYON HOUSE

Driven by the client's passion for sustainability, this house has an energy-conscious soul. While it is sustainably responsible, it has a 'life is meant to be fun' attitude, expressed by a playfulness between light and colour depending on the change of seasons. Integral to the sustainable design is its 200 m² footprint that can adapt as the young urban family grows and changes.
The house features two contrasting, yet complimentary house forms. A warm grey metal shape sits close to a timber form, and the glass entry blurs the lines between inside and outside. The metal house contains cooking, eating and socialising spaces.
The timber house is organised by a lofty corridor with high-level openable windows and contains two bedrooms and a utilities block that slides into a study. The garden design circles the house creating beautiful backdrops and functional outdoor living.

Angetrieben von der Leidenschaft des Kunden für Nachhaltigkeit, hat dieses Haus eine energiebewusste Seele. Obwohl nachhaltig und verantwortungsbewusst, hat sie eine Haltung, die sich durch eine Verspieltheit zwischen Licht und Farbe ausdrückt, die vom Wechsel der Jahreszeiten abhängt. Integral für das nachhaltige Design ist die 200 m² große Wohnfläche, die sich an das Wachstum und die Veränderungen der jungen Stadtfamilie anpassen kann.
Das Haus verfügt über zwei kontrastierende, aber sich dennoch ergänzende Formen: Eine warme graue Metallform liegt in der Nähe einer Holzform und der Glaseingang verwischt die Linien zwischen innen und außen. Das Metallhaus enthält Koch-, Ess- und Sozialräume.
Das Holzhaus wird von einem hohen Flur mit hoch aufklappbaren Fenstern organisiert und beinhaltet zwei Schlafzimmer und einen Hauswirtschaftsblock, der in ein Arbeitszimmer gleitet. Die Gartengestaltung umgibt das Haus und schafft schöne Kulissen und funktionales Wohnen im Freien.

Animée par la passion du client pour la durabilité, cette maison a une âme soucieuse de l'énergie. Si elle est durablement responsable, elle a une attitude « la vie est ludique », qui s'exprime par un jeu entre la lumière et les couleurs des différentes saisons. L'empreinte au sol de 200 m², qui peut s'adapter à mesure que la jeune famille urbaine grandit et change, fait partie intégrante du design durable.
La maison présente deux formes de maison contrastées, mais complémentaires. Une forme en métal gris chaud se trouve près d'une forme en bois, et l'entrée en verre brouille les lignes entre l'intérieur et l'extérieur. La maison en métal contient des espaces pour cuisiner, manger et socialiser.
La maison en bois est organisée par un haut couloir avec des fenêtres ouvrables de haut niveau et contient deux chambres à coucher et un bloc utilitaire qui glisse dans un bureau. La conception du jardin entoure la maison créant de beaux décors et une vie extérieure fonctionnelle.

Impulsada por la pasión del cliente por la sostenibilidad, esta casa tiene un alma consciente de la energía. Si bien es sosteniblemente responsable, tiene una actitud de «la vida es para divertirse», expresada por una actitud de juego entre la luz y el color, dependiendo del cambio de estaciones. Una parte integral del diseño sostenible es este espacio de 200 m² que puede adaptarse a medida que la joven familia urbana crece y cambia.
La casa cuenta con dos formas de casa que contrastan, pero que son complementarias. Una cálida forma de metal gris se asienta cerca de una forma de madera, y la entrada de vidrio difumina las líneas entre el interior y el exterior. La casa de metal contiene espacios para cocinar, comer y socializar.
La casa de madera está organizada por un elevado pasillo con ventanas de alto nivel que se abren y contiene dos dormitorios y un bloque de utilidades que se desliza en un estudio. El diseño del jardín rodea la casa creando hermosos telones de fondo y una vida funcional al aire libre.

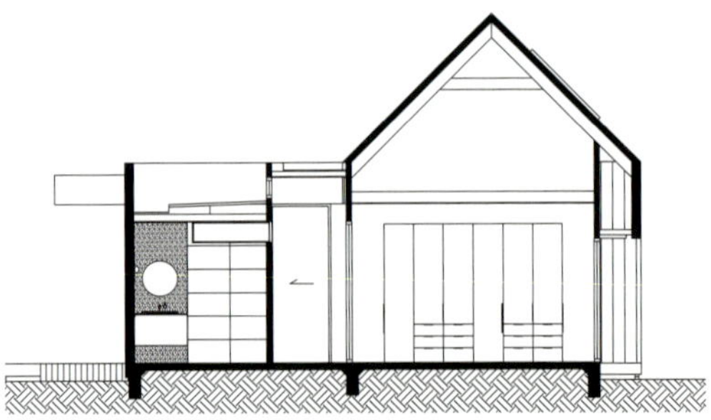

Section A

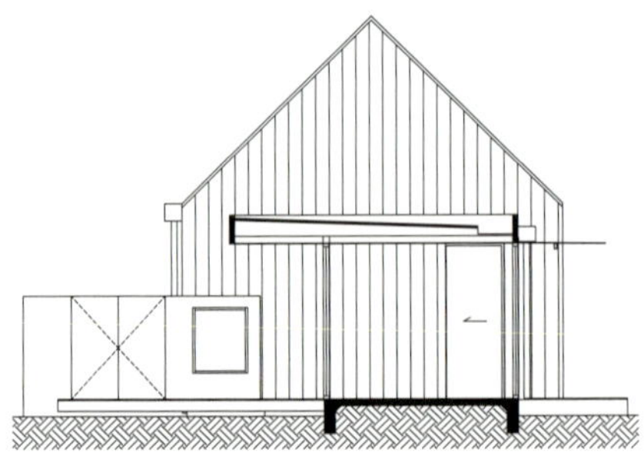

Section B

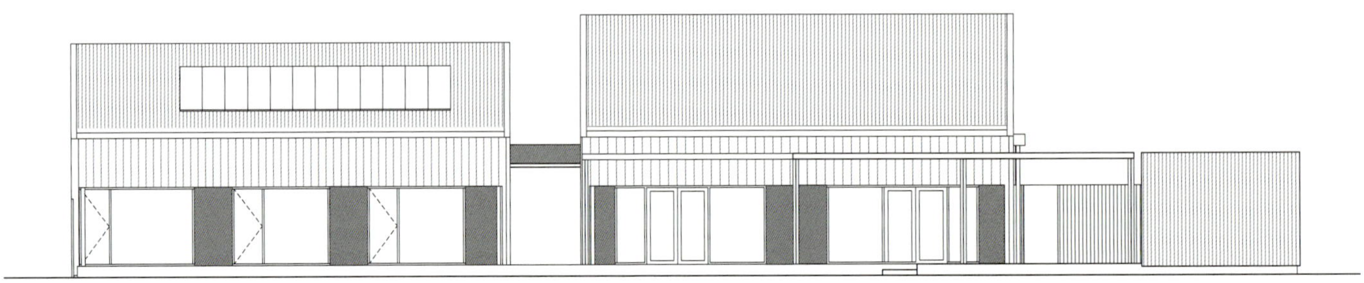

Elevation

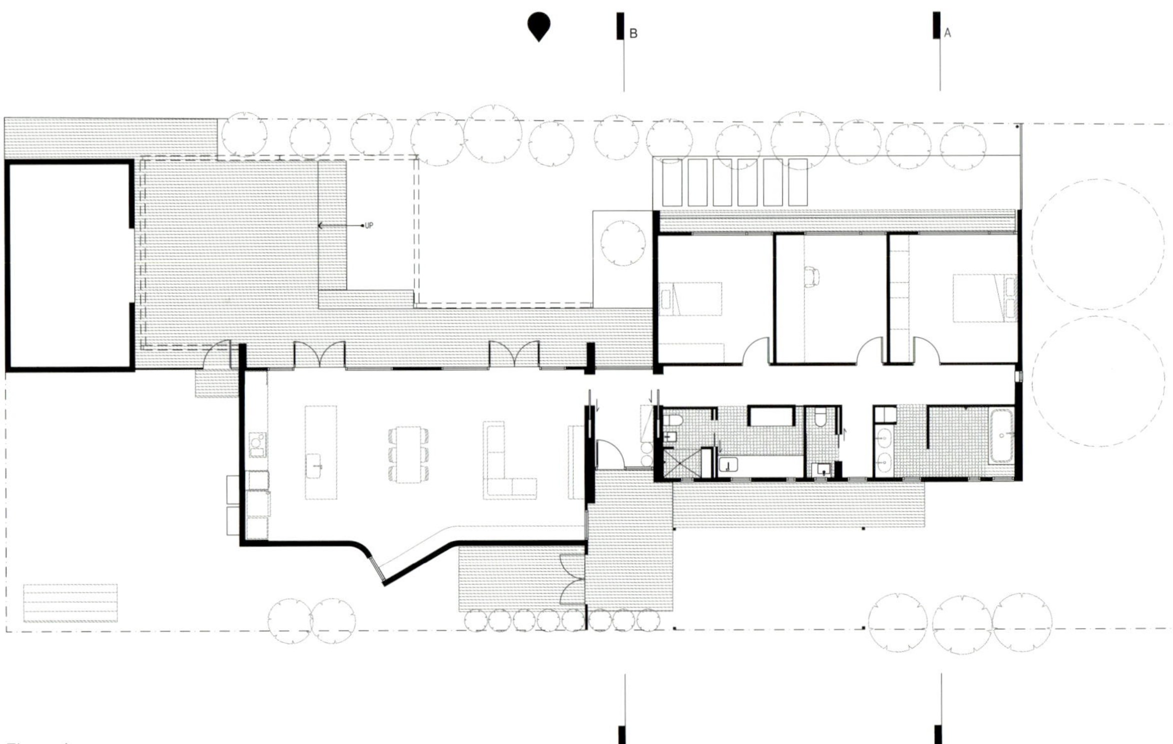

Floor plan

GOOLWA BEACH HOUSE

This house is nestled into the coastal dunes 250 m from the surf at Goolwa Beach in South Australia. Its design maximises the relationship and connection to this wonderful, yet harsh dune landscape.
The climatic conditions are extremely variable with strong winds bearing sand, salt and rain, cooling on-shore breezes, hot northerly winds and occasional breathless warm nights. Timber decks to the north and south provide outdoor living opportunities in almost every kind of weather. Flexible hand-controlled shading to the northern deck provides good amenity in both winter and summer, while solar panels provide shade to the southern deck.
This project proves that air conditioning is unnecessary if houses can be designed to work with their environment, and by employing simple principles of well-controlled cross ventilation, good insulation, external shading and sun control.

Dieses Haus liegt, eingebettet in die Stranddünen, 250 m von der Brandung am Goolwa Beach in Südaustralien. Sein Design maximiert die Beziehung und Verbindung zu dieser wunderbaren, aber dennoch rauen Dünenlandschaft.
Die klimatischen Bedingungen sind extrem unterschiedlich, geprägt von starken Winden mit Sand, Salz und Regen, kühlenden Brisen vom Land, heißen Nordwinden und gelegentlich atemlos warmen Nächten. Holzterrassen im Norden und Süden bieten Lebensräume im Freien bei fast jedem Wetter. Die flexible, handgesteuerte Beschattung des Norddecks bietet sowohl im Winter als auch im Sommer viel Annehmlichkeit, während Solarmodule die Südterrasse beschatten.
Dieses Projekt beweist, dass eine Klimatisierung unnötig ist, wenn die Häuser so gestaltet werden können, dass sie mit ihrer Umgebung harmonieren – und zwar durch einfache Prinzipien wie gut kontrollierte Querlüftung, gute Isolierung, Außenbeschattung und Sonnenschutz.

Cette maison est nichée dans les dunes côtières à 250 m du surf à Goolwa Beach en Australie du Sud. Sa conception maximise la relation et la connexion avec ce paysage dunaire merveilleux, mais rude.
Les conditions climatiques sont extrêmement variables avec des vents forts, du sable, du sel et de la pluie, des brises fraîches sur la côte, des vents chauds du nord et parfois des nuits à couper le souffle. Les terrasses en bois au nord et au sud offrent des possibilités de vie en plein air par presque tous les temps. La commande manuelle flexible de l'ombrage du pont nord offre un bon confort en hiver comme en été, tandis que les panneaux solaires procurent de l'ombre au pont sud.
Ce projet prouve que la climatisation n'est pas nécessaire si les maisons peuvent être conçues pour s'adapter à leur environnement et en utilisant des principes simples de ventilation transversale bien contrôlée, de bonne isolation, d'ombrage extérieur et de contrôle solaire.

Esta casa está enclavada en las dunas costeras a 250 metros de las olas de la playa de Goolwa Beach en el sur de Australia. Su diseño maximiza la relación y la conexión con este maravilloso y duro paisaje de dunas.
Las condiciones climáticas son extremadamente variables, con fuertes vientos de arena, sal y lluvia, brisas frescas en tierra, vientos calientes del norte y ocasionalmente noches extremadamente calurosas. Las cubiertas de madera al norte y al sur proporcionan oportunidades de vida al aire libre en casi cualquier tipo de clima. Los paneles de madera adaptables controlados a mano que proporcionan sombra de la cubierta norte funcionan tanto en invierno como en verano, mientras que los paneles solares proporcionan sombra a la cubierta sur.
Este proyecto demuestra que el aire acondicionado es innecesario si las casas pueden ser diseñadas para trabajar con su entorno, y empleando principios sencillos de ventilación cruzada bien controlada, buen aislamiento, paneles protectores exteriores y control solar.

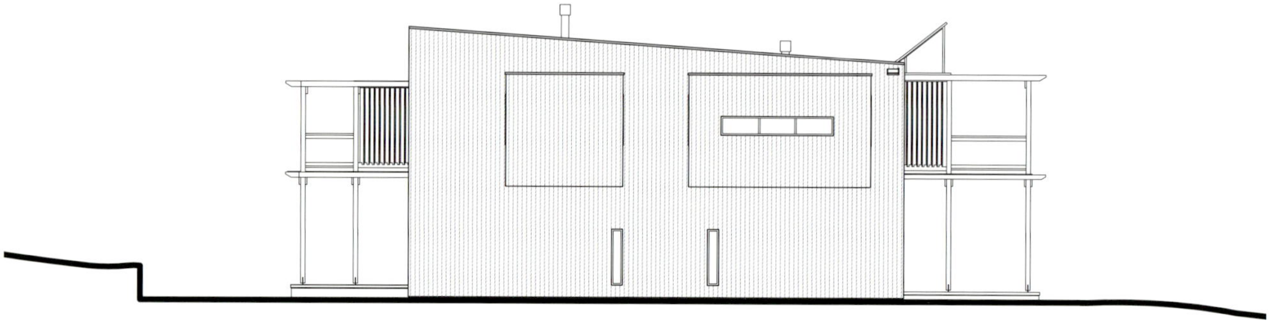

Elevation

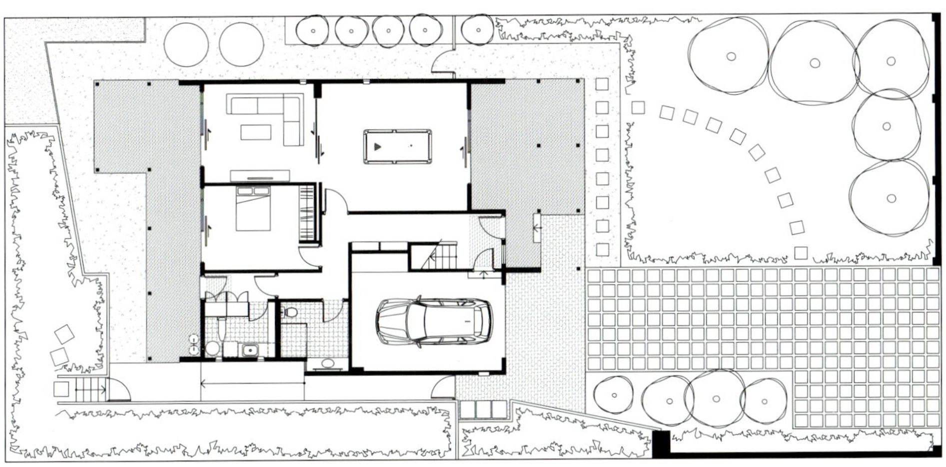

Ground floor plan

First floor plan

HARTREE + ASSOCIATES ARCHITECTS

As an individual winner of state and national architectural awards, the Perth office of Hartree + Associates Architects (est. 1992) has established a reputation for delivering innovative and thoughtfully crafted architecture and interior design of outstanding merit. Completed projects include numerous private luxury homes, multiple residential accommodation, commercial buildings and interiors, heritage and conservation work, retail and hospitality interiors.
H+AA seeks to capture the attention of building occupants, visitors and passing public, challenging predictable construction methods and outcomes, engaging to provoke enlightened thought processes —incorporating efficient construction systems and promoting sustainable design principles as a basic requirement. We take a holistic view of sustainability, not only concerned with physical issues, our focus is aimed at social, aesthetic and economic concerns.

En tant que lauréat individuel de prix d'architecture d'État et nationaux, le bureau de Perth de Hartree + Associates Architects (est. 1992) s'est forgé une réputation de fournisseur d'architecture et de design d'intérieur novateurs et bien conçus d'une valeur exceptionnelle. Les projets achevés comprennent de nombreuses maisons privées de luxe, des logements résidentiels multiples, des édifices commerciaux et des intérieurs, des travaux de conservation du patrimoine et de conservation, ainsi que des intérieurs de commerce de détail et d'hôtellerie.
H+AA cherche à capter l'attention des occupants des bâtiments, des visiteurs et du public de passage, en défiant les méthodes de construction prévisibles et les résultats, en s'engageant à provoquer des processus de réflexion éclairés - en intégrant des systèmes de construction efficaces et en promouvant les principes de conception durable comme une exigence fondamentale. Nous adoptons une vision holistique de la durabilité, ne nous préoccupant pas seulement des questions physiques, mais aussi des préoccupations sociales, esthétiques et économiques.

Als einzelner Gewinner von staatlichen und nationalen Architekturpreisen hat sich das Perther Büro von Hartree + Associates Architects (gegründet 1992) den Ruf erworben, innovative und durchdachte Architektur und Innenarchitektur von herausragender Qualität zu liefern. Zu den realisierten Projekten gehören zahlreiche private Luxushäuser, mehrere Wohnhäuser, Geschäftsgebäude und Innenräume, Denkmalpflege, Einzelhandels- und Gastronomieeinrichtungen.
H+AA möchte die Aufmerksamkeit von Gebäudenutzern, Besuchern und Passanten auf sich ziehen, vorhersehbare Baumethoden und -ergebnisse in Frage stellen, zu aufgeklärten Denkprozessen anregen, effiziente Bausysteme integrieren und nachhaltige Gestaltungsprinzipien als Grundvoraussetzung fördern. Wir betrachten Nachhaltigkeit ganzheitlich, nicht nur im Hinblick auf physische Probleme, sondern richten unseren Fokus auf soziale, ästhetische und wirtschaftliche Belange.

Como ganador individual de premios de arquitectura estatales y nacionales, la oficina de Perth de Hartree + Associates Architects, creada en 1992, se ha ganado la reputación de ofrecer una arquitectura y un diseño de interiores innovadores y bien pensados, con un mérito excepcional. Los proyectos terminados incluyen numerosas casas privadas de lujo, múltiples alojamientos residenciales, edificios comerciales e interiores, trabajos de patrimonio y conservación, tiendas e interiores de hostelería.
H+AA busca captar la atención de los ocupantes de los edificios, los visitantes y el público en general, desafiando métodos y resultados de construcción predecibles, comprometiéndose a provocar procesos de pensamiento abierto, incorporando sistemas de construcción eficientes y promoviendo los principios de diseño sostenible como un requisito básico. Tenemos una visión holística de la sostenibilidad, no solo en lo que se refiere a las cuestiones físicas, sino también a las sociales, estéticas y económicas.

GOLDTREE HOUSE

ARTHOUSE SWANBOURNE

GOLDTREE HOUSE

This reform and extension of a 1950s house promulgates the authenticity and regeneration of the original building as a declaration of time and place. Its composition uses a local language based on an eclectic mix of forms, textures, colours and plays of proportions that offer distinctive and articulated elevations.
The intervention preserves the imprint of the building and its structure to create an open and luminous design, in which the inhabitable spaces are related to the landscape and the views over the harbour. The original roof was dismantled to add a new level that houses the common spaces and the master bedroom. In contrast, the dynamic ground floor is dedicated to the family's teenage children. In addition to the photovoltaic panels, the project incorporates various measures aimed at promoting the sustainability of the home.

Dieser Umbau und Erweiterung eines Hauses aus den 1950er Jahren verkündet die Authentizität und Regeneration des ursprünglichen Gebäudes als Erklärung an Zeit und Ort. Die Komposition verwendet eine lokale Sprache, die auf einer eklektischen Mischung aus Formen, Texturen, Farben und Spielen von Proportionen basiert, die markante und artikulierte Höhen bieten.
Die Intervention bewahrt die Prägung des Gebäudes und seiner Struktur, um ein offenes und helles Design zu schaffen, in dem die bewohnbaren Räume mit der Landschaft und dem Blick über den Hafen verbunden sind. Das ursprüngliche Dach wurde demontiert, um eine neue Etage hinzuzufügen, die die Gemeinschaftsräume und das Hauptschlafzimmer beherbergt. Das dynamische Erdgeschoss hingegen ist den Teenagerkindern der Familie gewidmet. Neben den Photovoltaikmodulen umfasst das Projekt verschiedene Maßnahmen zur Förderung der Nachhaltigkeit des Hauses.

Cette réforme et l'agrandissement d'une maison des années 1950 promulguent l'authenticité et la régénération du bâtiment d'origine comme une déclaration du temps et du lieu. Sa composition utilise un langage local basé sur un mélange éclectique de formes, de textures, de couleurs et de jeux de proportions qui offrent des élévations distinctes et articulées.
L'intervention préserve l'empreinte du bâtiment et de sa structure pour créer un design ouvert et lumineux, dans lequel les espaces habitables sont liés au paysage et aux vues sur le port. Le toit d'origine a été démonté pour ajouter un nouveau niveau qui abrite les espaces communs et la chambre principale. En revanche, le rez-de-chaussée dynamique est dédié aux enfants adolescents de la famille. Outre les panneaux photovoltaïques, le projet intègre diverses mesures visant à promouvoir la durabilité de l'habitat.

Esta reforma y ampliación de una casa de los años 50 promulga la autenticidad y regeneración del edificio original como una declaración de tiempo y lugar. Su composición utiliza un lenguaje local basado en una mezcla ecléctica de formas, texturas, colores y juegos de proporciones que ofrecen elevaciones distintivas y articuladas.
La intervención conserva la huella del edificio y su estructura para crear un diseño abierto y luminoso, en el que los espacios habitables se relacionan con el paisaje y las vistas sobre el puerto. La cubierta original fue desmontada para añadir un nuevo nivel que alberga los espacios comunes y el dormitorio principal. Por el contrario, la dinámica planta baja está dedicada a los hijos adolescentes de la familia. Además de los paneles fotovoltaicos, el proyecto incorpora diversas medidas encaminadas a fomentar la sostenibilidad de la vivienda.

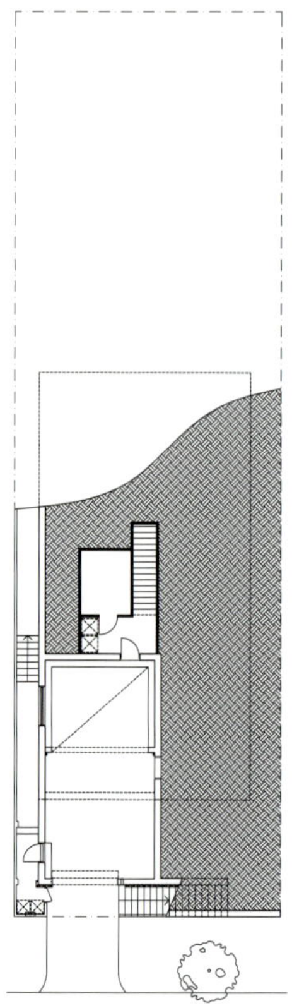

Basement level

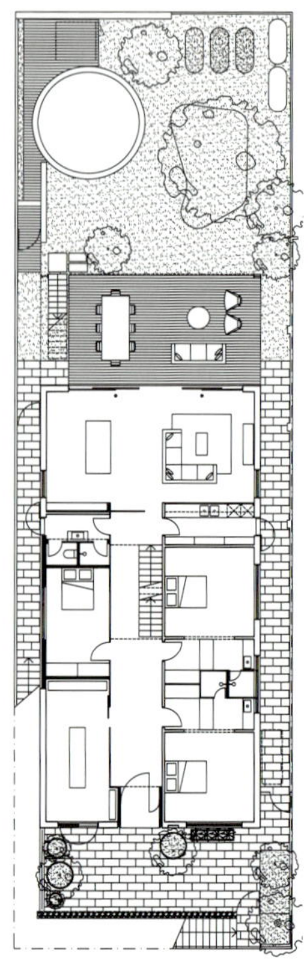

Ground floor level

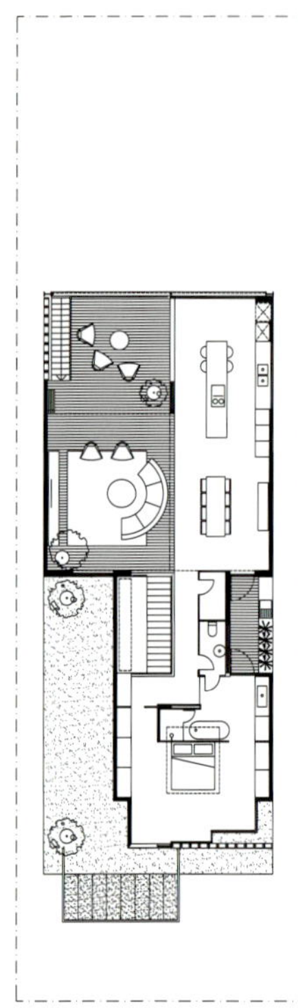

First floor level

ARTHOUSE SWANBOURNE

This house is organized in a series of layers and experiences located according to the client's priorities: privacy, views, protection from the harsh climate, entry of natural light and breezes, and the exhibition of an art collection.
Its open design integrates interior and exterior, adapts to climatic conditions and generates framed perspectives towards gardens and works of art. The key to the project is the agility of the terrace as a filter between the common areas and the exterior by means of sliding glass panels and a mobile roof configured to respond to the elements.
The sustainable aspects of the house also include photovoltaic panels, the use of low-maintenance materials, the management of energy and water through orientation, the selection of suitable accessories and low water consumption landscaping.

Dieses Haus ist in einer Reihe von Ebenen und Erfahrungen organisiert, die sich nach den Prioritäten des Kunden richten: Privatsphäre, Aussicht, Schutz vor dem rauen Klima, Eintritt von natürlichem Licht und Brisen und die Ausstellung einer Kunstsammlung.
Das offene Design integriert Innen- und Außenbereich, passt sich den klimatischen Bedingungen an und schafft gerahmte Perspektiven auf Gärten und Kunstwerke. Der Schlüssel zum Projekt ist die Wendigkeit der Terrasse als Filter zwischen den Gemeinschaftsräumen und dem Äußeren mittels Schiebeglasscheiben und einem mobilen Dach, das auf die Elemente abgestimmt ist.
Zu den nachhaltigen Aspekten des Hauses gehören auch Photovoltaikmodule, die Verwendung pflegeleichter Materialien, das Management von Energie und Wasser durch günstige Ausrichtung, die Auswahl geeigneter Accessoires und die Landschaftsgestaltung mit geringem Wasserverbrauch.

Cette maison est organisée en une série de couches et d'expériences situées selon les priorités du client : intimité, vues, protection contre le climat rigoureux, entrée de la lumière naturelle et de la brise, exposition d'une collection d'art.
Sa conception ouverte intègre l'intérieur et l'extérieur, s'adapte aux conditions climatiques et génère des perspectives encadrées vers les jardins et les œuvres d'art. La clé du projet est l'agilité de la terrasse comme filtre entre les parties communes et l'extérieur au moyen de panneaux vitrés coulissants et d'un toit mobile configuré pour répondre aux éléments.
Les aspects durables de la maison comprennent également les panneaux photovoltaïques, l'utilisation de matériaux nécessitant peu d'entretien, la gestion de l'énergie et de l'eau par l'orientation, le choix d'accessoires appropriés et un aménagement paysager à faible consommation d'eau.

Esta casa se organiza en una serie de capas y experiencias ubicadas de acuerdo a las prioridades del cliente: privacidad, vistas, protección ante el riguroso clima, entrada de la luz natural y de las brisas, y la exhibición de una colección de arte.
Su diseño abierto integra interior y exterior, se adapta a las condiciones climáticas y genera unas perspectivas enmarcadas hacia los jardines y las obras de arte. La clave del proyecto es la agilidad de la terraza como filtro entre las zonas comunes y el exterior mediante unos paneles deslizantes de vidrio y un techo móvil configurados para responder a los elementos.
Los aspectos sostenibles de la vivienda incluyen también paneles fotovoltaicos, el uso de materiales de bajo mantenimiento, la gestión de la energía y el agua a través de la orientación, la selección de accesorios adecuados y el paisajismo de bajo consumo de agua.

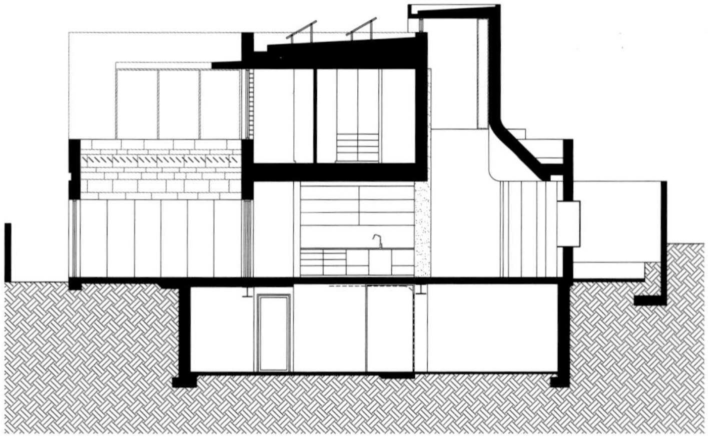

Section

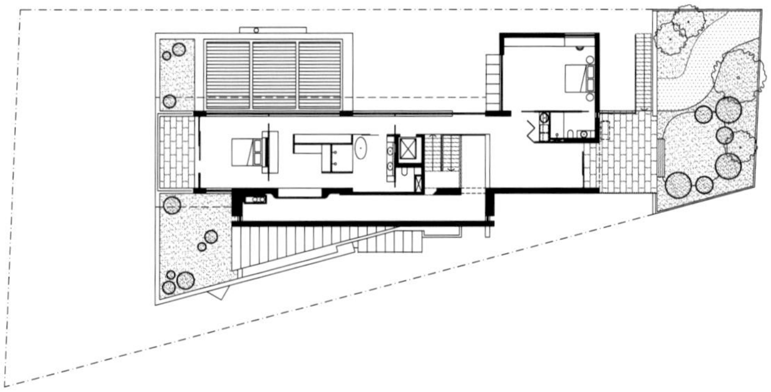

First floor plan

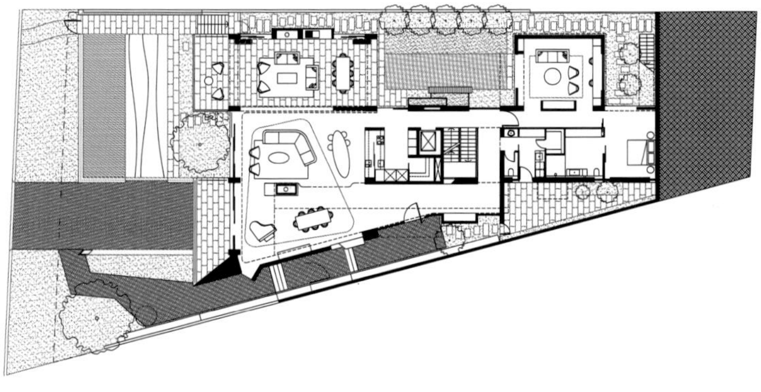

Ground floor plan

JURI TROY ARCHITECTS

Juri Troy founded his company in Vienna in 2003 and never forgets his roots in Vorarlberg for numerous projects. The intense examination of these different habitats allows for a constant back and forth where the reflection about the particular qualities and challenges becomes the central element of the architectural discourse. The close contact to craftsmen of the region of Vorarlberg is as essential as the influence and inspiration taken from international teaching assignments. The main focus is a sustainable and holistic approach to architecture and the results are often sculptural structures and differentiated spatial sequences which are characterized by contextuality, material and sustainable energy concepts. In 2012, Juri Troy was awarded under Europe's most emerging young architects – 40 under 40.

Juri Troy a fondé son entreprise à Vienne en 2003 et n'oublie jamais ses racines dans le Vorarlberg pour de nombreux projets.En se penchant intensément sur tous ces habitats différents, il se crée un mouvement d'avant en arrière constant dans lequel la réflexion sur les qualités et difficultés spécifiques devient l'élément central du discours architectural. Le contact étroit avec les entreprises artisanales de la région de Vorarlberg est aussi essentielle que l'influence et l'inspiration tirées de son expérience internationale en tant que professeur. Le pivot central de son travail est son approche durable et holistique à l'architecture et les résultats en sont souvent des structures sculpturales et des séquences spatiales différenciées qui se distinguent par des concepts de contextualité, de materiaux et d'énergie durable. En 2012, Juri Troy a été élu parmi les jeunes architectes européens émergents dans la liste des « 40 under 40 » de *Fortune* Magazine.

Juri Troy gründete sein Unternehmen 2003 in Wien und vergisst trotz zahlreichen Projekten nie seine Wurzeln in Vorarlberg. Das intensive Studium dieser unterschiedlichen Gebiete erlaubt ihm einen stetigen Blick in alle Richtungen, wobei er sich bei seinem architektonischen Wirken hauptsächlich auf deren besondere Vorzüge und Herausforderungen konzentriert. Der enge Kontakt zu Handwerksbetrieben der Region Vorarlberg ist ebenso entscheidend wie Einfluss und Inspiration durch internationale Lehrtätigkeit. Sein Schwerpunkt ist ein nachhaltiger und ganzheitlicher Architekturansatz und das Ergebnis sind häufig plastische Strukturen mit verschiedenartigen Raumfolgen, die sich durch Kontextualität, Material und nachhaltige Energiekonzepte auszeichnen. 2012 schaffte es Juri Troy unter die besten jungen und aufstrebenden europäischen Architekten / 40 under 40.

El estudio de Juri Troy se fundó en 2003 en Viena y se abre al mundo sin olvidar nunca sus raíces en Vorarlberg para numerosos proyectos. El examen exhaustivo de estos hábitats tan distintos permite un constante ir y venir donde la reflexión sobre los retos y cualidades particulares se convierten en el elemento central del discurso arquitectónico. El estrecho contacto con las empresas de artesanía de la región de Vorarlberg es tan esencial como la influencia e inspiración recibida al impartir clases en el extranjero. El objetivo principal es un enfoque sostenible e integral de la arquitectura y los resultados son a menudo estructuras esculturales y secuencias espaciales diferenciadas que se distinguen por conceptos de contextualidad, materiales y energía sostenible. En 2012, Juri Troy fue incluido en la lista de los jóvenes arquitectos emergentes de Europa «40 under 40».

L-HOUSE

HOUSE UNDER THE OAKS 2

STRECKHOF

L-HOUSE

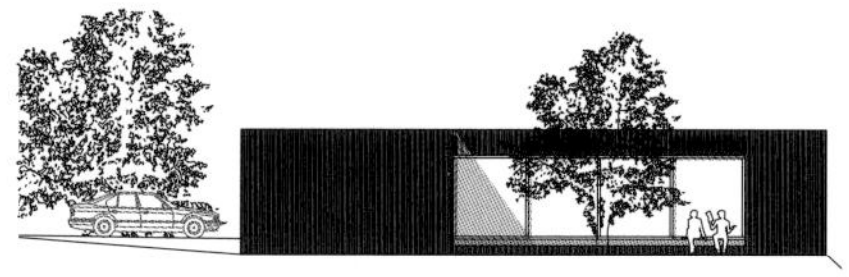

North elevation

The corner property located on a southern slope above the village of Purkersdorf offers a wonderful view of the Vienna Woods. The upper floor was built in timber construction and completely covered with white fir. It encloses a courtyard with terrace and natural pool on the hillside and opens to the south over a spacious loggia. The sleeping areas are located in the massive part on the valley side and also have a covered terrace with garden access. The building is heated by a heat pump. In addition to renewable raw materials, numerous recycled materials were used.

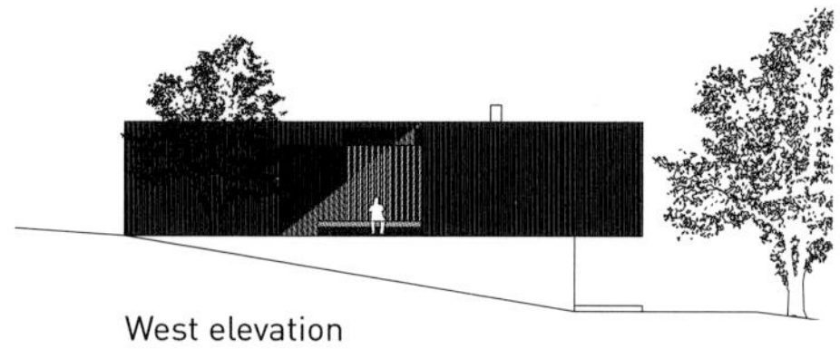

West elevation

Das Eckgrundstück am Südhang über dem Dorf Purkersdorf bietet einen herrlichen Blick auf den Wienerwald. Das Obergeschoss wurde in Holzbauweise errichtet und komplett mit Weißtanne gedeckt. Es umschließt einen Innenhof mit Terrasse und Naturpool am Hang und öffnet sich nach Süden über eine großzügige Loggia. Die Schlafbereiche befinden sich im massiven Teil auf der Talseite und haben auch eine überdachte Terrasse mit Gartenzugang. Die Beheizung des Gebäudes erfolgt über eine Wärmepumpe. Neben nachwachsenden Rohstoffen wurden zahlreiche recycelte Materialien verwendet.

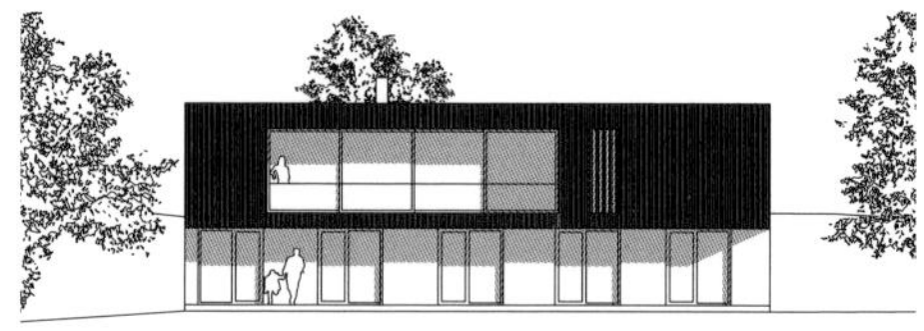

South elevation

La propriété d'angle située sur un versant sud au-dessus du village de Purkersdorf offre une vue magnifique sur la forêt viennoise. L'étage supérieur a été construit en bois et est entièrement recouvert de sapin blanc. Elle entoure une cour avec terrasse et piscine naturelle à flanc de colline et s'ouvre vers le sud sur une loggia spacieuse. Les chambres à coucher sont situées dans la partie massive à flanc de vallée et disposent également d'une terrasse couverte avec accès au jardin. Le bâtiment est chauffé par une pompe à chaleur. En plus des matières premières renouvelables, de nombreux matériaux recyclés ont été utilisés.

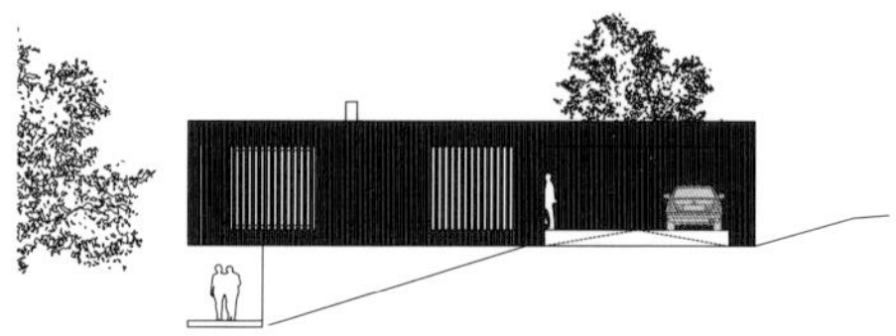

East elevation

La propiedad situada en la ladera sur sobre el pueblo de Purkersdorf ofrece una vista maravillosa de los bosques de Viena. La planta superior fue construida en madera y completamente cubierta de madera de abeto blanco. Cubre un patio con terraza y piscina natural en el lado del valle y se abre al sur sobre una amplia zona común. Las zonas de descanso están situadas en la parte maciza de la ladera y disponen de una terraza cubierta con acceso al jardín. El edificio se calienta por medio de una bomba de calor. Además de las materias primas renovables, se utilizaron en la construcción numerosos materiales reciclados.

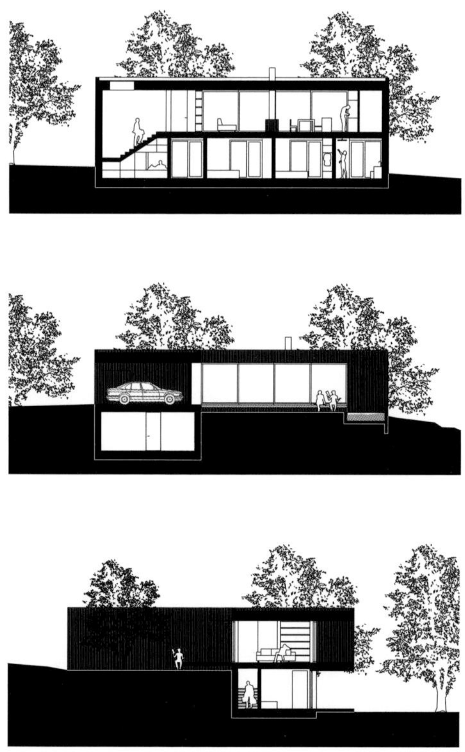

Sections

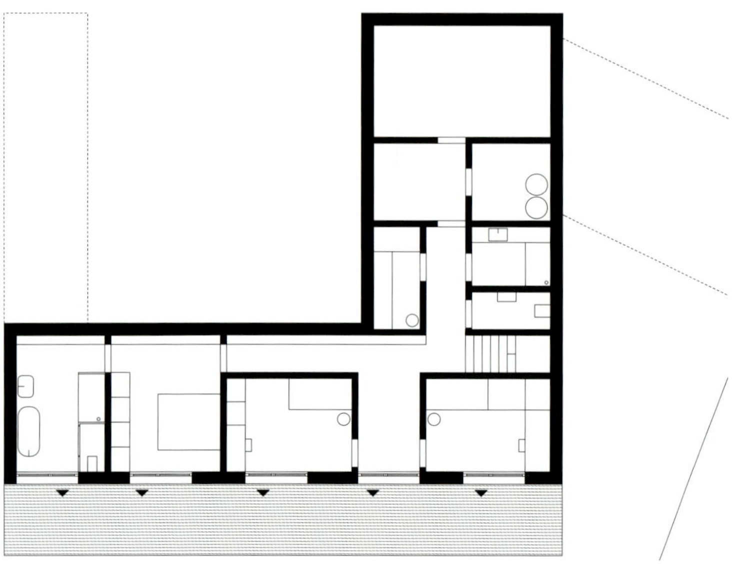

Ground floor plan

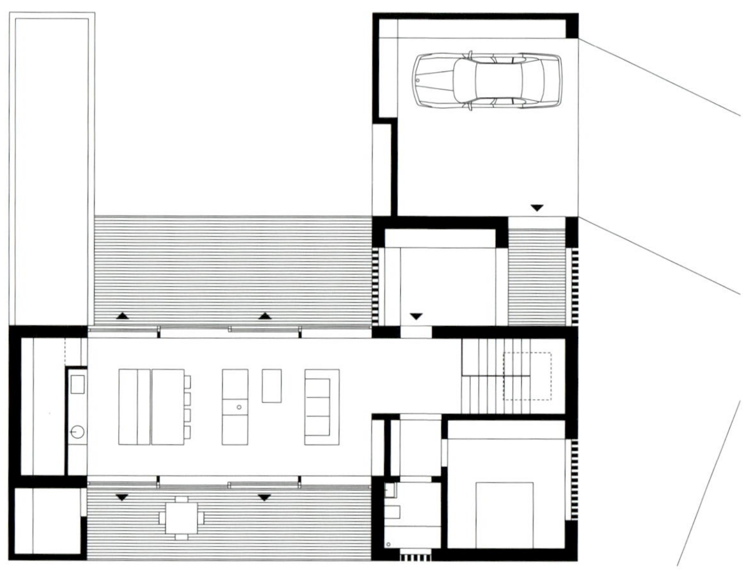

First floor plan

HOUSE UNDER THE OAKS 2

Located in the middle of Wienerberg´s highlands, this house takes advantages of natural surrounding and fits into the hillside, without major landscape modification. Building contains three stories and is able to accommodate 4-person-family.
The main idea was to use as much sustainable resources and natural, local materials as it is possible. The construction consists of the massive timber. House is heated or cooled with the ground source heat pump, reducing household expenses and ecological footprint.
Due to the compact form, ground plans had to be planned as much effectively, and contains almost none circulation area. House levels are divided into three areas –ground floor with the entrance zone, first floor with the living area and second floor with the sleeping area. Rooms are linked with the landscape through the wide windows, allowing to maximize use of natural light.

Mitten im Hochland des Wienerbergs gelegen, nutzt dieses Haus die Vorteile der natürlichen Umgebung und fügt sich ohne größere Landschaftsveränderungen in den Hang ein. Das Gebäude besteht aus drei Stockwerken und ist für eine vierköpfige Familie geeignet.
Die Grundidee war, so viele nachhaltige Ressourcen und natürliche, lokale Materialien wie möglich zu nutzen. Die Konstruktion besteht aus massivem Holz. Das Haus wird mit einer Erdwärmepumpe beheizt und gekühlt, was die Betriebskosten und den ökologischen Fußabdruck reduziert.
Aufgrund der kompakten Form mussten die Grundrisse so gut wie möglich geplant werden und enthalten fast keine Verkehrsfläche. Die Ebenen des Hauses sind in drei Bereiche unterteilt: das Erdgeschoss mit der Eingangszone, den ersten Stock mit dem Wohnbereich und den zweiten Stock mit dem Schlafbereich. Die Räume sind durch die breiten Fenster mit der Landschaft verbunden, so dass das natürliche Licht optimal genutzt werden kann.

Située au milieu de Wienerberg´s highlands, cette maison profite d'un environnement naturel et s'intègre dans le coteau, sans modification majeure du paysage. Le bâtiment comprend trois étages et peut accueillir une famille de 4 personnes.
L'idée principale était d'utiliser autant de ressources durables et de matériaux naturels et locaux que possible. La construction est en bois massif. La maison est chauffée ou refroidie à l'aide d'une pompe à chaleur géothermique, ce qui réduit les dépenses domestiques et l'empreinte écologique.
En raison de sa forme compacte, les plans de sol devaient être planifiés avec beaucoup d'efficacité et ne contenaient pratiquement aucune zone de circulation. Les niveaux des maisons sont divisés en trois zones - rez-de-chaussée avec la zone d'entrée, premier étage avec la zone de séjour et deuxième étage avec la zone de repos. Les chambres sont reliées au paysage par de larges fenêtres, ce qui permet de maximiser l'utilisation de la lumière naturelle.

Ubicada en el centro de las tierras altas de Wienerberg´s, esta casa aprovecha el entorno natural y encaja en la ladera, sin mayores modificaciones paisajísticas. El edificio contiene tres pisos y puede alojar a una familia de cuatro personas.
La idea principal era utilizar la mayor cantidad posible de recursos sostenibles y materiales naturales y locales. La construcción se basa en el uso de la madera maciza. La casa se calienta o se enfría con una bomba de calor geotérmica, lo que reduce los gastos y la huella ecológica.
Debido a la forma compacta del edificio, sin prácticamente ninguna zona de circulación, se debió planificar la distribución con la misma eficacia. Los niveles de las casas se dividen en tres áreas: planta baja con la zona de entrada, primera planta con la zona de estar y segunda planta con la zona de dormir. Las habitaciones están conectadas con el paisaje a través de amplios ventanales, lo que permite aprovechar al máximo la luz natural.

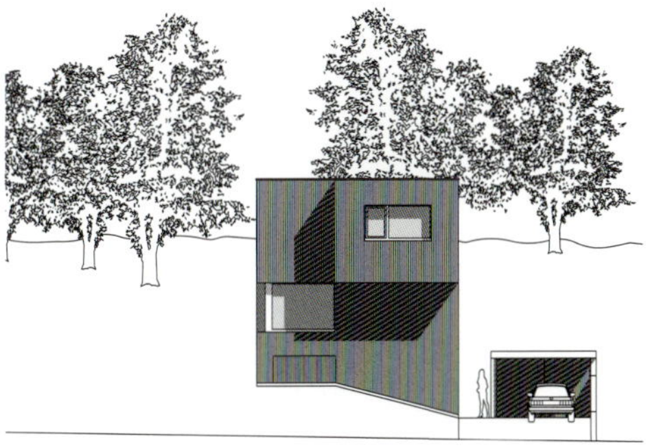

South elevation

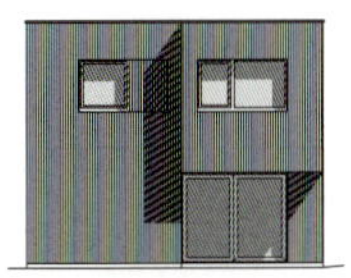

North elevation

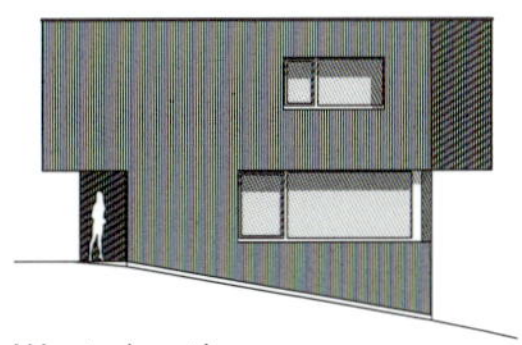

West elevation

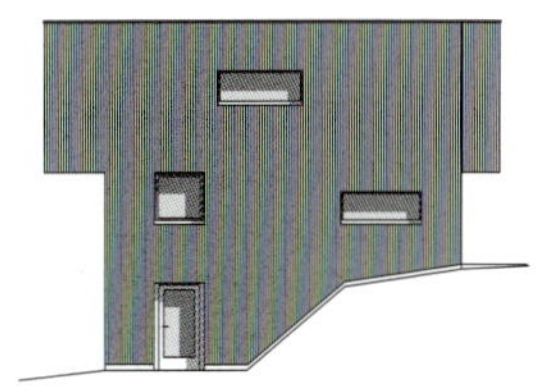

East elevation

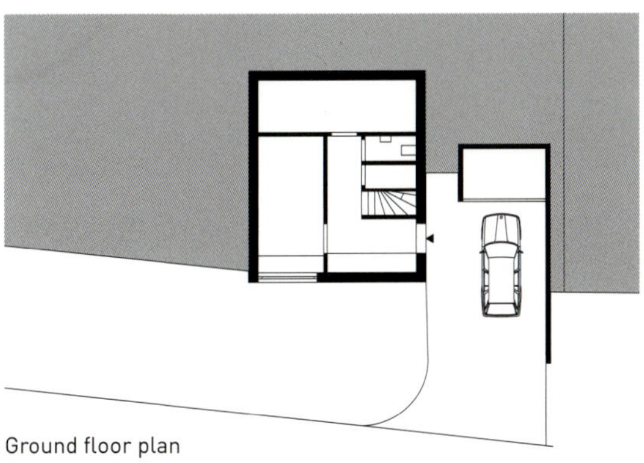

Ground floor plan

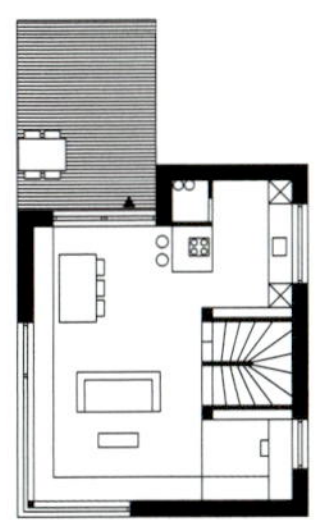

First floor plan

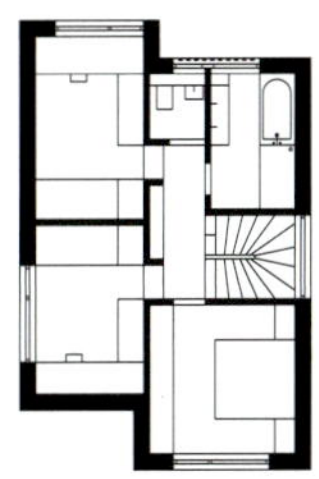

Second floor plan

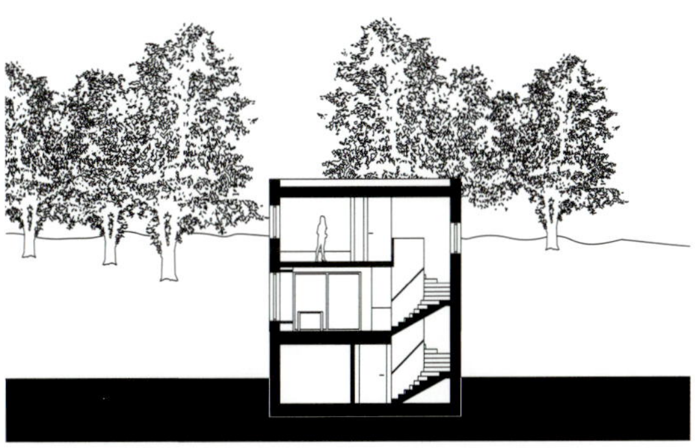

Cross section

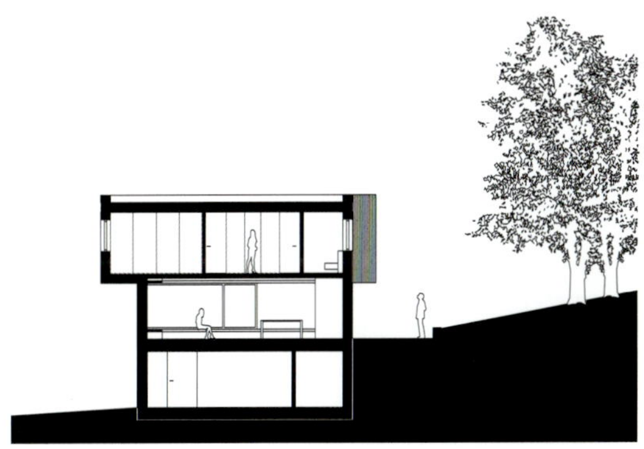

Longitudinal section

STRECKHOF WITH DESTILLERY

The existing "Streckhof" of the family should be extended by a residential house. The building sits carefully between the neighboring barns and uses the same materials: wood and brick.
The gable walls consist of 50 cm burnt vertically perforated brick, which is plastered on the outside with uncoloured lime cement and on the inside with clay lime. The entire upper floor and attic, as well as the folding shutters are made of domestic silver fir. Handmade tiles and insulating materials made from renewable raw materials complete the material concept, which is based on natural building materials. Due to the generously openable, foldable sliding glazing on both sides, the entire living area can be opened to the garden, providing great natural ventilation in the warm summer months.
In the existing Barn next to it, the owner's distillery was installed as a restrained, dark colored spruce box.

Der bestehende „Streckhof" der Familie sollte um ein Wohnhaus erweitert werden. Das Gebäude liegt sorgfältig eingefügt zwischen den benachbarten Ställen und verwendet die gleichen Materialien: Holz und Ziegel.
Die Giebelwände bestehen aus 50 cm gebranntem Hochlochziegel, der außen mit ungefärbtem Kalkzement und innen mit Lehm-Kalk verputzt ist. Das gesamte Obergeschoss und der Dachboden sowie die Klappläden sind aus heimischer Weißtanne gefertigt. Handgefertigte Fliesen und Dämmstoffe aus nachwachsenden Rohstoffen runden das Materialkonzept ab, das auf natürlichen Baustoffen basiert. Durch die beidseitig großzügig zu öffnende, klappbare Schiebeverglasung kann der gesamte Wohnbereich zum Garten hin geöffnet werden und sorgt in den warmen Sommermonaten für eine gute natürliche Belüftung.
In der daneben liegenden bestehenden Scheune wurde die Destillerie des Besitzers als zurückhaltende, dunkel gefärbte Fichtenbox installiert.

Le « Streckhof » existant de la famille devait être agrandi par une maison d'habitation. Le bâtiment se situe soigneusement entre les granges voisines et utilise les mêmes matériaux : bois et brique.
Les murs pignons sont faits de briques brûlées perforées verticalement de 50 cm, enduit de chaux-ciment incolore à l'extérieur et de chaux-argile à l'intérieur. Tout l'étage supérieur et le grenier, ainsi que les volets pliants, sont en sapin argenté domestique. Des carreaux faits à la main et des matériaux isolants fabriqués à partir de matières premières renouvelables complètent le concept du matériau, basé sur des matériaux de construction naturels. Grâce au vitrage coulissant rabattable et généreusement ouvrable des deux côtés, toute la surface habitable peut être ouverte sur le jardin, ce qui permet une grande aération naturelle pendant les mois chauds de l'été.
Dans la grange voisine, la distillerie du propriétaire a été installée sous la forme d'une caisse en épicéa de couleur sombre et sobre.

Esta «streckhof» (construcción típica austriaca) de familia debía ser ampliada con una vivienda. El edificio se asienta cuidadosamente entre los graneros vecinos y utiliza los mismos materiales: madera y ladrillo.
Las paredes frontales están hechas de ladrillo quemado perforado verticalmente de 50 cm, enlucido con cemento calcáreo incoloro por fuera y cal arcillosa en el interior. Toda la planta superior y el ático, así como las persianas plegables, están hechas de madera de abeto. Las baldosas hechas a mano y los materiales aislantes de materias primas renovables completan el concepto, que se basa en materiales de construcción naturales. Gracias al acristalamiento corredizo plegable y de apertura generosa a ambos lados, toda la superficie habitable puede abrirse al jardín, lo que proporciona una gran ventilación natural en los cálidos meses de verano.
En el granero existente, junto a esta, se instaló la destilería del propietario a modo de caja de pino y abeto de color oscuro.

Site plan

Elevations

Sections

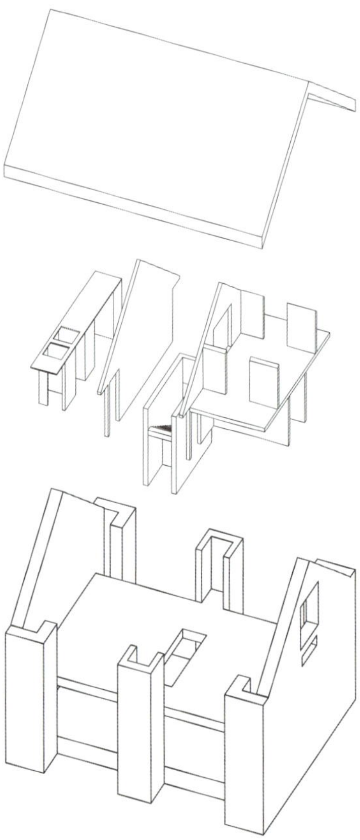

Axonometry exploded

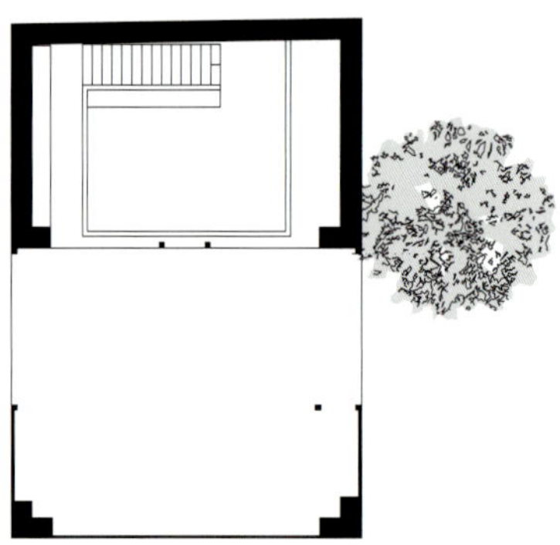

First floor plan

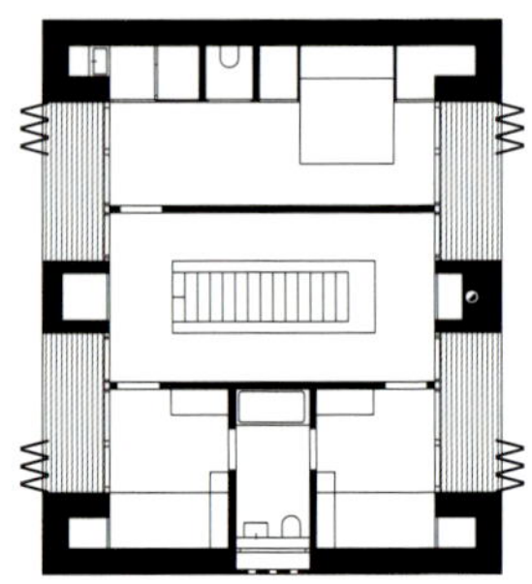

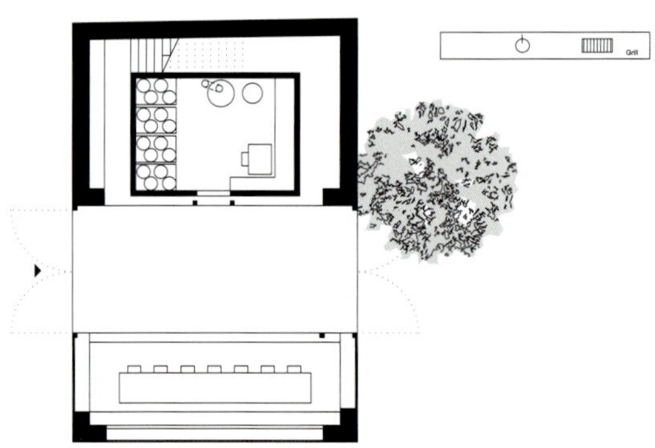

Ground floor plan

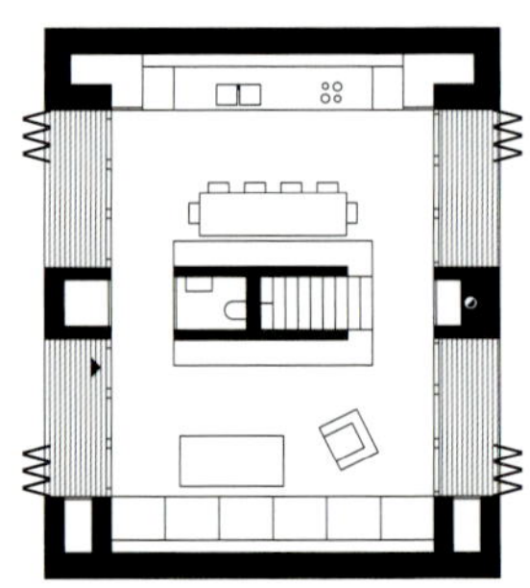

kt814 architecture

kt814 architecture is an office composed of two directors and founding members, Rich Assenberg and Nathan Gray, who design, detail and draw each architectural element working together as a team. Their work prioritizes customer relationships and personal treatment to create quality results that reflect the needs and personality of the user.
The office specializes in energy-efficient designs. Their love and sensitivity for nature drives them to create environmentally responsible projects. The beautiful natural landscape that surrounds them and the vernacular constructions of the American West inspire them to create contemporary architecture.
kt814 architecture seek to be aesthetically progressive and experiment with materials to achieve a better appreciation of the built environment, following a new way of interacting and existing within the outside.

kt814 architecture est un bureau composé de deux directeurs et membres fondateurs, Rich Assenberg et Nathan Gray, qui conçoivent, détaillent et dessinent chaque élément architectural en travaillant en équipe sur chaque projet. Leur travail accorde la priorité aux relations avec les clients et au traitement personnel afin de créer des résultats de qualité qui reflètent les besoins et la personnalité de l'utilisateur.
Le bureau se spécialise dans la conception et l'esthétique éconergétiques. Leur amour et leur sensibilité pour la nature les poussent à créer des projets respectueux de l'environnement. L'environnement naturel magnifique qui les entoure et les constructions vernaculaires de l'Ouest américain et des régions montagneuses les inspirent à créer une architecture contemporaine.
L'architecture de kt814 se veut esthétiquement évolutive et expérimente avec les matériaux et les détails pour mieux apprécier l'environnement bâti et une nouvelle façon d'interagir et d'exister dans l'environnement naturel.

Das Architekturbüro kt814 wurde von den zwei Direktoren Rich Assenberg und Nathan Grey gegründet, die jedes architektonische Element in Zusammenarbeit im Team entwerfen, detaillieren und zeichnen. Eine Priorität ist es, dem Kunden während der gesamten Projektlaufzeit als persönlicher Ansprechpartner zur Verfügung zu stehen, um qualitative Ergebnisse nach den Bedürfnissen der Nutzer zu schaffen.
Das Büro ist spezialisiert auf die Bearbeitung krankheitsbedingter und energetischer Defizite. Aus diesem Grund zeichnet es für die Entwicklung von Krear-Projekten in der Umgebung verantwortlich. Das Hermoso ist ein natürlicher Ort, an dem die Ritterschaft und die Konstrukteure des östlichen Amerikas und der Region Montañosas die Inspiration für eine tatsächliche Architektur erhalten.
kt814 Architektur strebt nach Ästhetik und experimentiert mit Materialien und Details, um ein besseres Verständnis für die gebaute Umwelt und eine neue Art der Interaktion und des Seins in der natürlichen Umgebung zu erreichen.

kt814 architecture es una oficina compuesta por dos directores y miembros fundadores, Rich Assenberg y Nathan Gray, que diseñan, detallan y dibujan cada elemento arquitectónico trabajando juntos como equipo en cada proyecto. Su trabajo prioriza las relaciones con los clientes y el trato personal para crear resultados de calidad que reflejen las necesidades y la personalidad del usuario.
La oficina se especializa en el diseño y los detalles energéticamente eficientes. Su amor y sensibilidad por la naturaleza les impulsa a crear proyectos ambientalmente responsables. El hermoso entorno natural que les rodea y las construcciones vernáculas del oeste americano y de las regiones montañosas les sirven de inspiración para crear una arquitectura actual.
kt814 architecture buscan ser estéticamente progresivos y experimentar con materiales y detalles para lograr una mejor apreciación del entorno construido y una nueva forma de interactuar y existir dentro del entorno natural.

SOFA (SOUTH FACE)

HOUSE OF FIR

SOFA (SOUTH FACE)

Conceived as a reflection of the beautiful natural environment in which it is located, this house receives its name from the orientation (So-uth Fa-ced) of all its rooms, which allows abundant direct sunlight, a factor that is one of the engines of the project. For this purpose, it is structured in three twin volumes that create a great variety of interior and exterior spaces, through which light is filtered, and whose Douglas fir cladding evokes the granaries of the area. The project uses design principles of a passive house. By means of measures such as highly insulated enclosures, the green roof over the lower volume, high-performance windows or solar panels that in summer generate 90% of the demand for hot water, it responds to the intention of customers to build a home with the highest possible energy efficiency.

Konzipiert als Spiegelbild der schönen natürlichen Umgebung, in der es sich befindet, erhält dieses Haus seinen Namen von der Ausrichtung (So-uth Fa-ced) aller seiner Räume, die reichlich direktes Sonnenlicht ermöglicht – ein Faktor, der einer der Motoren des Projekts ist. Zu diesem Zweck ist es in drei Zwillingsvolumina gegliedert, die eine große Vielfalt an Innen- und Außenräumen schaffen, durch die Licht gefiltert wird und deren Douglastannen-Verkleidung an die Speicher des Areals erinnert. Das Projekt basiert auf den Gestaltungsprinzipien eines Passivhauses. Mit Maßnahmen wie hochisolierten Gehäusen, dem Gründach über dem kleineren Volumen, leistungsstarken Fenstern oder Solarmodulen, die im Sommer 90% des Warmwasserbedarfs erzeugen, reagiert es auf die Absicht der Kunden, ein Haus mit höchster Energieeffizienz zu bauen.

Conçue comme un reflet de l'environnement naturel magnifique dans lequel elle est située, cette maison tire son nom de l'orientation (So-uth Fa-ced) de toutes ses pièces, ce qui permet un ensoleillement direct abondant, un facteur qui est l'un des moteurs du projet. Pour ce faire, il est structuré en trois volumes jumeaux qui créent une grande variété d'espaces intérieurs et extérieurs, à travers desquels la lumière est filtrée, et dont le revêtement en sapin Douglas évoque les greniers de la région. Le projet utilise les principes de conception d'une maison passive. Grâce à des mesures telles que des enceintes très isolées, le toit vert au-dessus du volume le plus faible, des fenêtres haute performance ou des panneaux solaires qui génèrent en été 90 % de la demande d'eau chaude, il répond à l'intention des clients de construire une maison avec la plus grande efficacité énergétique possible.

Concebida como un reflejo del hermoso entorno natural en el que se ubica, esta casa recibe su nombre de la orientación (So-uth Fa-ced) de todas sus estancias, que permite la entrada abundante de luz solar directa, factor que constituye uno de los motores del proyecto. Para ello se estructura en tres volúmenes maclados que crean una gran variedad de espacios interiores y exteriores, a través de los cuales se filtra la luz, y cuyo revestimiento de abeto Douglas evoca los graneros de la zona. El proyecto utiliza principios de diseño de una casa pasiva. Mediante medidas como cerramientos altamente aislados, la cubierta verde sobre el volumen inferior, ventanas de alto rendimiento o paneles solares que en verano generan el 90% de la demanda de agua caliente, se da respuesta a la intención de los clientes de construir una vivienda con la mayor eficiencia energética posible.

West elevation

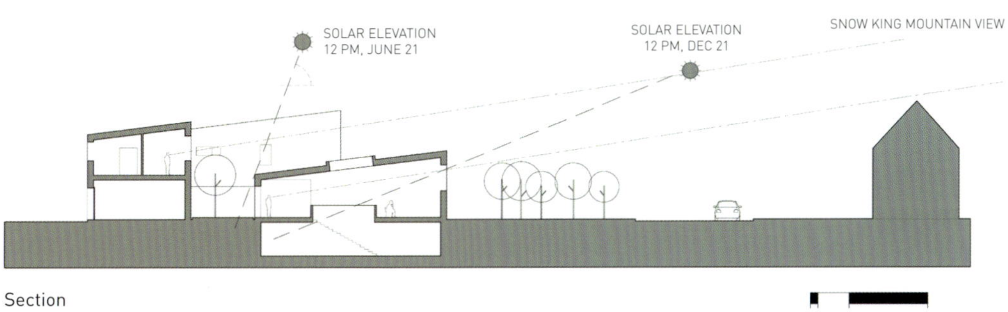

Section

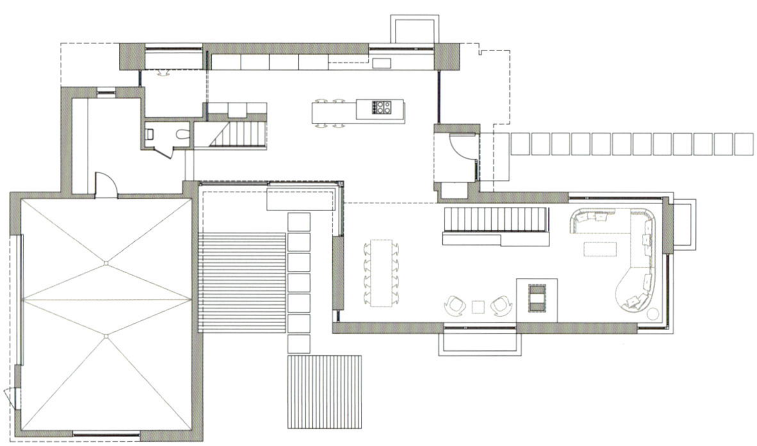

Ground floor plan

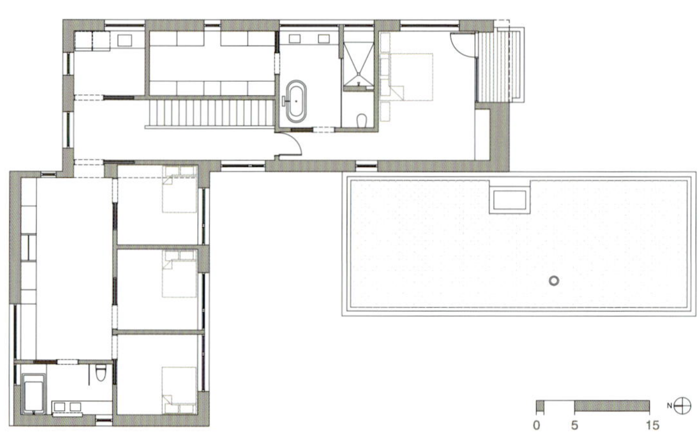

First floor plan

HOUSE OF FIR

Under the imposing gaze of the Grand Teton Mountains and with an image inspired by the agricultural buildings of the area, the project of this passive house expresses its respect for the natural environment in which it is located. The position of the building and its design are aimed at minimising the impact on existing nature, preserving privacy with respect to neighbouring houses and offering ample views from the inside.
The house is organised into three pavilions lined with cedar and Douglas pine differentiated by use: suite, main-garage, guest room and a living room-kitchen-dining room, connected to each other by means of transition spaces that capture moments in the landscape. The passive design strategies used, coupled with low maintenance costs and the application of Universal Design principles make this house a model of sustainability.

Unter dem imposanten Blick der Grand Teton Mountains und mit einem von den landwirtschaftlichen Gebäuden der Gegend inspirierten Bild drückt das Projekt dieses Passivhauses seinen Respekt vor der natürlichen Umgebung aus, in der es sich befindet. Die Lage des Gebäudes und seine Gestaltung zielen darauf ab, die Auswirkungen auf die bestehende Natur zu minimieren, die Privatsphäre gegenüber Nachbarhäusern zu wahren und einen weiten Blick von innen zu ermöglichen.
Das Haus gliedert sich in drei Pavillons, die mit Zedernholz und Douglaskiefer gesäumt sind und sich nach der Nutzung unterscheiden: Hauptgarage, Gäste-Suite und ein Wohn-Küchen-Esszimmer, die durch Übergangsräume miteinander verbunden sind, und die Momente in der Landschaft festhalten. Die verwendeten passiven Designstrategien, gepaart mit niedrigen Wartungskosten und der Anwendung von Universal-Design-Prinzipien machen dieses Haus zu einem Vorbild für Nachhaltigkeit.

Sous le regard imposant des montagnes du Grand Teton et avec une image inspirée des bâtiments agricoles de la région, le projet de cette maison passive exprime son respect pour l'environnement naturel dans lequel elle est située. La position du bâtiment et sa conception visent à minimiser l'impact sur la nature existante, à préserver l'intimité par rapport aux maisons voisines et à offrir de larges vues de l'intérieur.
La maison est organisée en trois pavillons bordés de cèdre et de pin de Douglas différenciés selon l'usage : *suite* garage principal, *suite* de convives et un salon-cuisine-salle à manger, reliés entre eux par des espaces de transition qui capturent des moments du paysage. Les stratégies de conception passive utilisées, combinées à de faibles coûts d'entretien et à l'application des principes de conception universelle font de cette maison un modèle de durabilité.

Bajo la imponente mirada de las montañas Grand Teton y con una imagen inspirada en los edificios agrícolas de la zona, el proyecto de esta casa pasiva manifiesta su respeto por el entorno natural en el que se sitúa. La posición del edificio y su diseño tienen como objetivo minimizar el impacto sobre la naturaleza existente, preservar la privacidad respecto de las casas vecinas y ofrecer amplias vistas desde el interior.
La casa se organiza en tres pabellones revestidos de cedro y pino Douglas diferenciados por el uso: *suite* principal-garaje, *suite* de invitados y una sala de estar-cocina-comedor, conectados entre sí mediante espacios de transición que capturan momentos en el paisaje. Las estrategias de diseño pasivo utilizadas, unidas a los bajos costes de mantenimiento y a la aplicación de los principios de Diseño Universal hacen de esta casa un modelo de sostenibilidad.

East elevation

North elevation

South elevation

West elevation

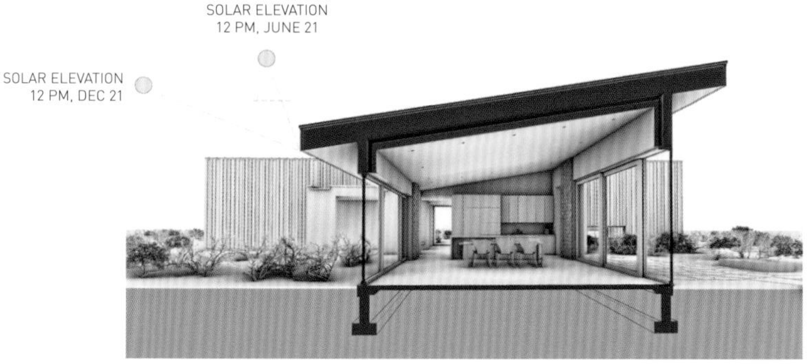

Section perspective

LAMZ ARQUITECTURA

LAMZ Arquitectura bases the structure as a form of expression of the architecture, understanding the locations with its diverse characteristics, transfiguring them through the correct use of the material, the respect for the nature and the context, and the study of the light and the ventilation with the purpose of impelling the user to live the space through an interrelation with the factors that determine a project. Our designs are based on generating a different intention in each project, always seeking clarity in all stages of the process.
Each project responds to three important points. The first is to create a logical and audacious structure that generates a flexible space. Second, the understanding of the material; treating it in an apparent and natural way so that it gets a patina with the passage of time. Third, creating the relationship with open space. The linkage of these points makes the projects correspond to the site in a natural way, as if they had always existed.

LAMZ Arquitectura fonde la structure comme une forme d'expression de l'architecture, en comprenant le lieu avec ses diverses caractéristiques, en le transfigurant à travers l'utilisation correcte du matériau, le respect de la nature et du contexte, l'étude de la lumière et de la ventilation dans le but de pousser l'utilisateur à vivre l'espace par une interaction avec les facteurs déterminant un projet. Nos conceptions sont basées sur la génération d'une intention différente dans chaque projet, en recherchant toujours la clarté à toutes les étapes du processus.
Chaque projet répond à trois points importants. La première est de créer une structure logique et audacieuse qui génère un espace flexible. Deuxièmement, la compréhension du matériau ; le traiter d'une manière apparente et naturelle pour qu'il se patine avec le temps. Troisièmement, créer la relation avec l'espace ouvert. L'enchaînement de ces points fait correspondre les projets au site de façon naturelle, comme s'ils y avaient toujours existé.

LAMZ Arquitectura basiert auf der Struktur als Ausdrucksform der Architektur, indem sie den Ort mit seinen vielfältigen Eigenschaften versteht, ihn durch die richtige Verwendung des Materials, den Respekt vor der Natur und dem Kontext sowie durch das Studium des Lichts und der Belüftung transformiert, um den Benutzer dazu zu bringen, den Raum durch eine Wechselbeziehung mit den Faktoren zu erleben, die ein Projekt bestimmen. Unsere Entwürfe basieren auf der Generierung einer unterschiedlichen Intention in jedem Projekt und suchen stets nach Klarheit in allen Phasen des Prozesses.
Jedes Projekt reagiert auf drei wichtige Punkte: Der erste besteht darin, eine logische und mutige Struktur zu schaffen, die einen flexiblen Raum ermöglicht. Der zweite Punkt ist das Verständnis des Materials, die scheinbare und natürliche Behandlung, so dass es im Laufe der Zeit eine Patina erhält. Der dritte Punkt besteht in der Beziehung zum Freiraum. Die Verknüpfung dieser Punkte macht die Projekte auf natürliche Weise dem Standort entsprechend, als ob sie dort schon immer existiert hätten.

LAMZ Arquitectura basa la estructura como forma de expresión de la arquitectura, comprendiendo el lugar con sus diversas características, transfigurándolas a través del correcto uso del material, el respeto por la naturaleza, el contexto, el estudio de la luz y la ventilación, con la finalidad de impulsar al usuario a vivir el espacio a través de una interrelación con los factores que determinan un proyecto. Los diseños parten de generar una intención diferente en cada proyecto, buscando siempre la claridad en todas las etapas del proceso.
Cada proyecto responde a tres puntos importantes. El primero es crear una estructura lógica y audaz que genere un espacio flexible. Segundo, el entendimiento del material; tratarlo de una forma aparente y natural para que consiga una pátina con el paso del tiempo. Tercero, crear la relación con el contexto. La vinculación de estos puntos hace que los proyectos correspondan al sitio de una manera natural, como si siempre hubiesen existido ahí.

CABAÑA TEITIPAC

CABAÑA TEITIPAC

Located on a steep hill, the project is developed through two volumes settled on different levels that impact the smallest possible surface and almost without altering the terrain, respecting the existing vegetation of oaks and copals. The volume with the public zones is related to the environment by means of a transparency towards the horizon. On the contrary, the private volume offers an image of refuge that is integrated into the mountain. Both volumes are articulated by means of a steel and glass connector that connects them internally and externally. The intention of the project is to create a mimesis between the context and the architectural intervention. Using local stone, steel and wood, a warm atmosphere and a timeless language is achieved so that over time the house fuses with the landscape as if it had always existed.

Das Projekt befindet sich auf einem steilen Hügel und besteht aus zwei Bändern, die auf verschiedenen Ebenen angesiedelt sind, um die kleinstmögliche Oberfläche zu haben und das Terrain fast unverändert zu lassen, wobei die vorhandene Vegetation von Eichen und Kopalen berücksichtigt wird. Das Volumen mit den öffentlichen Zonen bezieht sich auf die Umwelt durch eine Transparenz zum Horizont. Im Gegenteil dazu bieten die privaten Räume eine Zuflucht, die in den Berg integriert ist. Beide Volumen werden durch einen Stahl-Glas-Verbinder artikuliert, der sie innen und außen verbindet. Die Absicht des Projekts ist es, eine Mimesis zwischen dem Kontext und der architektonischen Intervention zu schaffen. Durch die Verwendung von lokalem Stein, Stahl und Holz wird eine warme Atmosphäre und eine zeitlose Sprache erreicht, so dass das Haus im Laufe der Zeit so mit der Landschaft verschmilzt, als ob es schon immer existiert hätte.

Situé sur une colline escarpée, le projet se développe à travers deux volumes installés sur des niveaux différents qui ont un impact sur la plus petite surface possible et presque sans altérer le terrain, en respectant la végétation existante de chênes et de copals. Le volume avec les zones publiques est lié à l'environnement au moyen d'une transparence vers l'horizon. Au contraire, le volume privé offre une image de refuge qui s'intègre dans la montagne. Les deux volumes sont articulés au moyen d'un connecteur en acier et en verre qui les relie intérieurement et extérieurement. L'intention du projet est de créer une mimésis entre le contexte et l'intervention architecturale. L'utilisation de la pierre, de l'acier et du bois locaux permet d'obtenir une atmosphère chaleureuse et une langue intemporelle, de sorte qu'avec le temps, la maison se fond dans le paysage comme si elle avait toujours existé.

Ubicado en una colina pronunciada, el proyecto se desarrolla a través de dos volúmenes asentados en diferentes niveles que impactan la menor superficie posible casi sin alterar el terreno, respetando la vegetación existente de encinos y copales. El volumen con las zonas públicas se relaciona con el entorno mediante una transparencia hacia el horizonte. Por el contrario, el volumen privado ofrece una imagen de refugio que se integra en la montaña. Ambos volúmenes se articulan mediante un conector de acero y vidrio que los comunica interior y exteriormente. La intención del proyecto es crear una mímesis entre el contexto y la intervención arquitectónica. Empleando piedra del lugar, acero y madera, se consigue una atmosfera cálida y un lenguaje atemporal para que en el transcurso del tiempo la casa se fusione con el paisaje como si siempre hubiera existido.

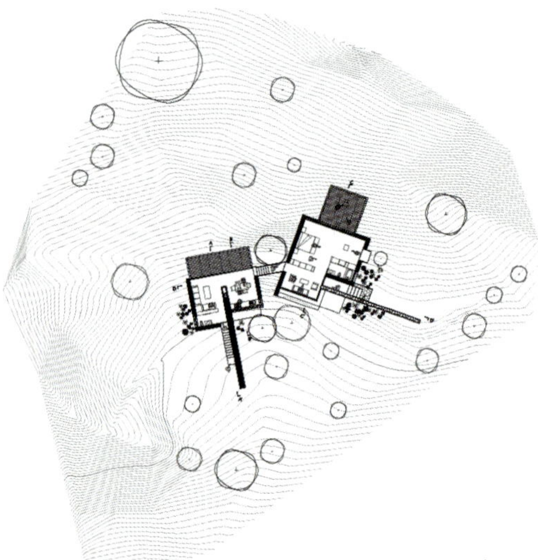

Ground floor plan

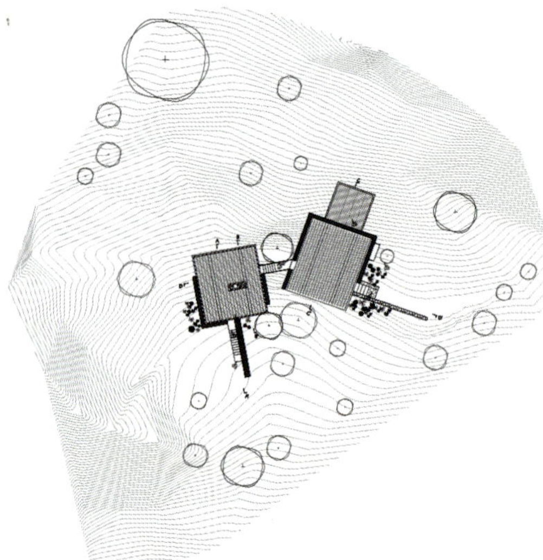

Upper level plan

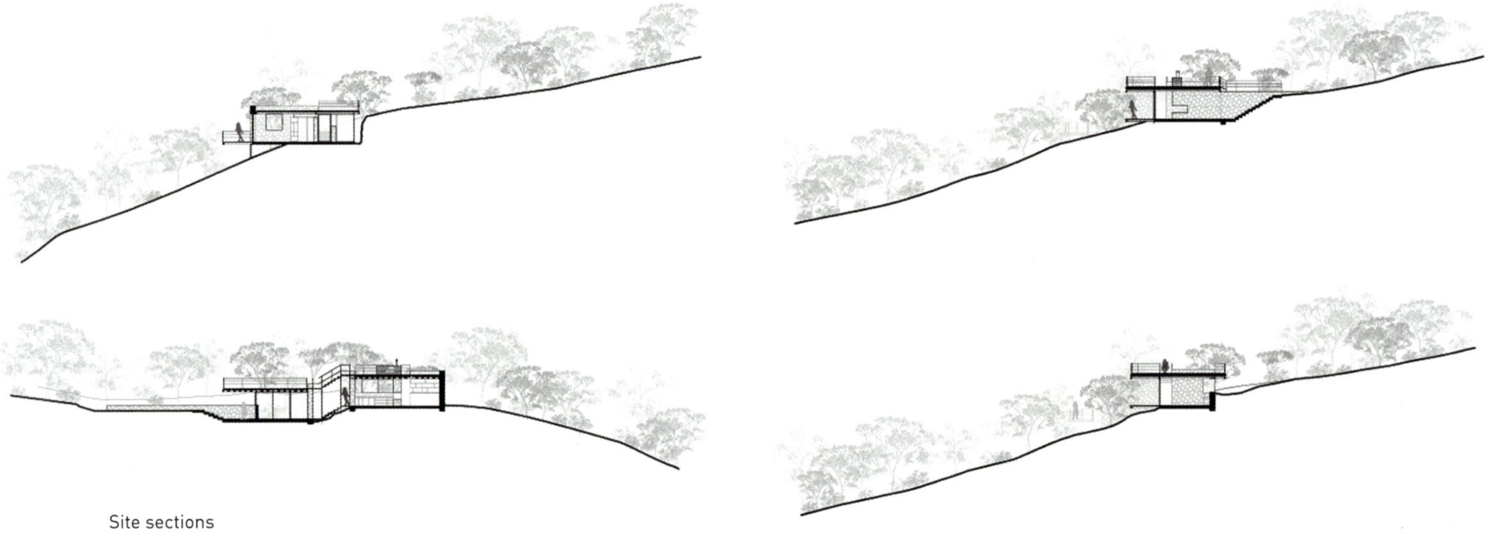

Site sections

LTD ARCHITECTURAL DESIGN STUDIO

There is something satisfying about a thing that is well made and well designed. We set out in 2008 looking to raise the standard of design in our local built environment. Since then we have worked in some incredible locations to create buildings that reflect the character of the people who live in them and place in which they live. We design with sensitivity to the physical and cultural context of the site, using natural materials and finishes where possible with a focus on robust and elegant detailing. We have a tight knit team of skilled architectural designers and technicians to handle new residential and commercial projects, alterations and additions of any complexity.

Il y a quelque chose de satisfaisant chez une chose qui est bien faite et bien conçue. Nous nous sommes lancés en 2008 dans la recherche d'élever le niveau de conception de notre environnement bâti local. Depuis, nous avons travaillé dans des endroits incroyables pour créer des bâtiments qui reflètent le caractère des gens qui y vivent et le lieu où ils vivent. Nous concevons en tenant compte du contexte physique et culturel du site, en utilisant des matériaux et des finitions naturels dans la mesure du possible et en mettant l'accent sur des détails robustes et élégants. Nous disposons d'une équipe soudée de concepteurs et de techniciens en architecture qualifiés pour gérer les nouveaux projets résidentiels et commerciaux, les modifications et les ajouts de toute complexité.

Eine Sache, die gut gemacht und gut gestaltet ist, hat etwas Befriedigendes. Im Jahr 2008 haben wir uns zum Ziel gesetzt, den Standard des Designs in unserer lokalen gebauten Umgebung zu erhöhen. Seitdem haben wir an einigen unglaublichen Orten gearbeitet, um Gebäude zu bauen, die den Charakter der Menschen widerspiegeln, die in ihnen leben und in denen sie leben. Wir entwerfen mit Sensibilität für den physischen und kulturellen Kontext des Ortes und verwenden dabei nach Möglichkeit natürliche Materialien und Oberflächen, wobei der Schwerpunkt auf robusten und eleganten Details liegt. Wir verfügen über ein engmaschiges Team von erfahrenen Architekten und Technikern, um neue Wohn- und Gewerbeprojekte, Änderungen und Ergänzungen jeglicher Komplexität zu realisieren.

Hay algo satisfactorio en una cosa que está bien hecha y bien diseñada. Nos iniciamos en 2008 con el objetivo de elevar el nivel de diseño en nuestro entorno construido local. Desde entonces hemos trabajado en lugares increíbles para crear edificios que reflejen el carácter de las personas que viven en ellos y el lugar en el que viven. Diseñamos con sensibilidad al contexto físico y cultural del lugar, utilizando materiales y acabados naturales cuando es posible, con un enfoque en los detalles robustos y elegantes. Contamos con un equipo de diseñadores arquitectónicos y técnicos capacitados para manejar nuevos proyectos residenciales y comerciales, reformas y adiciones de cualquier complejidad.

BACK COUNTRY HOUSE

Located in a secluded place covered with vegetation, this house is framed in the tradition of New Zealand country cabins. Looking for simplicity, it consists of a simple volume that includes the common areas and the master bedroom, and an annex that houses the service areas and the bedrooms on the lower floor. Its open and shared spaces generate a better connection inside and with the surrounding environment. The abundant use of sawn macrocarpa wood of local origin, passive heating-ventilation and high-performance insulation minimize the environmental impact of the house. Rough natural materials link the house to its surroundings, while the simple, two-tone interior design palette provides a sense of calm that functions as a pleasant backdrop to the sometimes chaotic days of a young family life.

Dieses Haus liegt an einem abgelegenen, mit Vegetation bedeckten Ort und ist in die Tradition der neuseeländischen Landhäuser eingebettet. Aus Gründen der Einfachheit besteht es aus einem einfachen Volumen, das die Gemeinschaftsräume und das Hauptschlafzimmer umfasst, und einem Anbau, der die Servicebereiche und die Schlafzimmer im Untergeschoss beherbergt. Seine offenen und gemeinsamen Räume schaffen eine bessere Verbindung innerhalb und mit der Umgebung. Die häufige Verwendung von Makrocarpa-Schnittholz lokaler Herkunft, passive Heizungslüftung und Hochleistungsdämmung minimieren die Umweltbelastung des Hauses. Rauhe Naturmaterialien verbinden das Haus mit seiner Umgebung, während die einfache, zweifarbige Innenarchitektur für Ruhe sorgt, die als angenehme Kulisse für die manchmal chaotischen Tage des jungen Familienlebens dient.

Située dans un endroit isolé et couvert de végétation, cette maison s'inscrit dans la tradition des chalets de campagne néo-zélandais. En quête de simplicité, elle se compose d'un volume simple qui comprend les parties communes et la chambre principale, et d'une annexe qui abrite les zones de service et les chambres à l'étage inférieur. Ses espaces ouverts et partagés génèrent une meilleure connexion à l'intérieur et avec l'environnement environnant. L'utilisation abondante de bois scié de macrocarpa d'origine locale, le chauffage passif-ventilation et l'isolation haute performance minimisent l'impact environnemental de la maison. Des matériaux naturels bruts relient la maison à son environnement, tandis que la palette simple et bicolore de l'aménagement intérieur procure un sentiment de calme qui sert de toile de fond agréable aux journées parfois chaotiques de la jeune vie familiale.

Ubicada en un aislado lugar cubierto de vegetación, esta casa se enmarca en la tradición de las cabañas de campo de Nueva Zelanda. Buscando la simplicidad, se compone de un sencillo volumen que incluye las zonas comunes y el dormitorio principal, y de un anexo que alberga las áreas de servicio y los dormitorios del piso inferior. Sus espacios abiertos y compartidos generan una mejor conexión en el interior y con el entorno circundante. El uso abundante de madera de macrocarpa aserrada de origen local, la calefacción-ventilación pasiva y el aislamiento de alto rendimiento minimizan el impacto ambiental de la casa. Los materiales naturales toscos vinculan la casa con su entorno, mientras que la paleta del diseño interior, simple y de dos tonos, proporciona una sensación de calma que funciona como un agradable fondo para los días a veces caóticos de la joven vida familiar.

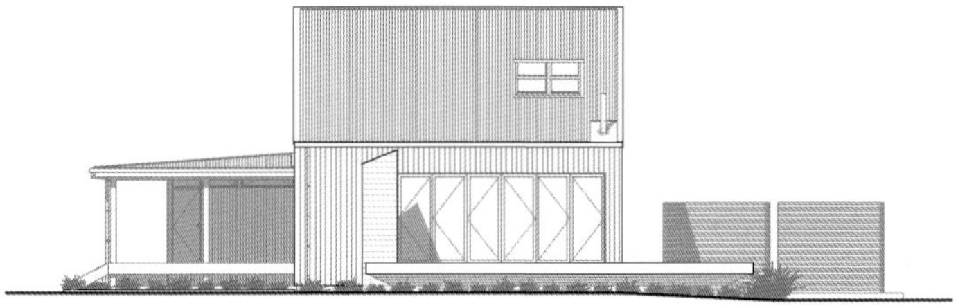

North east elevation

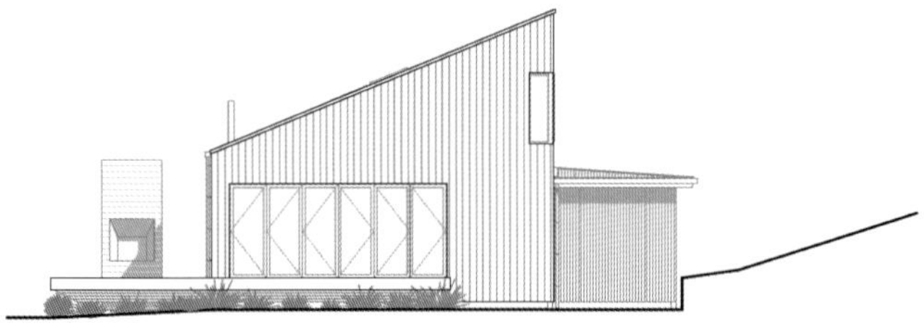

North west elevation

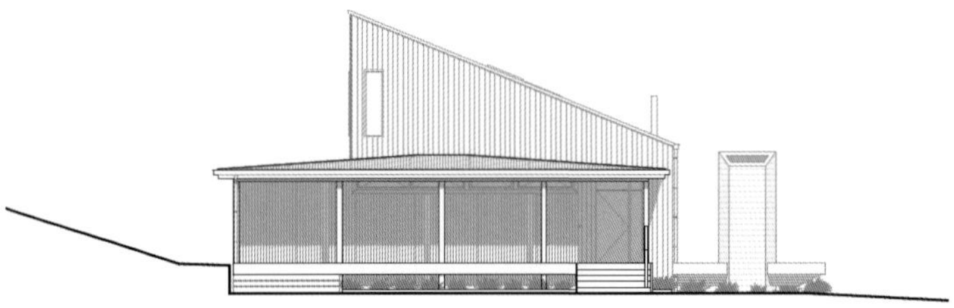

South east elevation

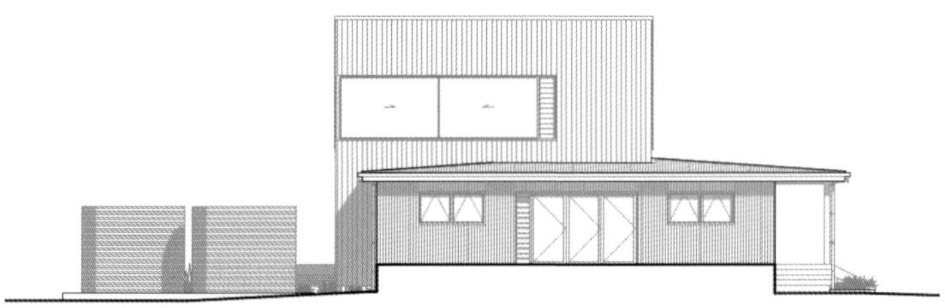

South west elevation

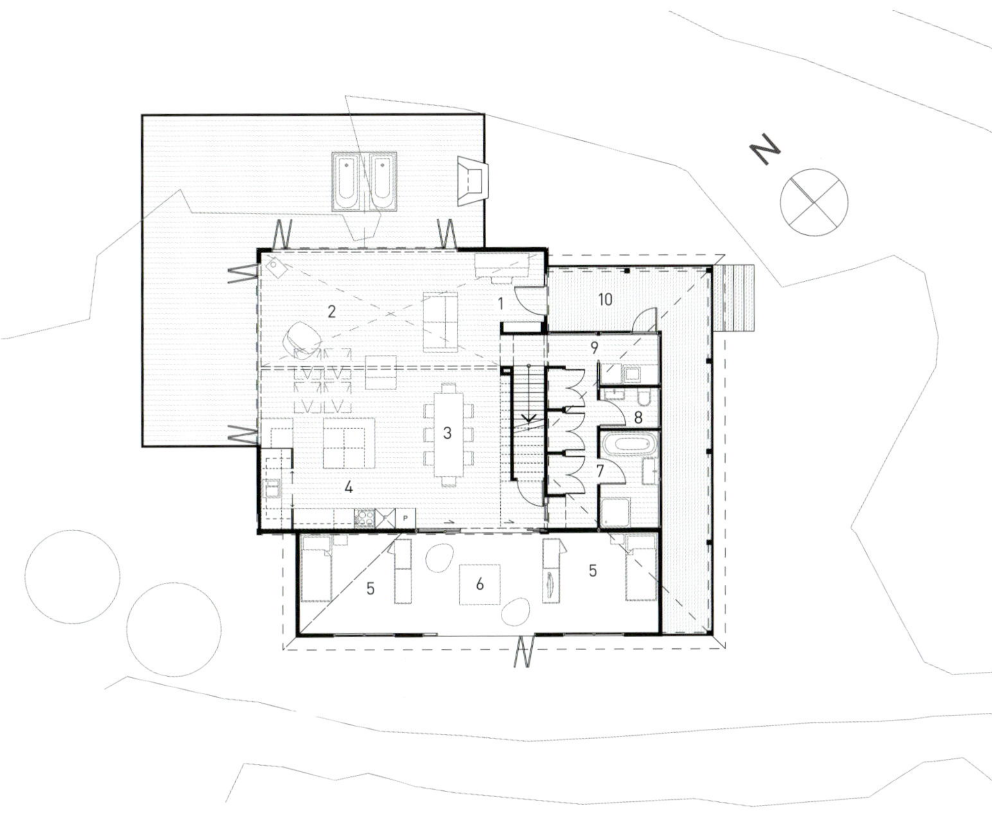

Ground floor site plan

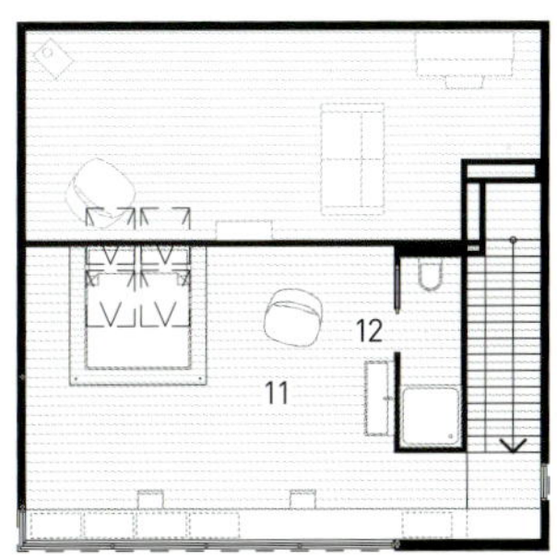

Mezzanine

1. Entry
2. Living
3. Living
4. Kitchen
5. Bedroom
6. Rumpus
7. Bathroom
8. Toilet
9. LDY
10. Porch
11. Master bedroom
12. Ensuite

enjoy
things

MWARCHITEKTEN

MWArchitekten is an architecture practice with more than 10 years of experience in the planning and execution of private residential buildings, as well as public and large-scale projects. Our focus is on ecological, customer-oriented architecture with a minimal impact on the environment. For our quality-conscious clients, we develop sustainable buildings with the highest level of precision.
Our claim to architecture is not only a rational and economic implementation developed from the construction method and the material, but it is also the creation of richness and diversity as we know it from grown structures such as medieval city centers or traditional farms. The human scale in terms of urban planning as well as the atmosphere and haptics inside are key issues of our planning.
To us a natural and renewable construction materials such as wood serves both of our needs. Wood not only sequesters carbon, preventing it from being released into the atmosphere but it also creates well-being.

MWArchitekten ist ein Architekturbüro mit mehr als 10 Jahren Erfahrung in der Planung und Ausführung privater Wohngebäuden sowie öffentlicher und großer Projekte. Unser Fokus liegt auf einer ökologischen, kundenorientierten Architektur mit minimalen Auswirkungen auf die Umwelt. Für unsere qualitätsbewussten Kunden entwickeln wir nachhaltige Gebäude mit höchster Präzision.
Unser Anspruch an die Architektur ist nicht nur eine rationale und wirtschaftliche Umsetzung, die sich aus der Bauweise und dem Material ergibt, sondern auch die Schaffung von Reichtum und Vielfalt, wie wir sie von gewachsenen Strukturen wie mittelalterlichen Stadtzentren oder traditionellen Bauernhöfen kennen. Die menschliche Dimension in Bezug auf die Stadtplanung sowie die Atmosphäre und Haptik im Inneren sind zentrale Themen unserer Planung.
Für uns sind natürliche und erneuerbare Baustoffe wie Holz für beide Bedürfnisse geeignet. Holz sequestriert nicht nur Kohlenstoff und verhindert dessen Freisetzung in die Atmosphäre, sondern schafft auch Wohlbefinden.

MWArchitekten est un cabinet d'architecture avec plus de 10 ans d'expérience dans la planification et l'exécution de bâtiments résidentiels privés, ainsi que de projets publics et à grande échelle. Nous mettons l'accent sur une architecture écologique, orientée client avec un impact minimal sur l'environnement. Pour nos clients soucieux de la qualité, nous développons des bâtiments durables avec le plus haut niveau de précision.
Notre revendication à l'architecture n'est pas seulement une mise en œuvre rationnelle et économique développée à partir de la méthode de construction et du matériau, mais c'est aussi la création de richesse et de diversité telles que nous les connaissons à partir de structures cultivées comme les centres-villes médiévaux ou les fermes traditionnelles. L'échelle humaine en termes d'urbanisme ainsi que l'atmosphère et l'haptique à l'intérieur sont des éléments clés de notre planification.
Pour nous, un matériau de construction naturel et renouvelable comme le bois répond à nos deux besoins. Non seulement le bois piège le carbone, l'empêchant d'être libéré dans l'atmosphère, mais il crée aussi du bien-être.

MWArchitekten es un estudio de arquitectura con más de diez años de experiencia en la planificación y ejecución de edificios residenciales privados, así como en proyectos públicos de gran escala. Nos centramos en la arquitectura ecológica, orientada al cliente y con un impacto mínimo en el medio ambiente. Para los clientes preocupados por la calidad, desarrollamos edificios sostenibles con el más alto nivel de precisión.
Nuestra arquitectura no es sólo una implementación racional y económica desarrollada a partir del método de construcción y del material, sino también la creación de riqueza y diversidad tal y como la conocemos a partir de estructuras existentes como los centros urbanos medievales o las granjas tradicionales. La escala humana en términos de planificación urbana, así como la atmósfera y un énfasis en el interior son temas clave en la planificación.
Para nosotros, un material de construcción natural y renovable como la madera satisface ambas necesidades. La madera no solo captura el carbono, evitando que se libere a la atmósfera, sino que también crea bienestar.

HILLSIDE DOUPLEX

HILLSIDE DOUPLEX

Based on the budget and the desire to create sustainable housing, the decision was made to build a semi-detached house of two entities. The goal was to create an ecological architecture that does not fall into sterility and artificiality. As a model for this purpose the architects studied housing typologies that have been developed over generations. The facade design is based on the atmospheric qualities of these traditional structures. In the interior space, the hillside becomes noticeable in steps towards the living room and the terrace. Despite its simple timber frame structure insulated with cellulose the compact volume causes the house an excellent energy balance. The low-energy house is heated by a geothermal heat pump. Instead of an artificial ventilation there is a fully programmable skylight at the highest point of the staircase providing fresh air and night cooling.

Basierend auf dem Budget und dem Wunsch, nachhaltigen Wohnraum zu schaffen, wurde beschlossen, ein Doppelhaus aus zwei Einheiten zu bauen. Das Ziel war eine ökologische Architektur, die nicht in Sterilität und Künstlichkeit verfällt. Als Modell für diesen Zweck untersuchten die Architekten Wohnbautypologien, die über Generationen entwickelt wurden. Die Fassadengestaltung basiert auf den atmosphärischen Qualitäten dieser traditionellen Bauwerke. Im Innenraum macht sich der Hang in Stufen zum Wohnzimmer und zur Terrasse bemerkbar. Trotz seiner einfachen, mit Zellulose gedämmten Holzrahmenkonstruktion bewirkt das kompakte Volumen eine hervorragende Energiebilanz des Hauses. Das Niedrigenergiehaus wird mit einer Erdwärmepumpe beheizt. Anstelle einer künstlichen Belüftung befindet sich am höchsten Punkt des Treppenhauses ein voll programmierbares Oberlicht, das für Frischluft und Nachtkühlung sorgt.

En se basant sur le budget et la volonté de créer des logements durables, la décision a été prise de construire une maison jumelée de deux entités. L'objectif était de créer une architecture écologique qui ne tombe pas dans la stérilité et l'artificialité. Comme modèle à cet effet, les architectes ont étudié des typologies de logements qui se sont développées au fil des générations. La conception de la façade est basée sur les qualités atmosphériques de ces structures traditionnelles. Dans l'espace intérieur, le flanc de la colline se fait remarquer par des marches vers le salon et la terrasse. Malgré sa structure simple à ossature bois isolée avec de la cellulose, le volume compact de la maison lui confère un excellent bilan énergétique. La maison basse consommation est chauffée par une pompe à chaleur géothermique. Au lieu d'une ventilation artificielle, il y a un puits de lumière entièrement programmable au point le plus haut de l'escalier qui fournit de l'air frais et un refroidissement nocturne.

Basándose en el presupuesto y en el deseo de crear una vivienda sostenible, se decidió construir una casa adosada de dos usos. El objetivo era crear una arquitectura ecológica que no cayera en la esterilidad y la artificialidad. Como modelo para este propósito, los arquitectos estudiaron las tipologías de viviendas que se han desarrollado a lo largo de generaciones. El diseño de la fachada se basa en las cualidades atmosféricas de estas estructuras tradicionales. En el espacio interior, la ladera se hace visible en pasos hacia el salón y la terraza. A pesar de su sencilla estructura de madera aislada con celulosa, el volumen compacto hace que la casa tenga un excelente balance energético. La casa de bajo consumo de energía es calentada por una bomba de calor geotérmica. En lugar de ventilación artificial, se instaló una claraboya totalmente programable en el punto más alto de la escalera que proporciona aire fresco y refrigeración nocturna.

Site plan

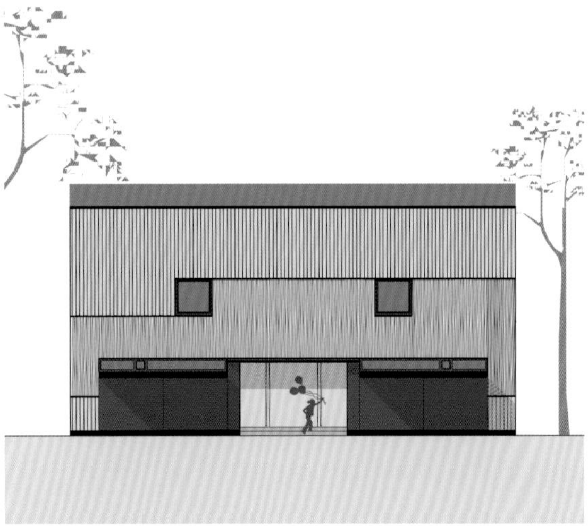

Back elevation

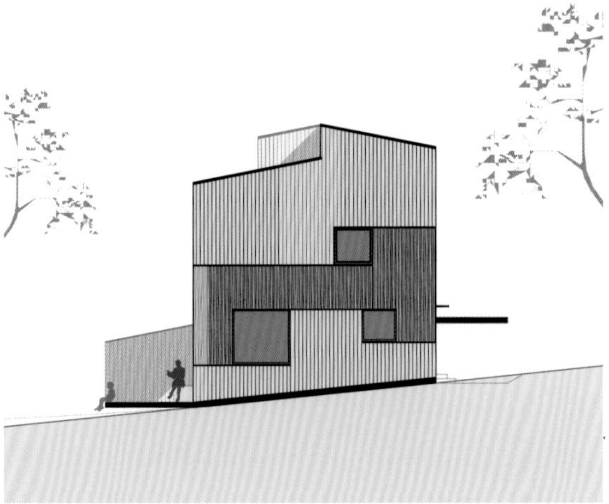

Side elevation

Front elevation

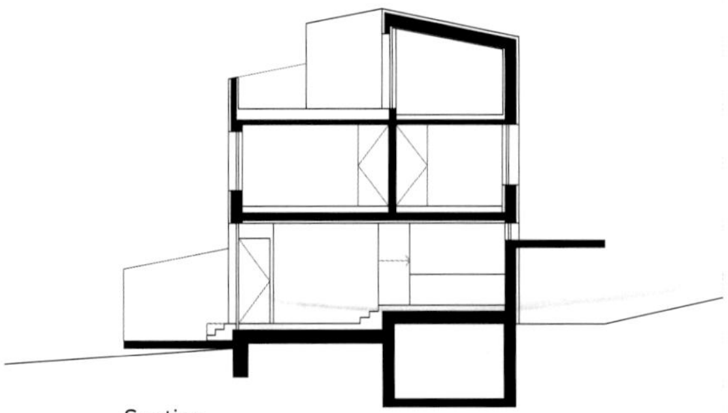

Section

NBA/ACA/NAA06

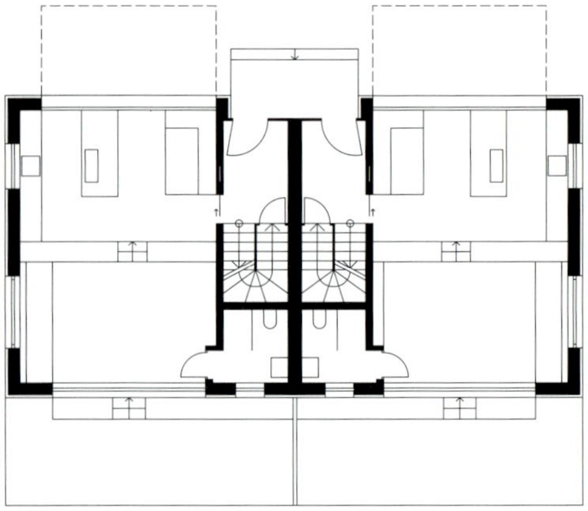

Ground floor plan

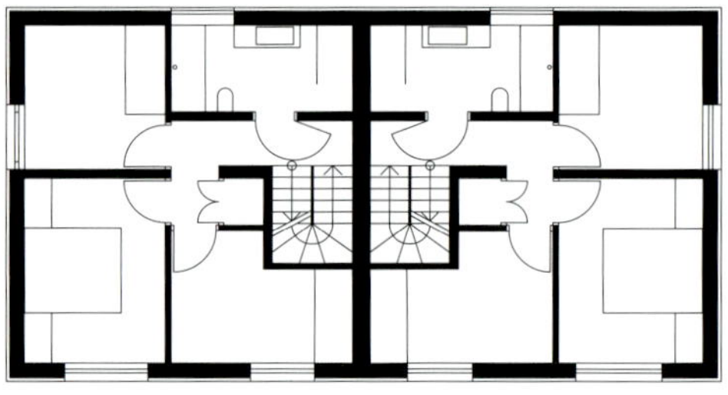

First floor plan

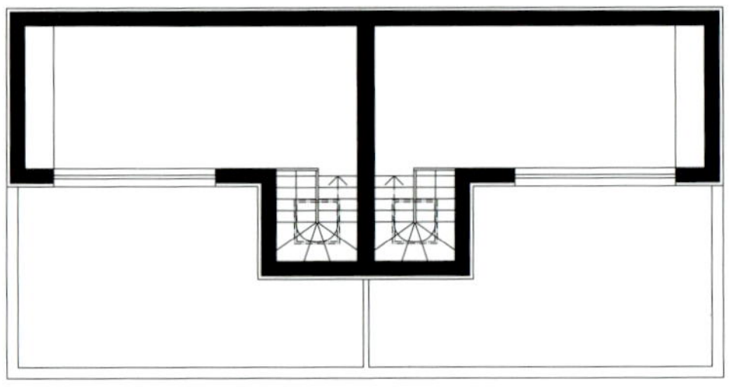

Second floor plan

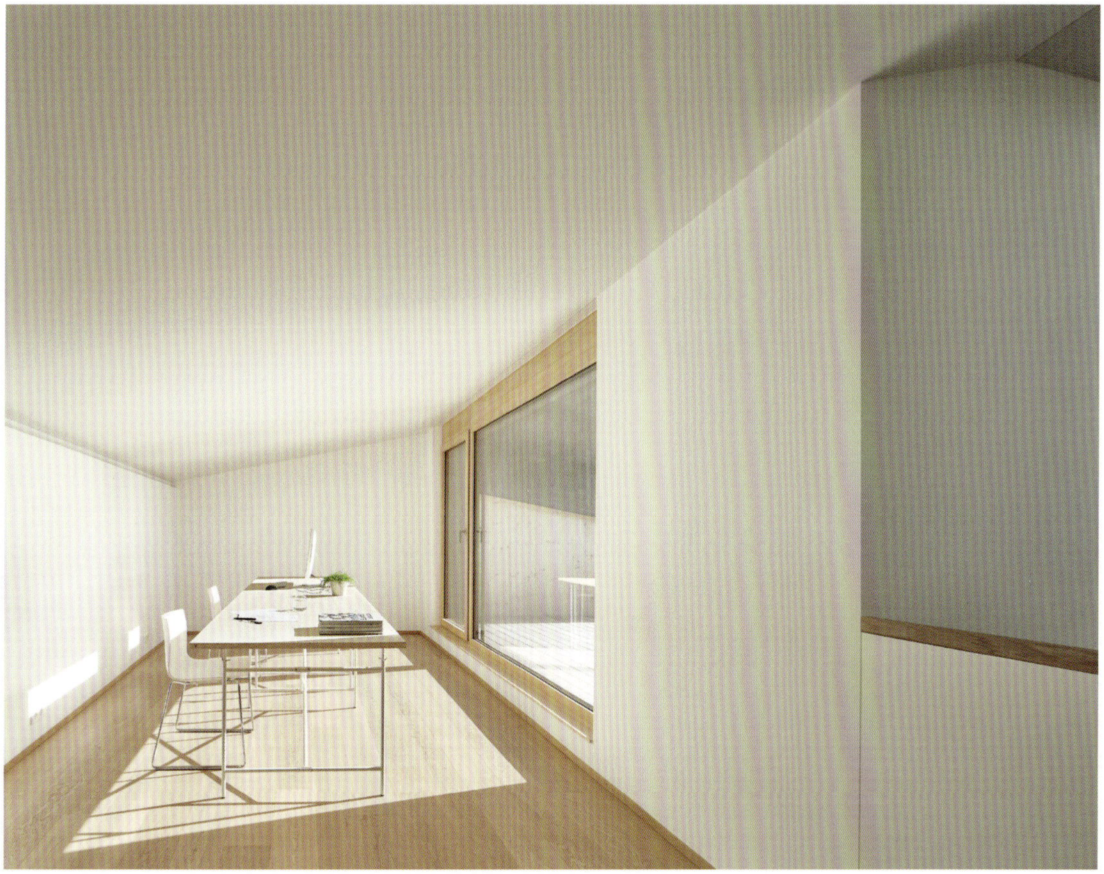

NATRUFIED

Natrufied Architecture designs projects in the Netherlands and abroad. With a team of international architects and designers, Natrufied is working on a wide range of projects in the areas of housing, work, leisure and relaxation. The company's aim is to be intensively involved in all stages of the projects, from the first sketch to the last screw. Through meticulous detail and the involvement of specialized companies in the first stages of projects, the balance between ambition and budget can generate the highest quality. The Natrufied team combines the dynamics of a young creative office with two decades of high-level architectural experience. The combination of architects and technical staff trained in both the design and construction phases leads to an ideal result.

Natrufied Architecture conçoit des projets aux Pays-Bas et à l'étranger. Avec une équipe d'architectes et de designers internationaux, Natrufied travaille sur un large éventail de projets dans les domaines du logement, du travail, des loisirs et de la détente. L'objectif de l'entreprise est de s'impliquer intensivement dans toutes les étapes des projets, de la première esquisse à la dernière vis. Grâce à un travail minutieux et à l'implication d'entreprises spécialisées dans les premières étapes des projets, l'équilibre entre l'ambition et le budget peut générer un résultat de la plus haute qualité. L'équipe de Natrufied combine la dynamique d'un jeune bureau créatif avec deux décennies d'expérience en architecture de haut niveau. La combinaison d'architectes et de techniciens formés à la fois à la conception et à la construction permet d'obtenir un résultat idéal.

Natrufied Architecture entwirft Projekte im In- und Ausland. Natrufied arbeitet mit einem Team von internationalen Architekten und Designern an einer Vielzahl von Projekten in den Bereichen Wohnen, Arbeit, Freizeit und Erholung. Ziel des Unternehmens ist es, intensiv in alle Phasen der Projekte eingebunden zu sein, von der ersten Skizze bis zur letzten Schraube. Durch die sorgfältige Detaillierung und die Einbeziehung von spezialisierten Unternehmen in die ersten Phasen der Projekte kann das Gleichgewicht zwischen Ehrgeiz und Budget zu einem Ergebnis höchster Qualität führen. Das Natrufied-Team verbindet die Dynamik eines jungen Kreativbüros mit zwei Jahrzehnten hochwertiger Architekturerfahrung. Die Kombination aus Architekten und technischem Personal, das sowohl in der Planungs- als auch in der Bauphase geschult ist, führt zu einem optimalen Ergebnis.

Natrufied Architecture diseña proyectos en los Países Bajos y en el extranjero. Con un equipo de arquitectos y diseñadores internacionales, Natrufied está trabajando en un amplio abanico de proyectos en las áreas de vivienda, trabajo, ocio y descanso. El objetivo de la empresa es involucrarse intensamente en todas las etapas de los proyectos, desde el primer boceto hasta el último tornillo. A través de un minucioso detalle y la participación de empresas especializadas en los primeros estados de los proyectos, el equilibrio entre ambición y presupuesto puede generar el máximo resultado de calidad. El equipo de Natrufied combina la dinámica de una joven oficina creativa con dos décadas de experiencia arquitectónica de alto nivel. La combinación de arquitectos y personal técnico formado tanto en el diseño como en las fases de construcción conduce a un resultado idóneo.

BOSVILLA

The project includes the construction of a house, a garden house, a car park and another for bicycles, designed to preserve and capture the natural environment. The house has a completely open upper floor with the common áreas. This area textends the natural environment towards the interior. The ground floor, which contains the bedrooms, is embedded in the land providing greater privacy. The different types of wood that make up the main structure, together with the rest of the materials used, generate a soft palette of natural tones. In addition to using materials that absorb CO_2 such as wood and bamboo, the house has great thermal insulation in its enclosures and openings, along with a green roof that also collects rainwater and houses 35 solar panels.

Das Projekt umfasst den Bau eines Hauses, eines Gartenhauses, eines Park- und eines Fahrradstellplatzes, um die natürliche Umwelt zu erhalten und zu erfassen. Das Haus hat ein komplett offenes Obergeschoss, das für die Gemeinschaftsräume bestimmt ist, unter dem Dach eines Flugzeugs, das die natürliche Umgebung nach innen erweitert. Das Erdgeschoss, in dem sich die Schlafzimmer befinden, ist in das Grundstück eingebettet und bietet mehr Privatsphäre. Die verschiedenen Holzarten, aus denen die Hauptstruktur besteht, erzeugen zusammen mit den übrigen verwendeten Materialien eine weiche Palette von Naturtönen. Neben der Verwendung von Materialien, die CO_2 absorbieren, wie Holz und Bambus, verfügt das Haus über eine hervorragende Wärmedämmung in seinen Gehäusen und Öffnungen sowie ein Gründach, das auch Regenwasser sammelt und 35 Solarmodule beherbergt.

Le projet comprend la construction d'une maison, d'un abri de jardin, d'un parking et d'un autre pour vélos, conçus pour préserver et capter l'environnement naturel. L'étage supérieur de la maison est entièrement ouvert, destiné aux parties communes, présidé par un toit en vol qui prolonge l'environnement naturel vers l'intérieur. Le rez-de-chaussée, qui contient les chambres, est encastré dans le terrain offrant une plus grande intimité. Les différentes essences de bois qui composent la structure principale, ainsi que le reste des matériaux utilisés, génèrent une palette douce de teintes naturelles. En plus d'utiliser des matériaux qui absorbent le CO_2 comme le bois et le bambou, la maison possède une grande isolation thermique dans ses enceintes et ses ouvertures, ainsi qu'un toit vert qui recueille également l'eau de pluie et abrite 35 panneaux solaires.

El proyecto comprende la construcción de una vivienda, una casa de jardín, un aparcamiento de coches y otro para bicicletas, diseñados para preservar y capturar el entorno natural. La vivienda presenta una planta superior completamente abierta, destinada a las zonas comunes, presidida por una cubierta en vuelo que prolonga el entorno natural hacia el interior. La planta inferior, que contiene los dormitorios, se incrusta en el terreno brindando una mayor privacidad. Los diferentes tipos de maderas que conforman la estructura principal, junto al resto de materiales utilizados, generan una paleta suave de tonos naturales. Además de utilizar materiales que absorben CO_2 como la madera y el bambú, la casa presenta un gran aislamiento térmico en sus cerramientos y aberturas, conjuntamente con una cubierta verde que también recoge el agua de lluvia y alberga 35 paneles solares.

Site plan

Sketch

North elevation

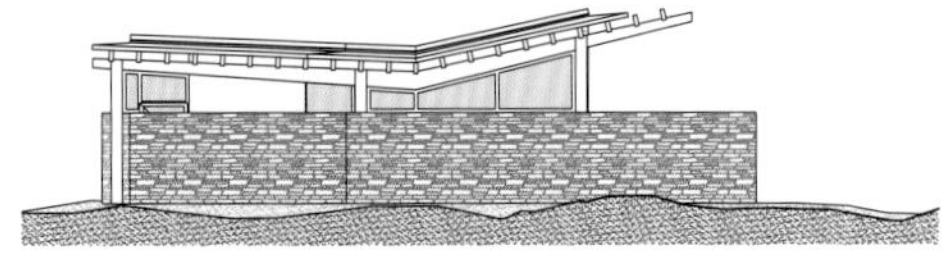

Garden house. North elevation

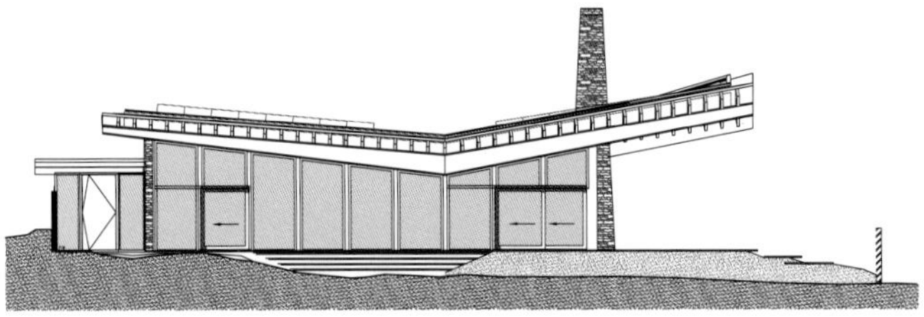

South elevation

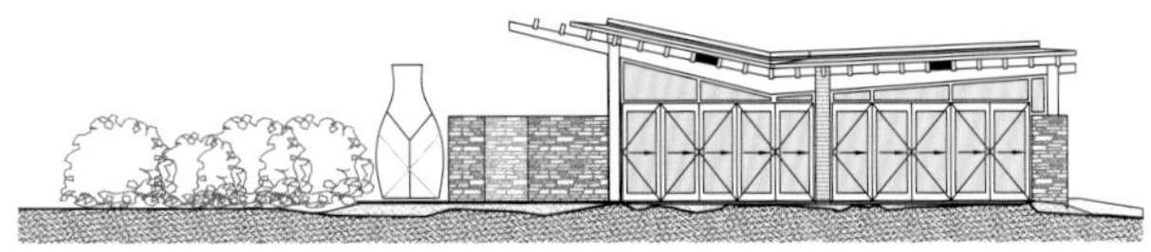

Garden house. South elevation

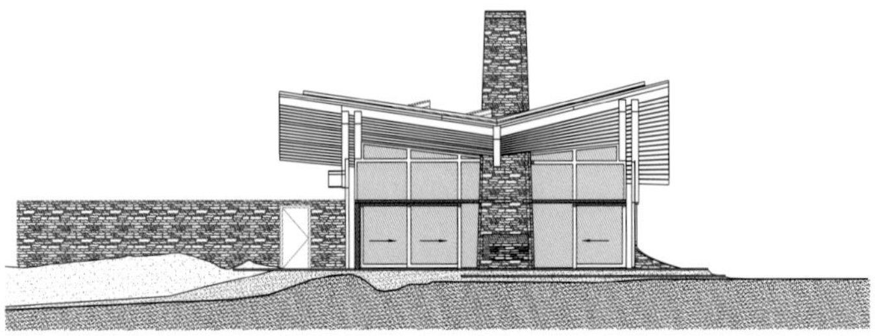

East elevation

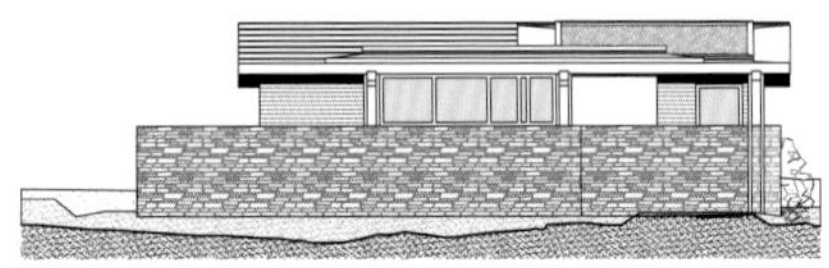

Garden house. East elevation

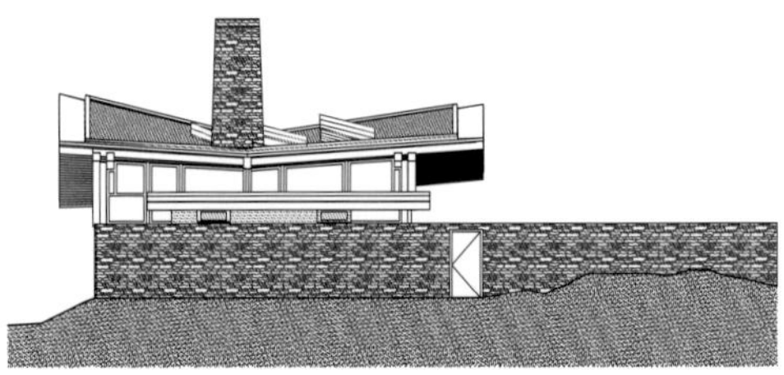

West elevation

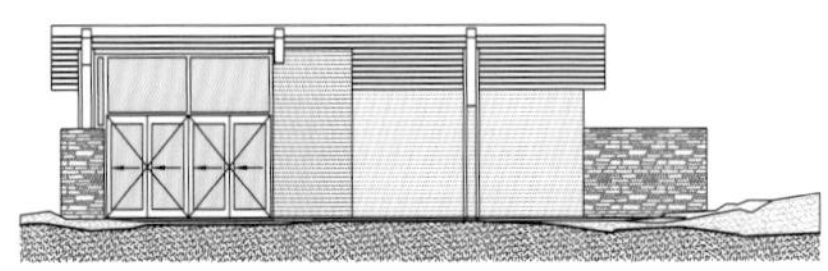

Garden house. West elevation

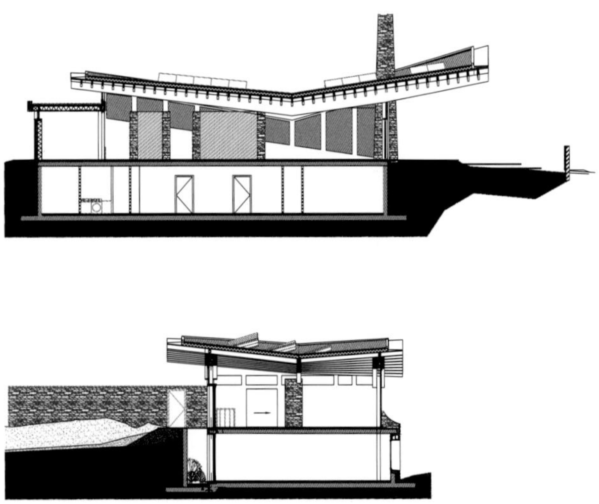

Sections

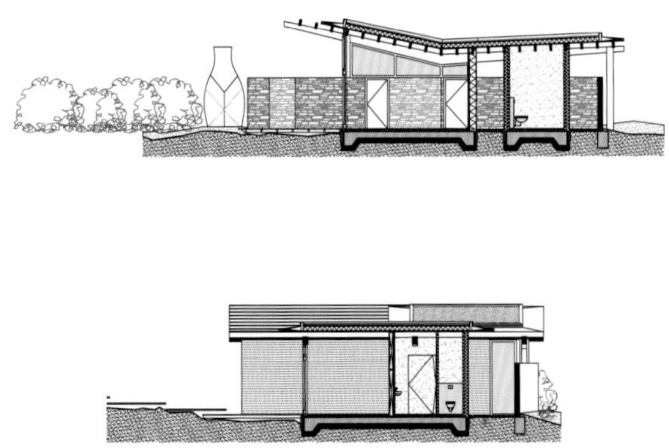

Garden house. Sections

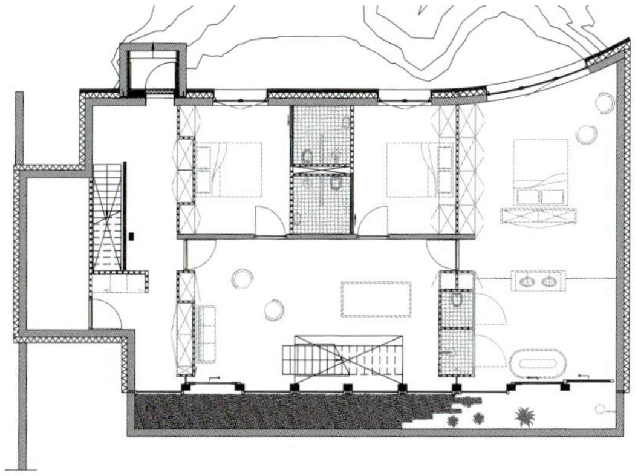

First floor plan

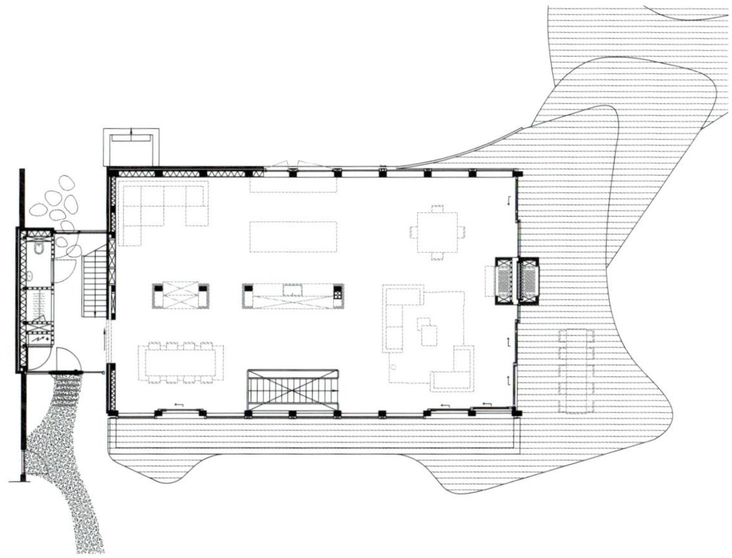

Ground floor plan

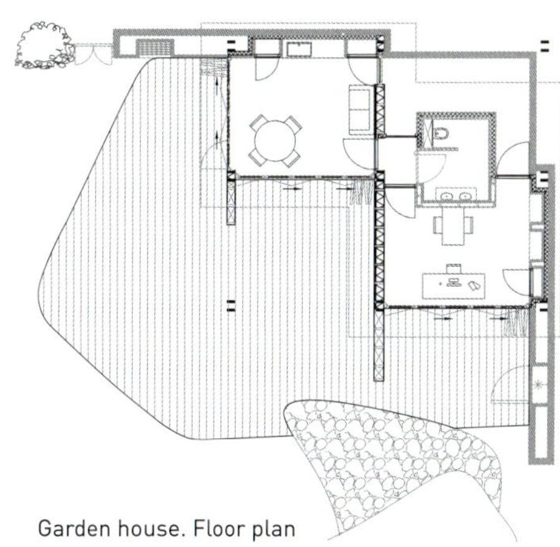

Garden house. Floor plan

PFENNIGER & ASOCIADOS

Pfenniger & Asociados is directed by Francis Pfenniger, architect,and his wife, Lorena González, graphic designer. They deal with works of different nature and scale, from editorial projects and books to interventions in urban space and the coastal edge, and have carried out architectural projects in residential, social housing, hotels and industry.
The object of their trade is to understand and respond to the needs of those who come to them, working for the quality of life of the people who inhabit and use the building. But architecture must also honor the conditions of the place and its time and this, inevitably and by extension, includes the environment in which life is inserted and developed.
In that sense, energy efficiency, environmental fitness, the use of available and low-impact resources as well as the possibility and opportunities to reuse materials are an integral part of their exploration of their way they understand architecture.

Pfenniger & Asociados est dirigé par Francis Pfenniger, architecte, et son épouse, Lorena González, graphiste. Nous traitons des travaux de nature et d'échelle différentes, depuis des projets éditoriaux et des livres jusqu'à des interventions dans l'espace urbain et le littoral. Nous avons réalisé des projets architecturaux dans le logement, le logement social, les hôtels et l'industrie.
Le but de notre métier est de comprendre et de répondre aux besoins de ceux qui viennent chez nous, en travaillant pour la qualité de vie des gens qui habitent et utilisent le batiment. Mais l'architecture doit aussi honorer les conditions du lieu et de son époque, ce qui, inévitablement et par extension, inclut l'environnement dans lequel cette vie est insérée et développée.
En ce sens, l'efficacité énergétique, l'aptitude à la protection de l'environnement, l'utilisation des ressources disponibles et à faible impact ainsi que la possibilité et les opportunités de réutiliser les matériaux font partie intégrante de notre exploration de notre réflexion et de notre action architecturale.

Pfenniger & Asociados wird von Francis Pfenniger, Architekt, und seiner Frau Lorena González, Grafikerin, geleitet. Wir beschäftigen uns mit Werken unterschiedlicher Art und Größenordnung, von redaktionellen Projekten und Büchern bis hin zu Interventionen im städtischen Raum und am Küstenrand. Wir haben Architekturprojekte in den Bereichen Wohnen, Sozialwohnungen, Hotels und Industrie durchgeführt.
Ziel unseres Handelns ist es, die Bedürfnisse derjenigen die zu uns kommen zu verstehen und auf sie einzugehen, , und für die Lebensqualität der Menschen zu arbeiten, die das Gebäude bewohnen und nutzen. Aber die Architektur muss auch die Bedingungen des Ortes und seiner Zeit berücksichtigen, und dazu gehört zwangsläufig und im weiteren Sinne auch die Umgebung, in der dieses Leben eingefügt und entwickelt wird.
In diesem Sinne sind Energieeffizienz, Umweltfitness, die Nutzung verfügbarer und schonender Ressourcen sowie die Möglichkeit der Wiederverwendung von Materialien ein integraler Bestandteil unserer Erforschung des architektonischen Denkens und Handelns.

Pfenniger & Asociados está dirigida por Francis Pfenniger, arquitecto, y su esposa, Lorena González, diseñadora gráfica. Abordamos trabajos de distinta índole y escala, desde proyectos editoriales y libros a intervenciones en el espacio urbano y borde costero,además de proyectos de arquitectura en vivienda, vivienda social, hotelería e industria.
El objeto de nuestro oficio es entender y dar respuesta a las necesidades de quienes acuden a nosotros, trabajando por la calidad de vida de las personas que habitan y usan la obra. Pero la arquitectura también debe honrar las condiciones del lugar y de su tiempo y esto, inevitablemente y por extensión, incluye al medio en que esa vida se inserta y se desarrolla.
En ese sentido la eficiencia energética, el acondicionamiento físico ambiental, el uso de recursos disponibles y de bajo impacto así como la posibilidad y oportunidades de reutilización de materiales son parte integral de nuestra exploración en nuestro hacer y pensar la arquitectura.

CASA HOLMES FUENTEALBA

The project is conceived as a refuge from the local climate and as a viewpoint over the Castro Channel. The building constitutes a simple volume with a common geometry in the area, which is located on a hillside and sits on piles, thus reducing its footprint on the ground.
The orientation of the house towards the views to the south made it necessary to foresee controlled openings in the rest of the façades to take advantage of sunlight. The construction reused waste materials from fish and mussels farming, abundant on the coast, and materials from domestic recycling.
Using a local strategy, a continuous watertight outer skin was proposed to facilitate the evacuation of rainwater. Indoor conditioning is achieved with a traditional Chiloé wood-burning stove and a low-consumption one, reinforced by the important insulation of the construction.

Das Projekt ist als Zufluchtsort vor dem lokalen Klima und als Blickwinkel auf den Castro-Kanal konzipiert. Das Gebäude bildet ein einfaches Volumen mit einer üblicher Geometrie mit dem Grundstück, das sich an einem Hang befindet. Es steht auf Pfählen, wodurch die Grundfläche reduziert wird.
Die Ausrichtung des Hauses nach Süden machte es notwendig, kontrollierte Öffnungen in den übrigen Fassaden vorzusehen, um das Sonnenlicht zu nutzen. Bei der Konstruktion wurden Abfälle aus der Fisch und Miesmuschelzucht die an der Küste reichlich vorhanden sind, sowie Materialien aus dem heimischen Recycling wiederverwendet.
Mit einer lokalen Strategie wurde eine durchgehende, wasserdichte Außenhaut vorgeschlagen, um die Ableitung von Regenwasser zu erleichtern. Die Raumheizung erfolgt mit einem traditionellen, verbrauchsarmen Chiloé-Holzofen, dessen Wirkung durch die wichtige Isolierung des Gehäuses verstärkt wird.

Le projet est conçu comme un refuge contre le climat local et comme un point de vue sur le canal Castro. Le bâtiment constitue un volume simple avec une géométrie commune dans la zone, qui est situé à flanc de colline et s'appuie sur des pieux, réduisant ainsi son empreinte au sol.
L'orientation de la maison vers le sud a nécessité de prévoir des ouvertures contrôlées dans le reste des façades pour profiter de la lumière du soleil. La construction a réutilisé des déchets issus de la pisciculture et de la culture des moulles abondants sur la côte, et des matériaux issus du recyclage domestique.
Dans le cadre d'une stratégie locale, on a proposé une enveloppe extérieure étanche continue pour faciliter l'évacuation de l'eau de pluie. La climatisation intérieure est réalisée avec un poêle à bois traditionnel Chiloé et un poêle à bois basse consommation, renforcé par l'importante isolation de l'enceinte.

El proyecto se concibe como refugio frente al clima local y como mirador sobre el canal de Castro. El edificio constituye un volumen simple con una geometría común en la zona, que se sitúa en una ladera y se asienta sobre pilotes, reduciendo así su huella sobre el terreno.
La orientación de la casa hacia las vistas al sur hizo necesario prever aberturas controladas en el resto de fachadas para aprovechar la luz solar. La construcción reutilizó materiales de desecho de la piscicultura y mitilicultura, abundantes en la costa, y materiales procedentes del reciclaje doméstico.
Usando una estrategia local, se propuso una piel exterior estanca continua que facilitase la evacuación del agua de lluvia. La climatización interior se consigue con una tradicional cocina a leña de Chiloé y una estufa de leña de bajo consumo, reforzadas por el importante aislamiento de la envolvente.

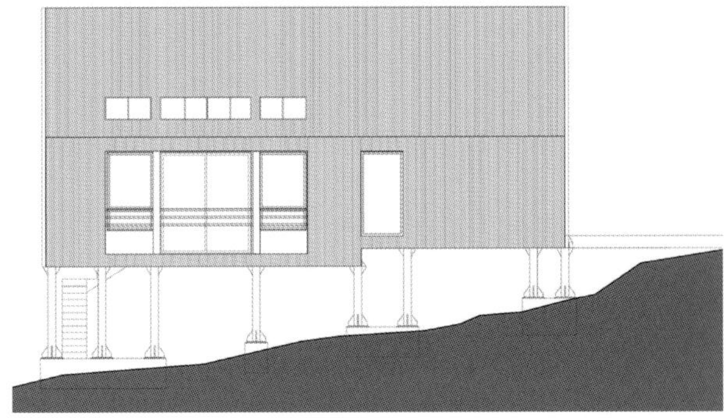

East elevation

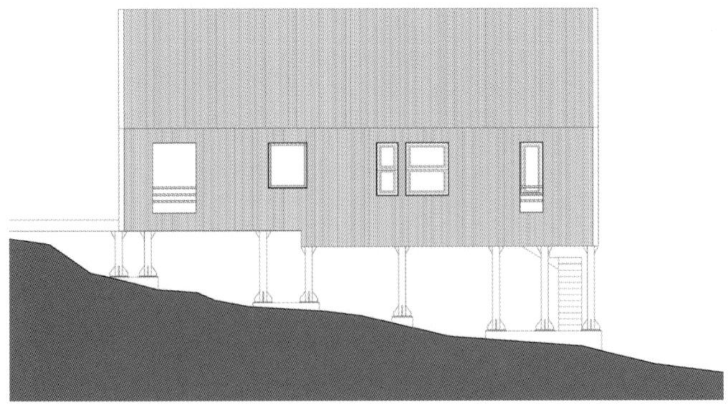

West elevation

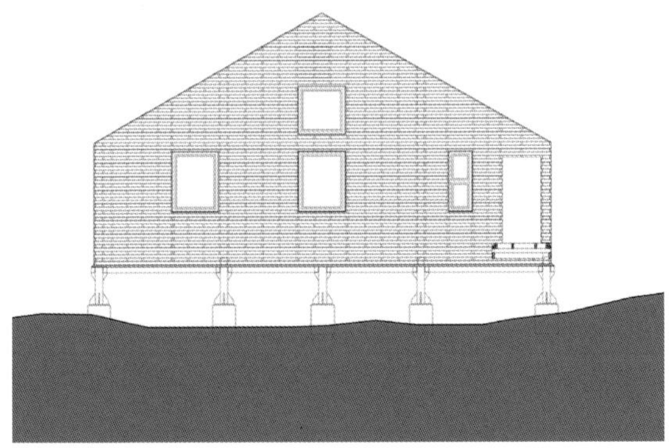

North elevation

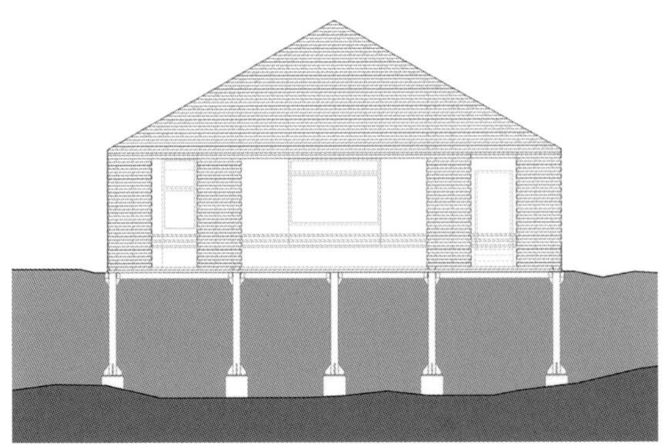

South elevation

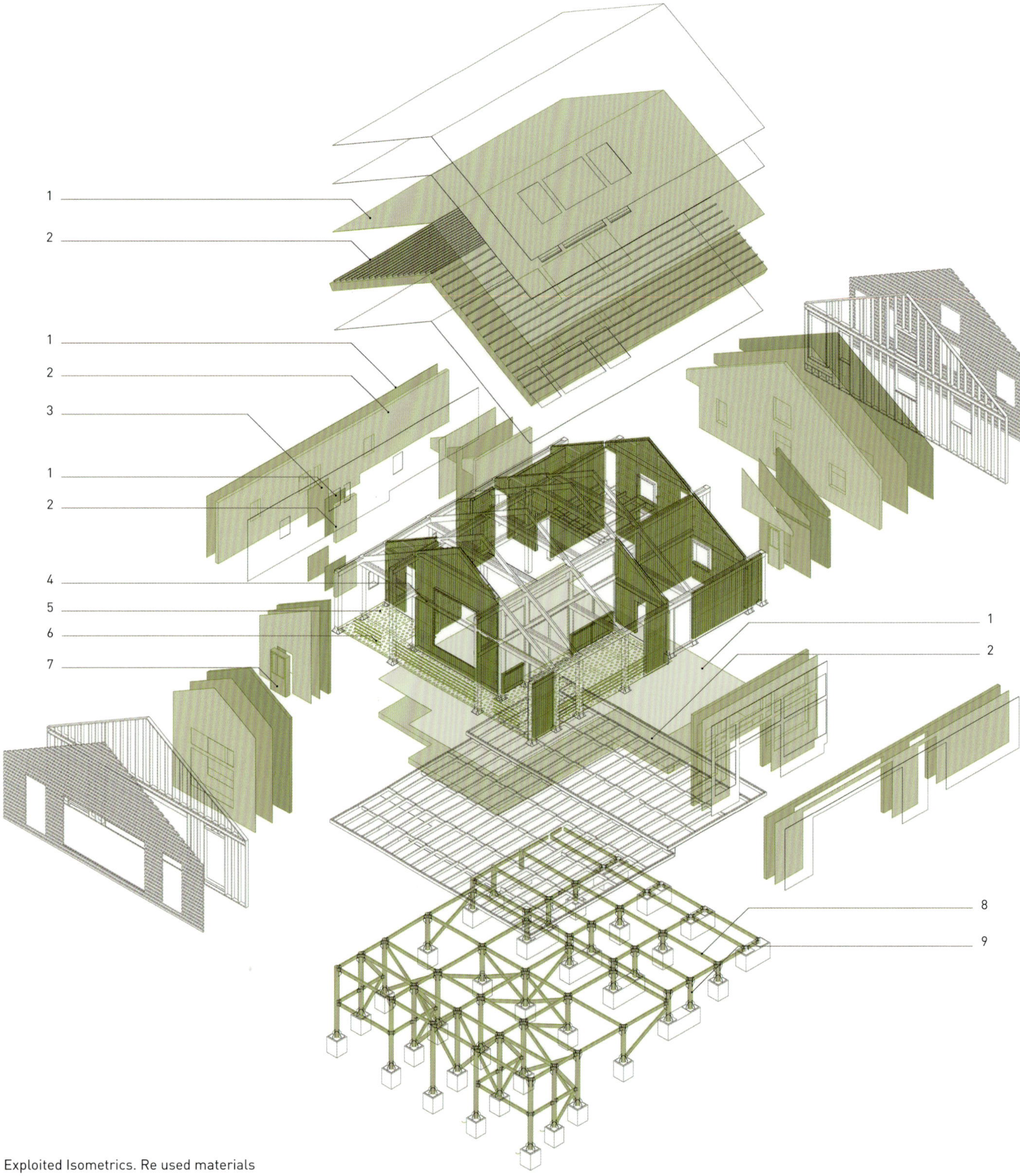

Exploited Isometrics. Re used materials

1. Tetrapack packaging
2. Expanded polystyrene
3. Wood recovered from spring
4. Wooden pallets
5. Salmon cage aisle
6. Salmon cage railing
7. Demolition doors
8. 150/50/4 mm galvanized beams with Weimaster type salmon cage structure.
9. Galvanized pillars d: 150 x 5mm structure salmon cage type Proma

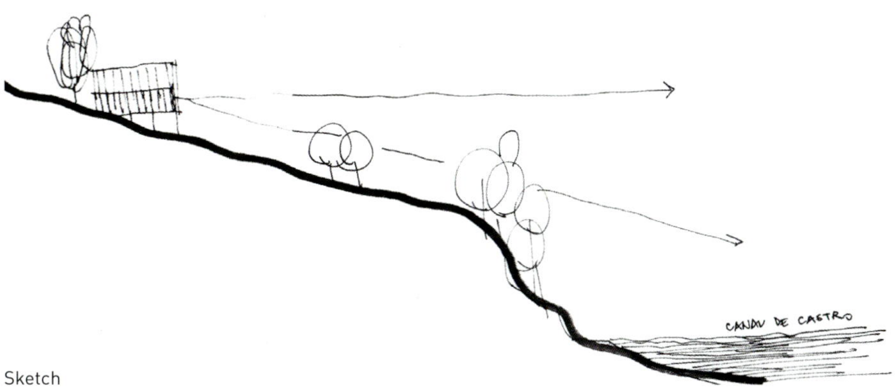

Sketch

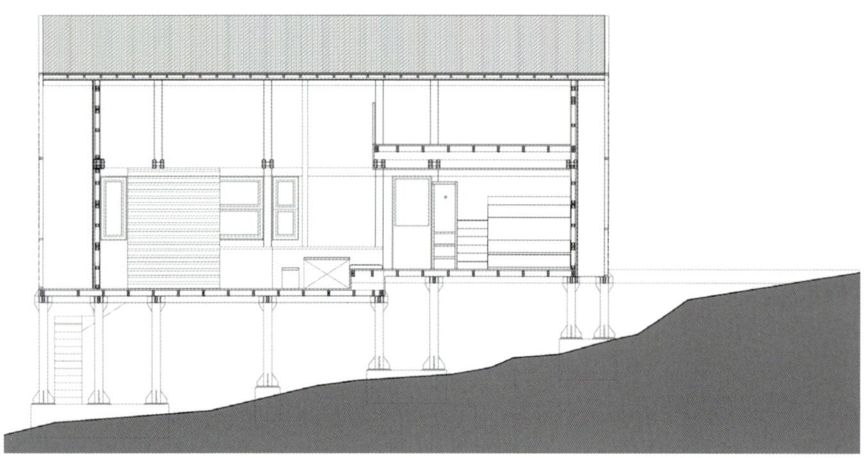

Longitudinal section

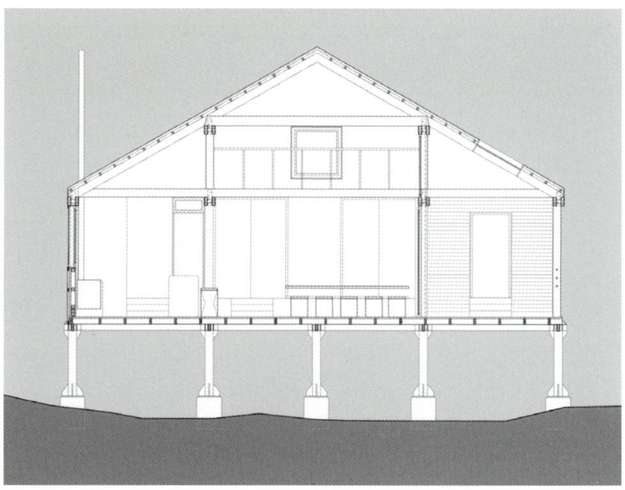

Cross section

Floor plan

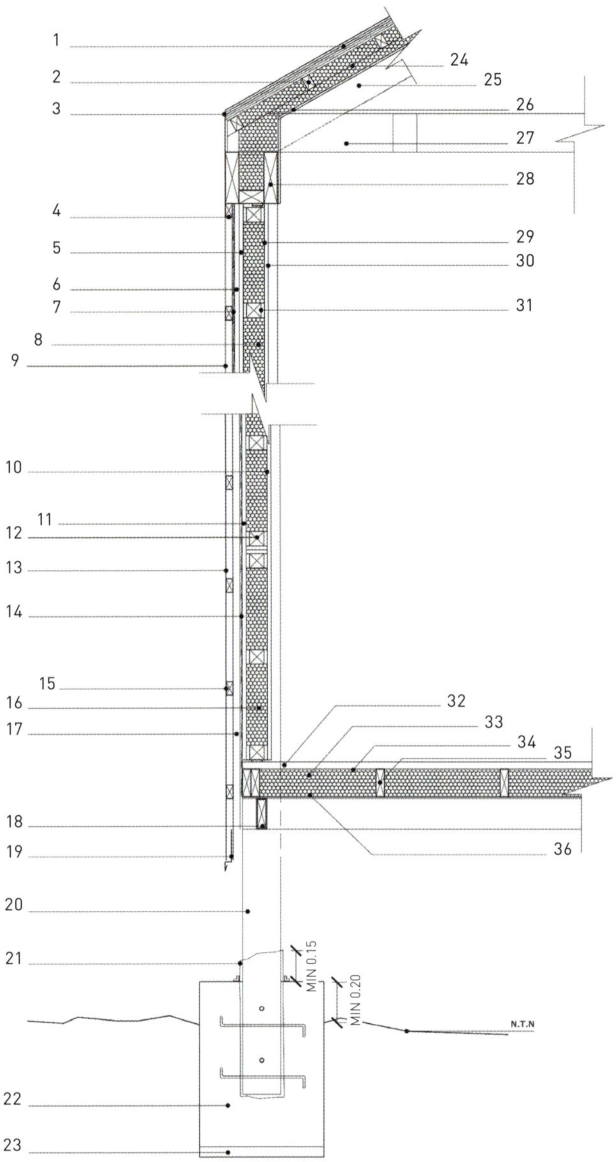

Detail: wall with Zincalum floor/coating

1. Tetrapack moisture barrier overlapped
2. Steep 5 × 7 cm @ 400 mm
3. Zincalum steel plate e=0.4 mm
4. Horizontal strip 2,5 × 7 cm @ 50 mm
5. Pallet boarding 2,5 × 7 cm (vertical)
6. Vertical strip 2,5 × 5 cm @ 50 mm
7. Tetrapack moisture barrier stapled to boarding with overlap. Aluminised face to exterior
8. Expanded polystyrene e=100 mm
9. External cladding plate Zincalum
10. Polyethylene vapour barrier 0.2 mm
11. Pallet boarding 2,5 × 7 cm (vertical)
12. Pallet frame
13. External cladding plate Zincalum e 0.4 m.
14. Tetrapack moisture barrier stapled to boarding with overlap. Aluminised face to exterior
15. Horizontal strip 2,5 × 7 cm @ 50 mm
16. Expanded polystyrene e=100 mm or total width
17. Vertical strip 2,5 × 5 cm @ 50 mm
18. Galvanized steel master beams 150 × 50 × 5 mm
19. Cutter profile zincalum e=0.4 mm
20. 20 × 20 cm post
21. Tarred sheathing
22. Foundation support 0,60 × 0,60 × 0,8 m
23. Planted poor concrete
24. 5 x 5 cm @60 cm under steep
25. 7 x 10 cm beam
26. Ceiling plywood 10 mm
27. Master Beam 2 (7 × 20 cm)
28. Master Beam 2 (5 × 25 cm)
29. Polyethylene vapour barrier 0.2 mm
30. Plywood cladding 10 mm
31. Pallet frame
32. Boarding 3,7 × 10 cm tongue and groove
33. Expanded polystyrene e=100 mm (min)
34. Polyethylene vapour barrier 0.3 mm
35. Beam 2 (2" × 6") @ 0,6 m (tip)
36. Felt paper moisture barrier

SEBASTIÁN CALERO LARREA
DANIEL MORENO FLORES

Sebastián Calero Larrea (1977) links independent professional practice with academic teaching, graphic exploration and urban photography. His works and projects seek to rethink the relationship between space, matter and structure. The reference for the formulation of his ideas is based on the virtues and rarities of anonymous architecture located above all in the worn, vulnerable and rural landscapes of geography, which seek to adapt to a contemporary technique and vision.

Daniel Moreno Flores (1984), dreamy architect who lives the profession with an attitude of search, innovation and discovery. He explores, experiments and links art with craftsmanship. His starting point is playful, poetic, practical and concrete thought. Under a free gaze, conscious and without prejudice of reality, he seeks to intensify aspects of context, establishing dialogues with matter, recycling, constructive technique, structure and clean systems that are thoughtful with the environment.

Sebastián Calero Larrea (1977) lie la pratique professionnelle indépendante à l'enseignement académique, l'exploration graphique et la photographie urbaine. Ses œuvres et projets cherchent à repenser la relation entre l'espace, la matière et la structure. La référence pour la formulation de ses idées s'appuie sur les vertus et les raretés de l'architecture anonyme située avant tout dans les paysages géographiques usés, vulnérables et ruraux, qui cherchent à s'adapter à une technique et une vision contemporaine.

Daniel Moreno Flores (1984), architecte rêveur qui vit la profession avec une attitude de recherche, d'innovation et de découverte. Il explore, expérimente et relie l'art à l'artisanat. Son point de départ est ludique, poétique, pratique et concret. Sous un regard libre, conscient et sans préjugé de la réalité, il cherche à intensifier les aspects du contexte, en établissant des dialogues avec la matière, le recyclage, la technique constructive, la structure et les systèmes propres qui sont réfléchis avec l'environnement.

Sebastián Calero Larrea (1977) verbindet die unabhängige Berufspraxis mit akademischer Lehre, grafischer Erkundung und Stadtfotografie. Seine Arbeiten und Projekte versuchen, die Beziehung zwischen Raum, Materie und Struktur zu überdenken. Die Referenz für die Formulierung seiner Ideen basiert auf den Vorzügen und Raritäten der anonymen Architektur, die sich vor allem in den abgenutzten, verwundbaren und ländlichen Landschaften der Geographie befinden, die versuchen, sich an eine zeitgenössische Technik und Vision anzupassen.

Daniel Moreno Flores (1984), traumhafter Architekt, der den Beruf mit einer Haltung der Suche, Innovation und Entdeckung lebt. Er erforscht, experimentiert und verbindet Kunst mit Handwerk. Sein Ausgangspunkt ist spielerisches, poetisches, praktisches und konkretes Denken. Im freien Blick, bewusst und ohne Beeinträchtigung der Realität, versucht er, Kontextaspekte zu intensivieren, indem er Dialoge mit Materie, Recycling, konstruktiver Technik, Struktur und sauberen Systemen etabliert, die auf die Umwelt achten.

Sebastián Calero Larrea (1977) vincula la práctica profesional independiente con la enseñanza académica, la exploración gráfica y la fotografía urbana. Sus obras y proyectos buscan repensar la relación entre el espacio, materia y estructura. La referencia para la formulación de sus ideas están basadas en las virtudes y rarezas de la arquitectura anónima localizada sobre todo en los paisajes desgastados, vulnerables y rurales de la geografía, que buscan adaptarse a una técnica y visión contemporánea.

Daniel Moreno Flores (1984), arquitecto soñador que vive la profesión con actitud de búsqueda, innovación y descubrimiento. Explora, experimenta y enlaza el arte con la artesanía. Su punto de partida es el pensamiento lúdico, poético, práctico y concreto. Bajo una mirada libre, consciente y sin prejuicio de la realidad, busca intensificar aspectos del contexto, estableciendo diálogos con la materia, reciclaje, técnica constructiva, estructura y sistemas limpios reflexivos con el medio ambiente.

EL CAMAROTE

EL CARRIZAL

EL CAMAROTE

SEBASTIÁN CALERO LARREA

This low-cost housing project on the outskirts of Quito attempts to reconstruct the idea of a local architecture that has been erased and replaced by an intrusive and serial housing typology. It consists of two elevated concrete platforms, a wooden skeleton and a mixed skin of brick, metal, glass and wood that encloses a topography of spaces that differentiates public from private areas. The relationship of the interior with the vegetation, and the fusion between structure, skin and space, always under the guidance of the manufacture of small details, are the main achievements of the project. As a consequence a great atlas of pieces and singular mechanisms emerges becoming an essential part of this project. These artisan conditions give the house an atmosphere of warmth and cosiness, very typical of a country home.

Dieses kostengünstige Wohnprojekt am Stadtrand von Quito versucht, die Idee einer lokalen Architektur zu rekonstruieren, die verdrängt und durch eine aufdringliche und serielle Wohntypologie ersetzt wurde. Es besteht aus zwei erhöhten Betonplattformen, einem Holzskelett und einer Mischhülle aus Ziegel, Metall, Glas und Holz, die eine Topographie der Räume umschließt, die öffentliche und private Bereiche voneinander unterscheidet. Die Beziehung des Innenraums zur Vegetation und die Verschmelzung von Struktur, Hülle und Raum, immer unter der Prämisse der Herstellung kleiner Details, sind die wichtigsten Ergebnisse des Projekts. Daraus ergibt sich ein großer Atlas von Stücken und Einzelmechanismen, die ein wesentlicher Bestandteil dieses Projekts sind. Diese handwerklichen Bedingungen verleihen dem Haus eine Atmosphäre von Wärme und Häuslichkeit, die sehr typisch für ein Landhaus ist.

Ce projet de logements bon marché en périphérie de Quito tente de reconstruire l'idée d'une architecture locale qui a été effacée et remplacée par une typologie de logements intrusifs et en série. Il se compose de deux plates-formes surélevées en béton, d'une ossature en bois et d'une peau mixte de brique, de métal, de verre et de bois qui renferme une topographie d'espaces qui différencie les espaces publics des espaces privés. La relation de l'intérieur avec la végétation et la fusion entre la structure, la peau et l'espace, toujours sous la direction de la fabrication de petits détails, sont les principales réalisations du projet. En conséquence, un grand atlas de pièces et de mécanismes singuliers émerge, qui sont une partie essentielle de ce projet. Ces conditions artisanales donnent à la maison une atmosphère de chaleur et de domesticité, très typique d'une maison de campagne.

El proyecto de esta vivienda de bajo coste en las afueras de Quito intenta reconstruir la idea de una arquitectura lugareña que se ha ido borrando y ha sido reemplazada por una tipología habitacional intrusa y en serie. Se compone de dos plataformas elevadas de hormigón, un esqueleto de madera y una piel mixta de ladrillo, metal, vidrio y madera que encierra una topografía de espacios que diferencia las áreas públicas de las privadas. La relación del interior con la vegetación, y la fusión entre estructura, piel y espacio, siempre bajo la guía de la manufactura de pequeños detalles, son los principales logros del proyecto. Como consecuencia surge un gran atlas de piezas y mecanismos singulares que son parte esencial de este proyecto. Estas condiciones artesanales imprimen a la vivienda una atmósfera de calidez y domesticidad, muy propias de una casa de campo.

Front view

Rear view

Right side vew

Left side view

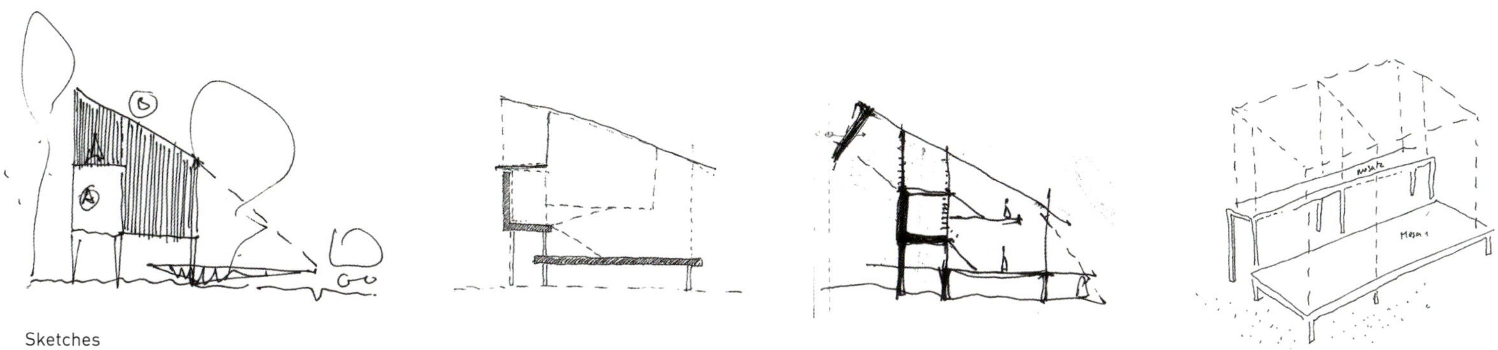

Sketches

EL CARRIZAL

SEBASTIÁN CALERO LARREA + DANIEL MORENO FLORES

The dwelling appears as a longitudinal strip that separates itself from the land, circling the existing vegetation and incorporating open green islands that are directly related to the interior. The project transmits an aesthetic of imperfection, old age and precariousness and reinterprets the conditions of local architecture, for which it uses materials from the area such as adobe, brick, wood and reeds. The interiors transmit harmony with the environment and are organised by means of an elongated central core of reeds that concentrates the circulations and in which the spaces are born and projected outwards. The project incorporates a rainwater collection system and a natural mechanism for treating black and grey water, a solar heating system for the water and the reuse of various disused materials.

Die Wohnung erscheint als ein Längsstreifen, der sich vom Land absetzt, die bestehende Vegetation umgeht und offene grüne Inseln mit direktem Bezug zum Inneren integriert. Das Projekt vermittelt eine Ästhetik von Abnutzung, Unvollkommenheit, Alter und Prekarität und interpretiert die Bedingungen einer lokalen Architektur neu, für die Materialien aus der Region wie Lehm, Ziegel, Holz und Schilf verwendet werden. Die Innenräume vermitteln Harmonie mit der Umgebung und werden durch einen länglichen zentralen Kern aus Schilfrohr organisiert, der die Zirkulationen bündelt und in dem die Räume geboren und nach außen projiziert werden. Das Projekt umfasst ein Regenwassersammelsystem und einen natürlichen Mechanismus zur Behandlung von Schwarz- und Grauwasser, eine Solaranlage zur Wassererwärmung und die Wiederverwendung verschiedener Altmaterialien.

L'habitation se présente sous la forme d'une bande longitudinale qui se sépare de la terre, contournant la végétation existante et incorporant des îles vertes ouvertes qui sont directement liées à l'intérieur. Le projet transmet une esthétique de l'usure, de l'imperfection, de la vieillesse et de la précarité et réinterprète les conditions d'une architecture locale, pour laquelle il utilise des matériaux de la région comme la terre battue, la brique, le bois et les roseaux. Les intérieurs transmettent l'harmonie avec l'environnement et sont organisés au moyen d'un noyau central allongé de roseaux qui concentre les circulations et dans lequel les espaces sont nés et projetés vers l'extérieur. Le projet comprend un système de collecte des eaux pluviales et un mécanisme naturel de traitement des eaux noires et grises, un système de chauffage solaire de l'eau et la réutilisation de divers matériaux non utilisés.

La vivienda aparece como una franja longitudinal que se separa del terreno sorteando la vegetación existente e incorporando islas verdes abiertas que se relacionan directamente con el interior. El proyecto transmite una estética de desgaste, imperfección, vejez y precariedad y reinterpreta las condiciones de una arquitectura local, para lo cual utiliza materiales de la zona tales como adobe, ladrillo, madera y carrizo. Los interiores transmiten armonía con el entorno y se organizan mediante un núcleo central alargado de carrizo que concentra las circulaciones y en el que nacen y se proyectan los espacios hacia el exterior. El proyecto incorpora un sistema de recolección para el agua de lluvia y un mecanismo natural para tratar las aguas negras y grises, un sistema de calentamiento solar para el agua y la reutilización de diversos materiales en desuso.

Front view

Rear view

Section

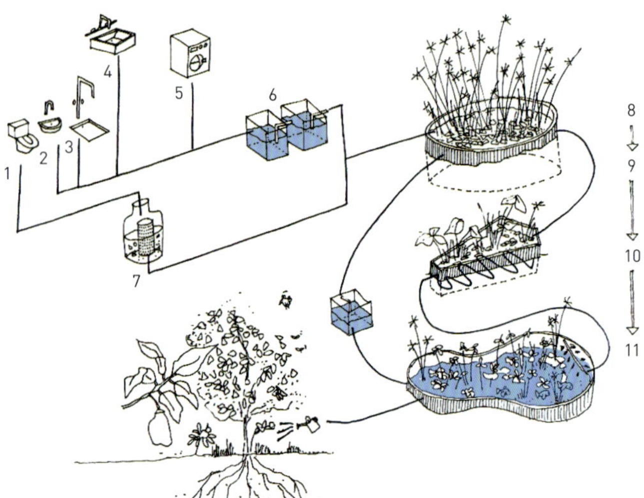

Vegetable filters

1. Toilet
2. Washbasin
3. Shower
4. Sink
5. Washing
6. Grease trap
7. Biomanager
8. Vegetable filter
   Native swamp plants for black water and grey water
9. Vertical filter
10. Horizontal filter
11. Lagoon with fish

SPARKS ARCHITECTS

Sparks Architects are a young dynamic architectural studio focused on sustainable, progressive architecture and is based at Peregian Beach on Australia's Sunshine Coast. The work of Sparks Architects is driven by the Client's brief and budget, the project's context and the firm's desire to create buildings which contribute true quality to the user experience - for both the individual and community in which they are placed. Their buildings respond to the climate in which they are located, the designs being inspired by and carefully integrated with the natural environment.
These buildings seek a balance between the built and natural environments and use form, materials, and systems that create spaces of comfort, calm, and beauty. The studio's work has been recognised by numerous awards from the Australian Institute of Architects, and published in national and international international journals and books.

Sparks Architects est un jeune studio d'architecture dynamique axé sur l'architecture durable et progressive, basé à Peregian Beach sur la Sunshine Coast en Australie. Le travail de Sparks Architects est guidé par la mission et le budget du client, le contexte du projet et le désir du cabinet de créer des bâtiments qui contribuent à la véritable qualité de l'expérience utilisateur - tant pour l'individu que pour la communauté dans laquelle ils sont placés. Leurs bâtiments répondent au climat dans lequel ils sont situés, les conceptions s'inspirant et s'intégrant avec soin à l'environnement naturel.
Ces bâtiments recherchent un équilibre entre l'environnement bâti et l'environnement naturel et utilisent des formes, des matériaux et des systèmes qui créent des espaces de confort, de calme et de beauté. Le travail de l'atelier a été reconnu par de nombreux prix de l'Australian Institute of Architects et publié dans des revues et livres nationaux et internationaux.

Sparks Architects ist ein junges und dynamisches Architekturstudio, das sich auf nachhaltige, fortschrittliche Architektur konzentriert und seinen Sitz am Peregian Beach an der Sunshine Coast Australiens hat. Die Arbeit von Sparks Architects wird durch den Auftrag und das Budget des Auftraggebers, den Kontext des Projekts und den Wunsch des Unternehmens bestimmt, Gebäude zu schaffen, die qualitativ hochwertige Nutzungserfahrungen bieten – sowohl für den Einzelnen als auch für die Gemeinschaft, in der sie sich befinden. Ihre Gebäude reagieren auf das Klima, in dem sie sich befinden, wobei die Entwürfe von der Natur inspiriert und sorgfältig in sie integriert sind.
Diese Gebäude suchen ein Gleichgewicht zwischen der gebauten und der natürlichen Umgebung und verwenden Formen, Materialien und Systeme, die Räume von Komfort, Ruhe und Schönheit schaffen. Die Arbeit des Studios wurde mit zahlreichen Preisen des Australian Institute of Architects ausgezeichnet und in nationalen und internationalen Fachzeitschriften und Büchern vorgestellt.

Sparks Architects es un estudio de arquitectura joven y dinámico centrado en la arquitectura sostenible y progresista, con sede en Peregian Beach, en la Sunshine Coast de Australia. El trabajo de Sparks Architects está impulsado por el *briefing* y el presupuesto del cliente, el contexto del proyecto y el deseo de la empresa de crear edificios que aporten una verdadera calidad a la experiencia del usuario, tanto para el individuo como para la comunidad en la que se encuentran. Sus edificios responden al clima en el que se encuentran, inspirándose los diseños en el entorno natural e integrándose cuidadosamente en él.
Estos edificios buscan un equilibrio entre el entorno construido y el natural y utilizan formas, materiales y sistemas que crean espacios de confort, tranquilidad y belleza. El trabajo del estudio ha sido reconocido con numerosos premios del Instituto Australiano de Arquitectos y publicado en revistas y libros nacionales e internacionales.

VALLEY HOUSE

TENT HOUSE

VALLEY HOUSE

The dramatic topography, bush setting of the Obi Obi Valley and Kondalilla Falls; and diverse climatic conditions of the hinterland were the driving forces for this design. A simple pavilion form was adopted which allowed for a rational approach to planning and structure.
Precast concrete rainwater tanks act as thermal buffers and spatial dividers. The tanks are partially buried in the site to allow for small plywood 'bed nests' to sit above them, regaining the lost space of the tanks footprint. The tanks and their hoop pine nests become 'precious objects', protected by the robust outer shell of masonry, steel and glass. The draped roof of the building, a subtle echo of the site topography, allows for appropriate pitch and northern orientation for the photovoltaic array, direct rainwater feed to the internal tanks and appopriate shading for winter and summer sun angles.

Die dramatische Topographie, die Buschlandschaft des Obi Obi Valley und der Kondalilla Falls sowie die unterschiedlichen klimatischen Bedingungen des Hinterlandes waren die treibenden Kräfte für diesen Entwurf. Es wurde eine einfache Pavillonform gewählt, die einen rationellen Planungs- und Strukturansatz ermöglicht.
Regenwasserspeicher aus Betonfertigteilen dienen als Wärmepuffer und Raumteiler. Die Tanks sind teilweise im Gelände vergraben, so dass kleine „Bettnester" aus Sperrholz über ihnen sitzen können, wodurch die durch die Tanks verlorene Fläche zurückgewonnen wird. Die Tanks und ihre Kiefernrahmen werden zu „Kostbarkeiten", geschützt durch die robuste Außenhülle aus Mauerwerk, Stahl und Glas. Das drapierte Dach des Gebäudes, ein subtiles Echo der Geländetopographie, ermöglicht eine angemessene Neigung und Nordorientierung der Photovoltaikanlage, eine direkte Regenwasserversorgung der internen Tanks und eine entsprechende Verschattung für Winter- und Sommersonneneinstrahlung.

La topographie spectaculaire, la végétation de la vallée de l'Obi Obi et des chutes Kondalilla, ainsi que les conditions climatiques diverses de l'arrière-pays ont été les moteurs de cette conception. Une forme simple de pavillon a été adoptée, ce qui a permis une approche rationnelle de la planification et de la structure.
Les réservoirs d'eau de pluie préfabriqués en béton font office de tampons thermiques et de séparateurs spatiaux. Les réservoirs sont partiellement enfouis dans le site pour permettre aux petits « nids de lit » en contreplaqué de s'asseoir au-dessus d'eux, regagnant ainsi l'espace perdu de l'empreinte des réservoirs. Les réservoirs et leurs nids de pins cerclés deviennent des « objets précieux », protégés par la robuste enveloppe extérieure en maçonnerie, en acier et en verre. Le toit drapé du bâtiment, un subtil écho de la topographie du site, permet d'orienter l'installation photovoltaïque vers le nord, d'acheminer directement l'eau de pluie vers les réservoirs internes et d'approprier l'ombrage pour les angles de soleil hiver et été.

La espectacular topografía, el entorno de arbustos del valle de Obi Obi y las cataratas de Kondalilla, y las diversas condiciones climáticas del interior fueron las fuerzas impulsoras de este diseño. Se adoptó una forma de pabellón sencilla que permitía un enfoque racional de la planificación y la estructura.
Los depósitos de agua de lluvia prefabricados de hormigón actúan como amortiguadores térmicos y divisores espaciales. Los tanques están parcialmente enterrados en el sitio para permitir que los pequeños «nidos de cama» de madera contrachapada se asienten sobre ellos, recuperando el espacio perdido de la huella del tanque. Los tanques y sus nidos de pino se convierten en «objetos preciosos», protegidos por el robusto armazón exterior de mampostería, acero y vidrio. El tejado del edificio, un sutil eco de la topografía del lugar, permite una adecuada inclinación y orientación norte para el conjunto fotovoltaico, alimentación directa de agua de lluvia a los tanques internos y sombra adecuada para los ángulos de sol de invierno y verano.

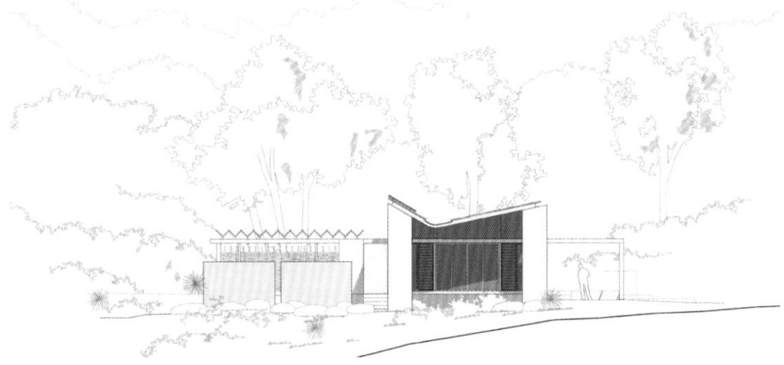
East elevation

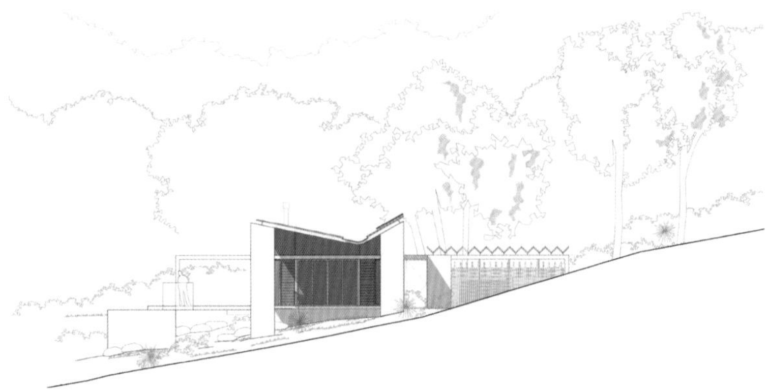
West elevation

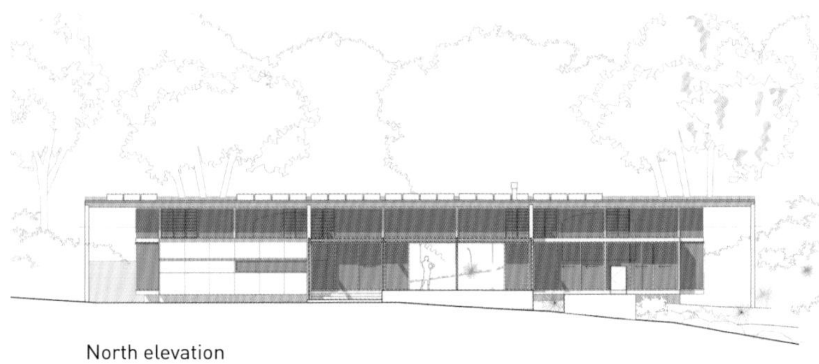
North elevation

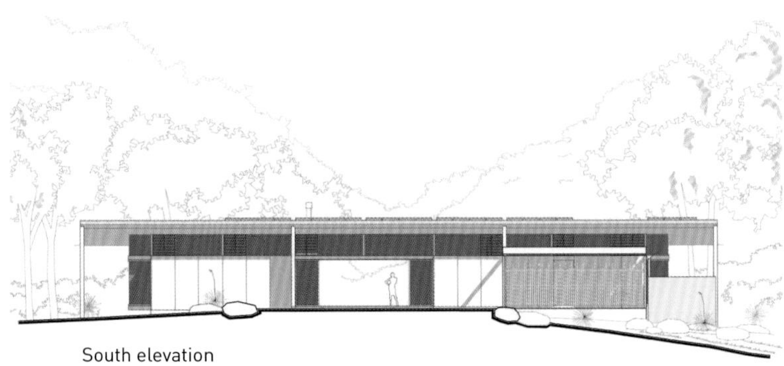
South elevation

Site plan

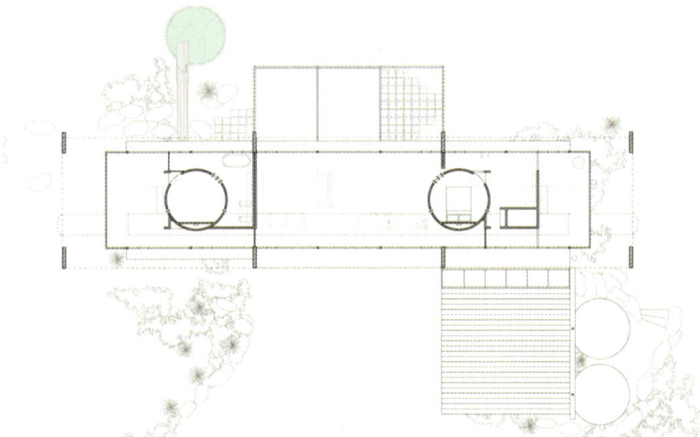

Mezzanine plan

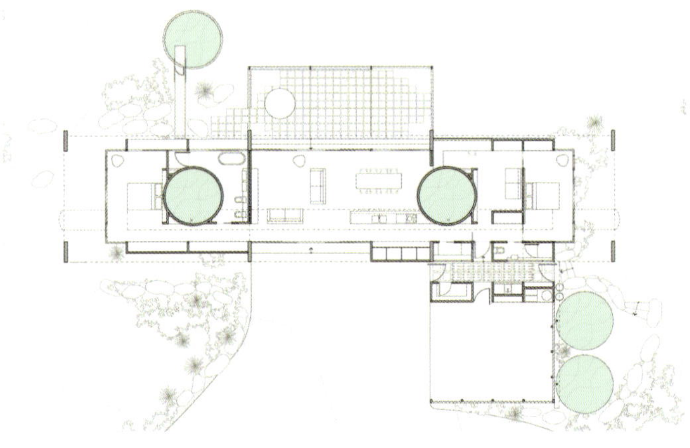

Ground floor plan

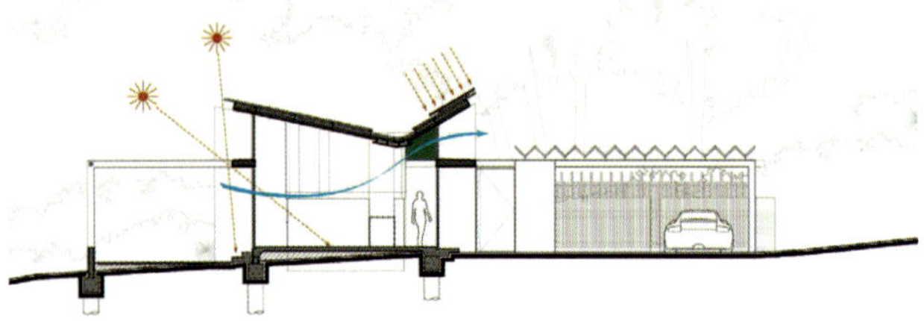

Cross section

TENT HOUSE

The architecture of this dynamic building is based on a dual concept whereby a closed and insulated box in the coldest months is transformed, by opening its enclosures in the warmest months, into a new volumetry presided over by a translucent membrane with the form of a tent that contrasts with the dark colour of the box.
The design integrates sustainable strategies adapted to the site. The plant, simple and open, is located on an east-west axis that allows you to enjoy the views over the rainforest and maximize solar gain in winter. The natural cross ventilation is complemented by the additional ventilation generated between the tent and the pavilion. Rainwater collected in tanks is used for the general purpose of the house and to maintain the orchard. Trees felled during construction were reused in various carpentry elements.

Die Architektur dieses dynamischen Gebäudes basiert auf einem dualen Konzept, bei dem eine geschlossene und isolierte Box in den kältesten Monaten durch das Öffnen ihrer Gehäuse in den wärmsten Monaten in ein neues Volumen umgewandelt wird, das von einer lichtdurchlässigen Membran wie einem Zelt überlagert wird, das mit der dunklen Farbe der Box kontrastiert.
Das Design integriert nachhaltige Strategien, die an den Standort angepasst sind. Die Anlage, einfach und offen, befindet sich auf einer Ost-West-Achse, die es den Bewohnern ermöglicht, den Blick über den Regenwald zu genießen und den Sonnenertrag im Winter zu maximieren. Die natürliche Querlüftung wird durch die zusätzliche Belüftung zwischen Zelt und Pavillon ergänzt. Das in Tanks gesammelte Regenwasser wird für den allgemeinen Zweck des Hauses und zur Pflege des Obstgartens verwendet. Die während des Baus gefällten Bäume wurden in verschiedenen Schreinerei-Elementen wiederverwendet.

L'architecture de ce bâtiment dynamique repose sur un double concept : une boîte fermée et isolée dans les mois les plus froids se transforme, en ouvrant ses enceintes dans les mois les plus chauds, en une nouvelle volumétrie présidée par une membrane translucide comme une tente qui contraste avec la couleur sombre de la boîte.
La conception intègre des stratégies durables adaptées au site. L'usine, simple et ouverte, est située sur un axe est-ouest qui permet de profiter de la vue sur la forêt tropicale et de maximiser le gain solaire en hiver. La ventilation transversale naturelle est complétée par la ventilation supplémentaire générée entre la tente et le pavillon. L'eau de pluie recueillie dans les citernes est utilisée pour l'usage général de la maison et pour l'entretien du verger. Les arbres abattus pendant la construction ont été réutilisés dans divers éléments de menuiserie.

La arquitectura de este dinámico edificio se basa en un concepto dual por el que una caja cerrada y aislada en los meses más fríos se transforma, al abrir sus cerramientos en los meses cálidos, en una nueva volumetría presidida por una membrana translúcida a modo de carpa que contrasta con el color oscuro de la caja.
El diseño integra estrategias sostenibles adecuadas al emplazamiento. La planta, simple y abierta, se sitúa sobre un eje este-oeste que permite disfrutar de las vistas sobre la selva tropical y maximizar la ganancia solar en invierno. La ventilación cruzada natural se complementa con la ventilación adicional generada entre la carpa y el pabellón. El agua de lluvia recolectada en tanques se utiliza para los fines generales de la casa y para mantener el huerto. Los árboles talados durante la construcción se reutilizaron en diversos elementos de carpintería.

North elevation

South elevation

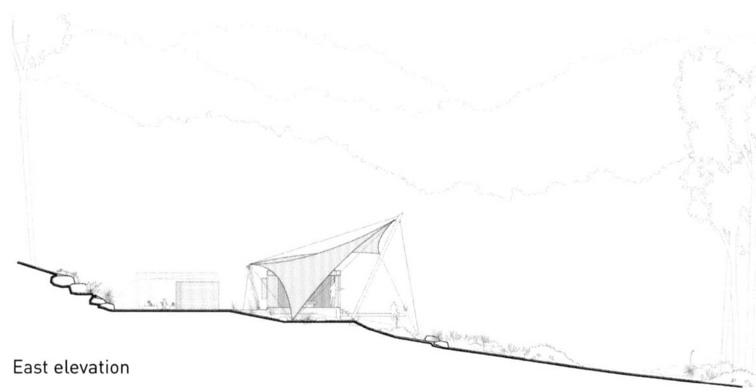

East elevation

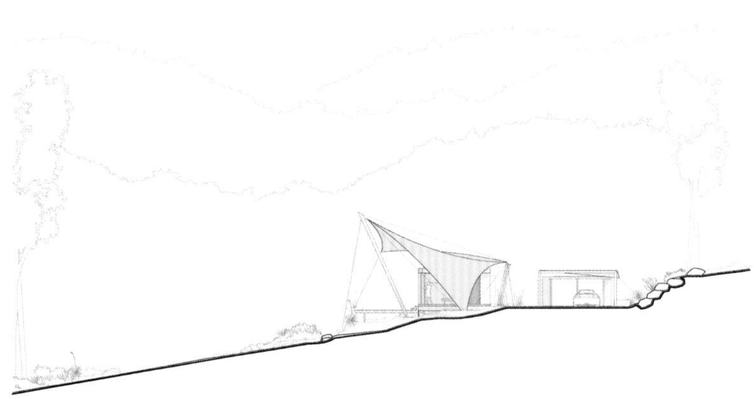

West elevation

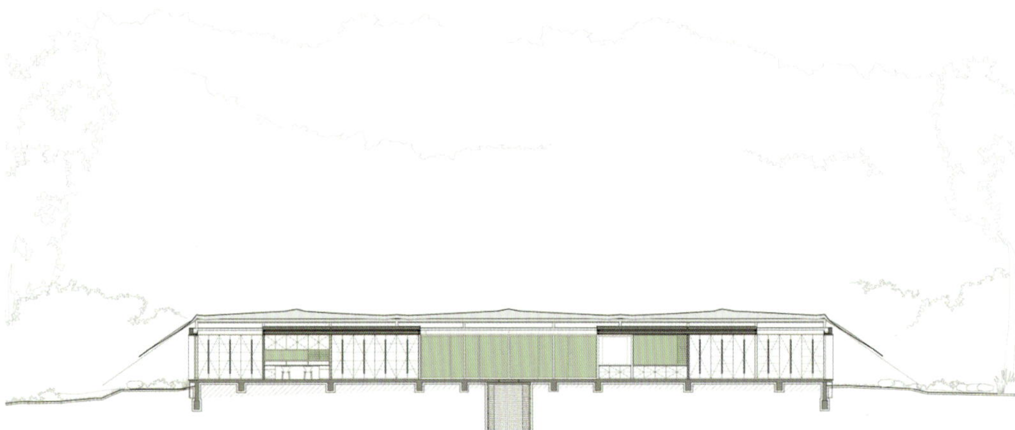

Section

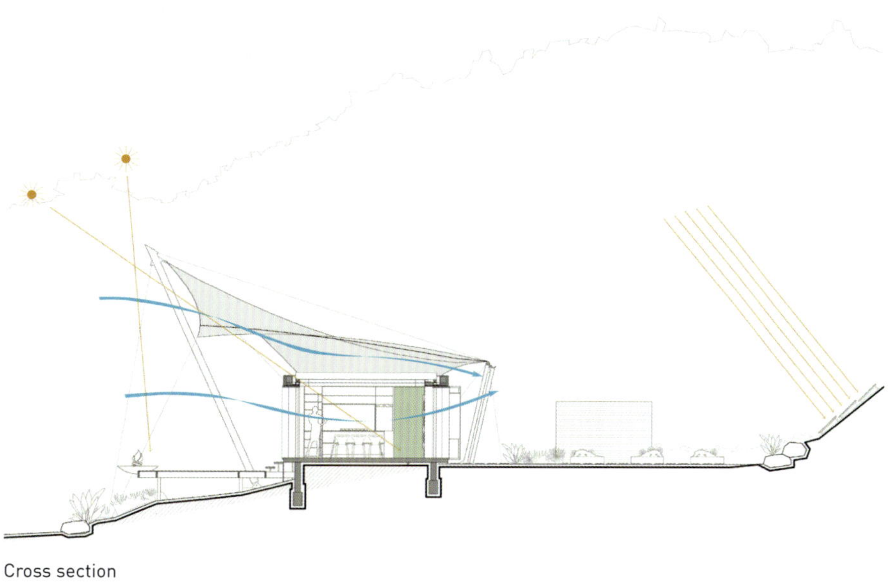

Cross section

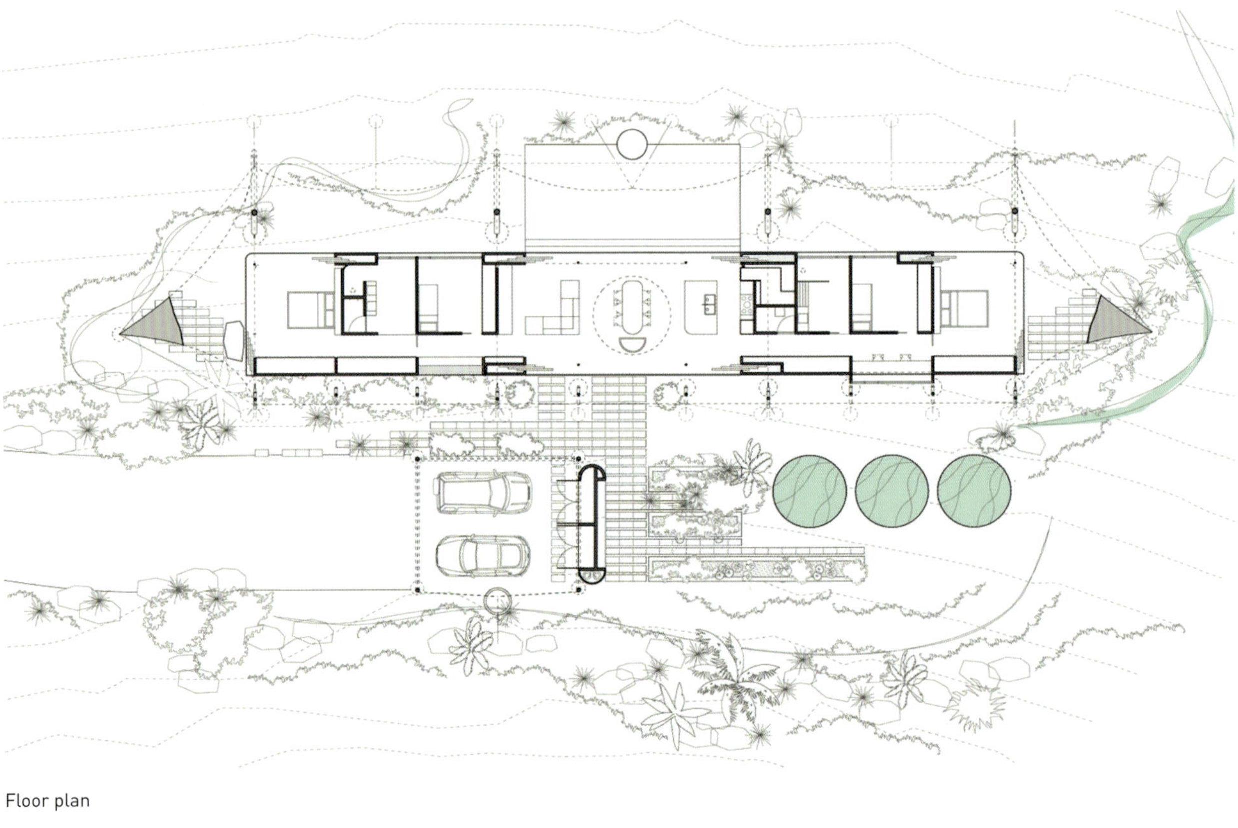

Floor plan

STEENDIJK

Brian Steendijk's bold and energetic work creatively conveys an emotive sculptural allure, exploring line, colour and form. The 'Steendijk' design studio synergises and engages a mixture of design disciplines, including architecture, interior and exhibition design, landscape, planning and urban design, and product design. The practice is engaged in 'convergent design' where a perceptive, interdisciplinary approach is applied to resolve project complexities. The success of this approach has been recognised through numerous awards, exhibitions and publications.
The studio's designs possess a free-spirited Australian larrikinism that provides robust product solutions for design focused clientele. "Our design practice is passionate about the creation of designs that are sustainable environmentally, functionally, and aesthetically. An emotive sculptural quality that possesses an underlying logic is imbued in each design resulting in pertinent objects that combine elegance with panache."

Le travail audacieux et énergique de Brian Steendijk transmet de façon créative une allure sculpturale émotive, explorant lignes, couleurs et formes. Le studio de design « Steendijk » crée des synergies et fait appel à un mélange de disciplines du design, notamment l'architecture, le design d'intérieur et d'exposition, le paysage, la planification et le design urbain, et le design de produits. La pratique est engagée dans une « conception convergente » où une approche perceptive et interdisciplinaire est appliquée pour résoudre les complexités d'un projet. Le succès de cette approche a été reconnu par de nombreux prix, expositions et publications.
Les conceptions du studio possèdent un larrikinisme australien libre d'esprit qui fournit des solutions de produits robustes pour une clientèle axée sur le design. « Notre pratique du design est passionnée par la création de designs qui sont durables sur le plan environnemental, fonctionnel et esthétique. Une qualité sculpturale émotive qui possède une logique sous-jacente s'imprègne à chaque dessin et donne naissance à des objets pertinents qui allient élégance et panache. »

Brian Steendijks mutige und energische Arbeit vermittelt kreativ eine emotionale skulpturale Verlockung und erforscht Linie, Farbe und Form. Das Designstudio „Steendijk" verbindet und verfolgt eine Mischung aus Designdisziplinen, darunter Architektur, Innenarchitektur und Ausstellungsdesign, Landschafts-, Planungs- und Städtebau sowie Produktdesign. Das Büro beschäftigt sich mit dem „konvergenten Design", bei dem ein wahrnehmender, interdisziplinärer Ansatz zur Lösung von Projektkomplexitäten angewendet wird. Der Erfolg dieses Ansatzes wurde durch zahlreiche Auszeichnungen, Ausstellungen und Publikationen gewürdigt.
Die Designs des Studios besitzen einen australischen Larrikinismus, der robuste Produktlösungen für designorientierte Kunden bietet. „Unsere Designpraxis ist leidenschaftlich an der Entwicklung von Designs interessiert, die ökologisch, funktional und ästhetisch nachhaltig sind. Eine emotionale skulpturale Qualität, die eine zugrundeliegende Logik besitzt, wird in jedem Design umgesetzt, was zu passenden Objekten führt, die Eleganz mit Eleganz und Eleganz verbinden."

La audaz y enérgica obra de Brian Steendijk transmite creativamente un emotivo encanto escultórico, explorando la línea, el color y la forma. El estudio de diseño Steendijk mezcla varias disciplinas de diseño, incluyendo arquitectura, diseño de interiores y exposiciones, paisajismo, planificación y diseño urbano y diseño de productos. El estudio se dedica a un «diseño convergente» en el que se aplica un enfoque perceptivo e interdisciplinario para resolver las complejidades del proyecto. El éxito de este enfoque ha sido reconocido a través de numerosos premios, exposiciones y publicaciones.
Los diseños del estudio poseen un estilo australiano de espíritu libre que proporciona soluciones de productos robustos para una clientela centrada en el diseño. «Nuestra empresa se apasiona por la creación de diseños que sean sostenibles desde el punto de vista medioambiental, funcional y estético. Una cualidad escultórica emotiva que posee una lógica subyacente se impregna en cada diseño, dando como resultado objetos pertinentes que combinan elegancia con garbo».

BELLBIRD RETREAT

This weekend home in a forest reserve fosters a dialogue between the natural and man-made environment through form and materials, climate sensitivity and the structure of views. Three pivoting brick walls define the organic shape of the house, shortening the perception of the façade and protecting it from southern winds, rain and fire. Inside, the space expands through a continuous boomerang shaped glass façade to blend in with the landscape. The thermal mass of the three-layer walls and the concrete slab minimizes temperature fluctuations in the interior. The pleated steel corten roof channels supply water to the house, offering a simple structural solution that allows for a north-facing overhang and has a maintenance-free finish.

Das Wochenendhaus in einem Waldreservat fördert den Dialog zwischen der natürlichen und der vom Menschen geschaffenen Umwelt durch Form und Material, Klimasensitivität und die Struktur der Ansichten. Drei schwenkbare Ziegelwände definieren die organische Form des Hauses, verkürzen die Wahrnehmung der Fassade und schützen sie vor Südwinden, Regen und Feuer. Im Inneren dehnt sich der Raum durch eine durchgehend bumerangförmige Glasfassade aus, die sich in die Landschaft einfügt. Die thermische Masse der dreischichtigen Wände und der Betonplatte minimiert Temperaturschwankungen im Innenraum. Das plissierte Cortenstahldach leitet das Wasser zu den Tanks, die das Haus versorgen, und bietet eine einfache konstruktive Lösung, die einen nach Norden gerichteten Überhang ermöglicht und wartungsfrei ausgeführt ist.

Cette maison de week-end dans une réserve forestière favorise le dialogue entre l'environnement naturel et l'environnement artificiel par la forme et les matériaux, la sensibilité climatique et la structure des vues. Trois murs de briques pivotants définissent la forme organique de la maison, réduisant la perception de la façade et la protégeant des vents du sud, de la pluie et du feu. À l'intérieur, l'espace s'agrandit grâce à une façade de verre en forme de boomerang continu pour s'intégrer dans le paysage. La masse thermique des murs à trois couches et de la dalle de béton minimise les fluctuations de température à l'intérieur. Le toit en corten d'acier plissé canalise l'eau vers les réservoirs qui alimentent la maison, offre une solution structurelle simple qui permet un porte-à-faux vers le nord et a une finition sans entretien.

Esta vivienda de fin de semana situada en una reserva forestal fomenta un diálogo entre el entorno natural y el creado por el hombre a través de la forma y los materiales, la sensibilidad climática y la estructura de las vistas. Tres muros de ladrillo pivotantes definen la forma orgánica de la casa, acortando la percepción de la fachada, y la protegen de los vientos del sur, la lluvia y los incendios. En el interior, el espacio se expande a través de una fachada continua de vidrio en forma de bumerán para mezclarse con el paisaje. La masa térmica de los muros de tres capas y de la losa de hormigón minimiza las fluctuaciones de temperatura en el interior. La cubierta plisada de acero corten canaliza el agua hacia los tanques que abastecen la casa, ofrece una solución estructural simple que permite un voladizo orientado a norte y presenta un acabado sin mantenimiento.

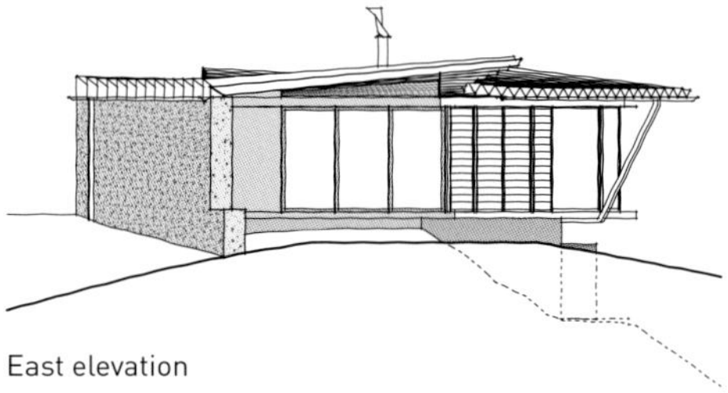
East elevation

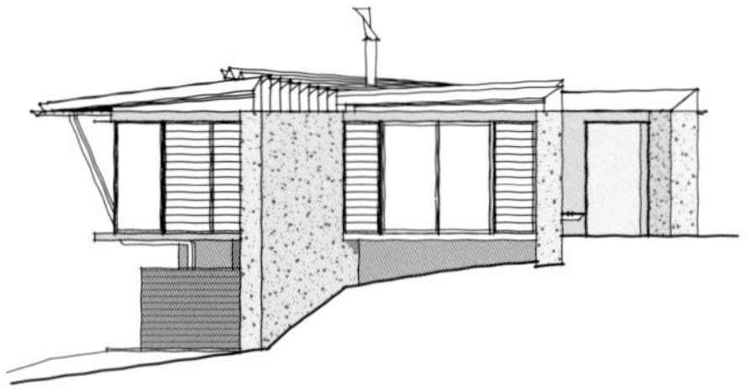
West elevation

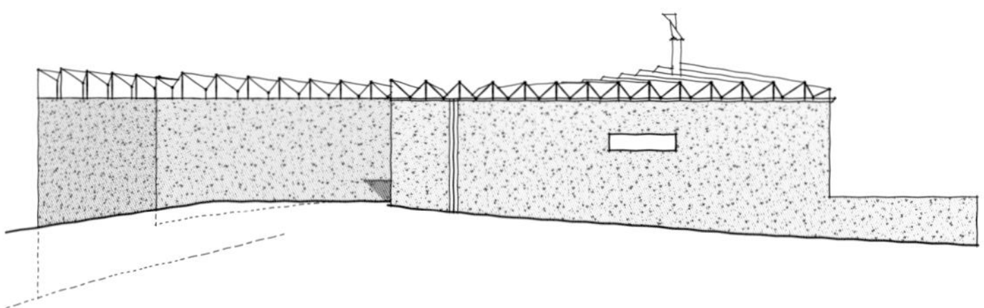
South elevation

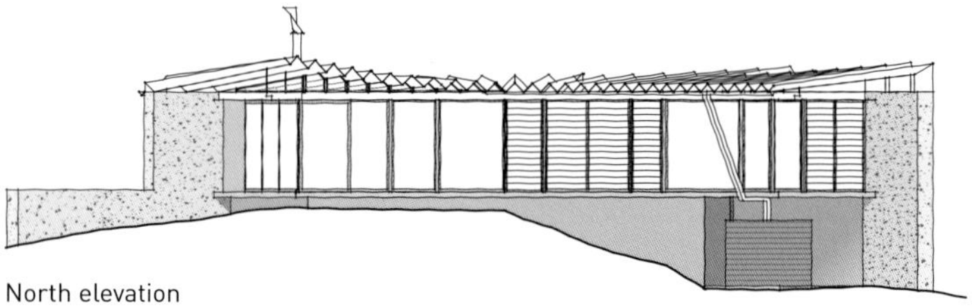
North elevation

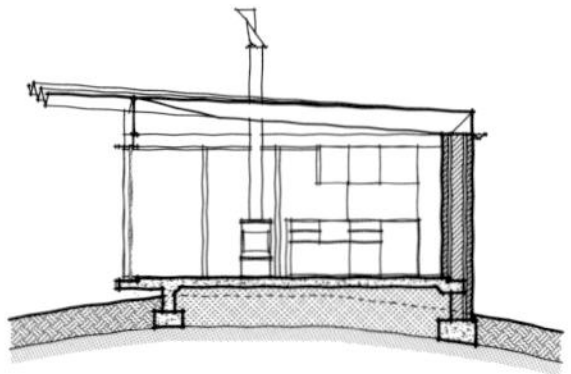
Cross section

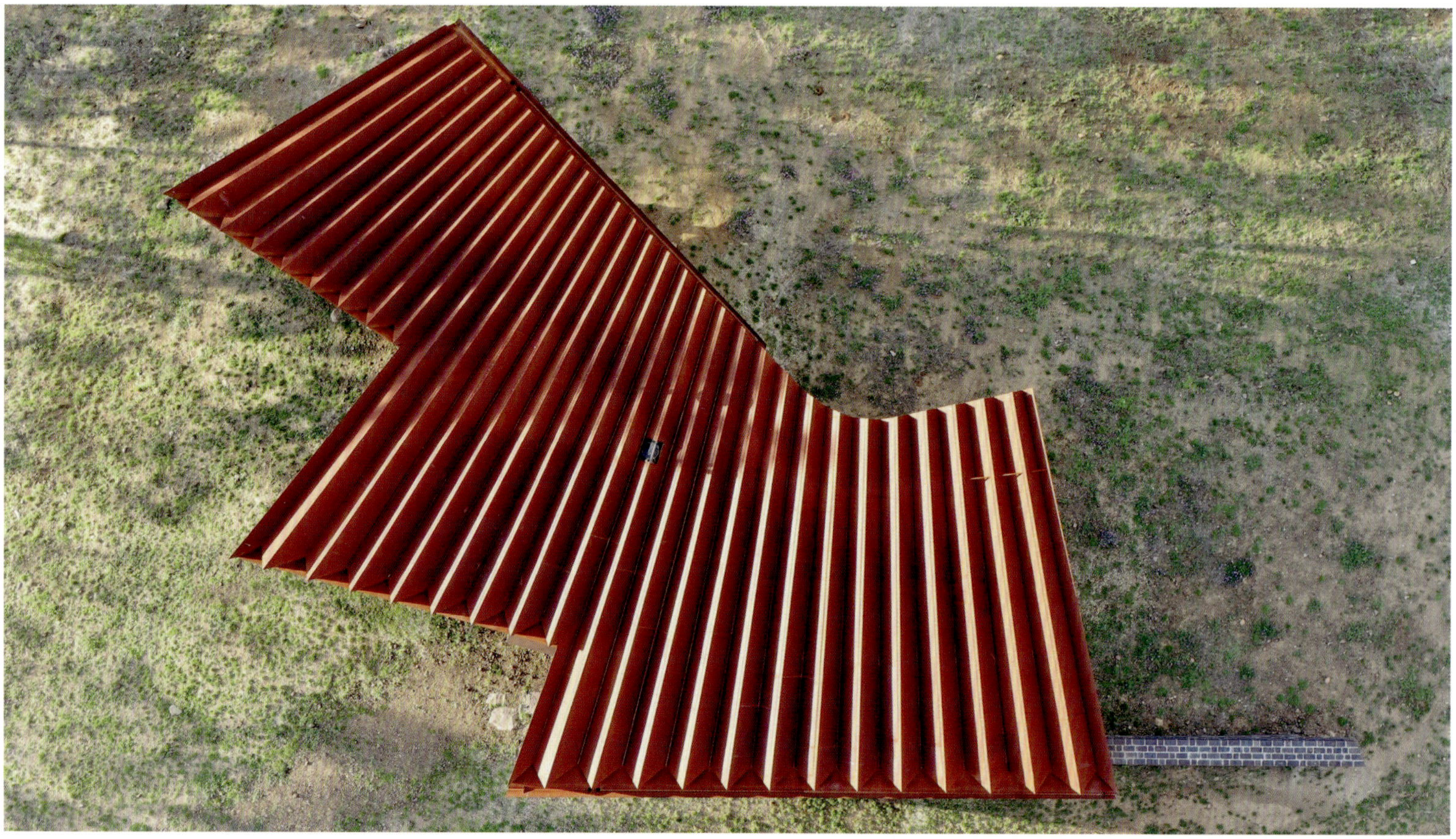

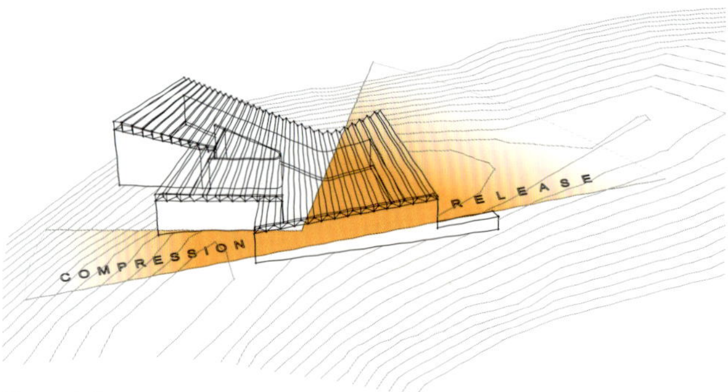

Concept diagram

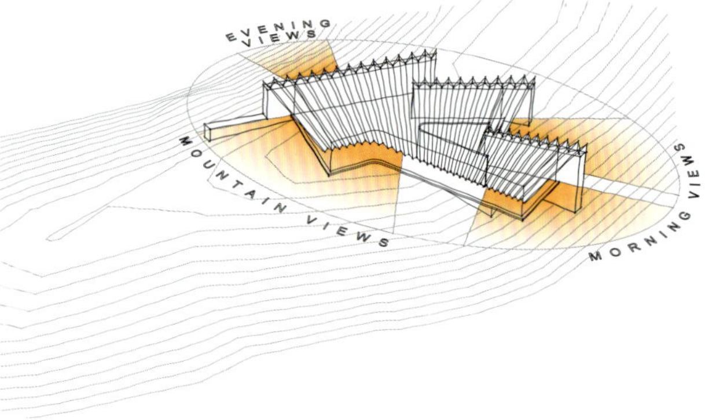

View diagram

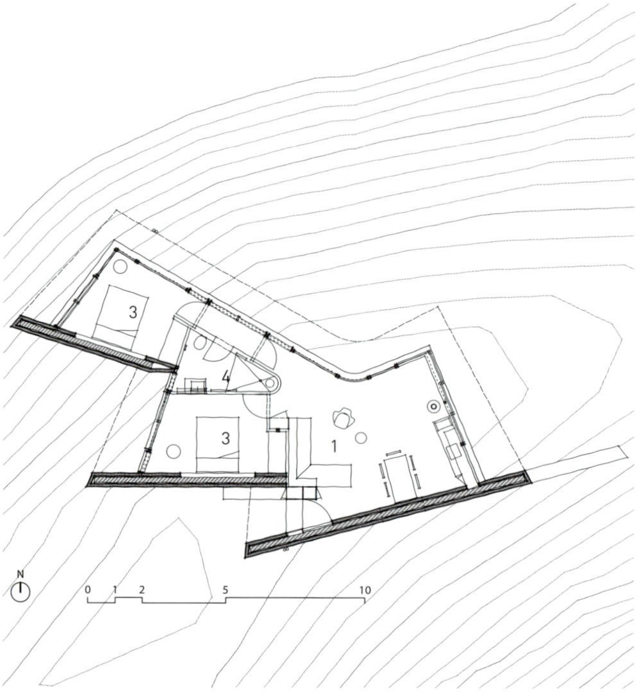

Floor plan

1. Living
2. Kitchen
3. Bedroom
4. Bathroom

STEMPEL TESAŘ ARCHITEKTI

Stempel Tesař architekti is an architectural office based in Prague and founded in 2008 by prof. Ing. arch. Ján Stempel and Ing. arch. Jan Jakub Tesař, Ph.D.
Our aim is for Stempel & Tesař architects to be associated with beautiful, elegant, and original buildings that serve their inhabitants perfectly, down to the very last detail. Every house reflects the unique character of its builder and its location. We aim to incorporate these qualities into our buildings with the greatest level of responsibility towards society and the landscape. For us, a house is like a child. You cannot abandon it at any phase of its existence, not even after it has been finished. We are interested in how a house serves its users and how it ages.

Stempel Tesař architekti est un bureau d'architecture basé à Prague et fondé en 2008 par le professeur Ing. arch. Ján Stempel et Ing. arch. Jan Jakub Tesař, Ph.D.
Notre objectif est d'associer les architectes de Stempel & Tesař à des bâtiments beaux, élégants et originaux qui servent parfaitement leurs habitants, jusque dans les moindres détails. Chaque maison reflète le caractère unique de son constructeur et de son emplacement. Notre objectif est d'intégrer ces qualités dans nos bâtiments avec le plus haut niveau de responsabilité envers la société et le paysage. Pour nous, une maison est comme un enfant. Vous ne pouvez l'abandonner à aucun moment de son existence, pas même lorsque celle-ci est terminée. Nous nous intéressons à la façon dont une maison sert ses utilisateurs et à la façon dont elle vieillit.

Stempel Tesař architekti ist ein Architekturbüro mit Sitz in Prag und wurde 2008 von Prof. Ing. Arch. Ján Stempel und Ing. Arch. Jan Jakub Tesař, Ph.D., gegründet.
Unser Ziel ist es, dass die Architekten von Stempel & Tesař mit schönen, eleganten und originellen Gebäuden in Verbindung gebracht werden, die ihre Bewohner bis ins kleinste Detail perfekt bedienen. Jedes Haus spiegelt den einzigartigen Charakter seines Bauherrn und seiner Lage wider. Diese Qualitäten wollen wir in unsere Gebäude integrieren, mit der größten Verantwortung gegenüber Gesellschaft und Landschaft. Für uns sind Häuser wie Kinder. Man kann sie in keiner Phase ihrer Existenz aufgeben, auch nicht nach ihrer Fertigstellung. Wir sind daran interessiert, wie ein Haus seine Nutzer bedient und wie es altert.

Stempel Tesař architekti es un estudio de arquitectura con sede en Praga fundado en 2008 por el profesor Ing. arch. Ján Stempel y el profesor Ing. arch. Jan Jakub Tesař, Ph.D.
Nuestro objetivo es que se asocie a los arquitectos de Stempel & Tesař con edificios bellos, elegantes y originales que sirvan a sus habitantes a la perfección, hasta el último detalle. Cada casa refleja el carácter único de su constructor y su ubicación. Pretendemos incorporar estas cualidades en nuestros edificios con el mayor grado de responsabilidad hacia la sociedad y el paisaje. Para nosotros una casa es como un niño; no puedes abandonarla en ninguna fase de su existencia, ni siquiera después de que haya sido terminada. Interesa saber cómo sirve una casa a sus usuarios y cómo envejece.

RENOVATION OF MILL AND CONVERSION INTO HOUSING

HOUSE ON WINDY PEAK

VSENORY

RENOVATION OF MILL AND CONVERSION INTO HOUSING

The reconversion into a house of this old mill located next to a pond was a radical action that revitalized the building but retained its charm. The main action consisted of creating a courtyard that allowed light to enter through a transverse glazed enclosure and interior ventilation, necessary to reduce the constant humidity that threatened the house. For this purpose, a strip of the central part was avoided thus preserving the original imprint of the building. The existing wooden structure of the roof was dismantled, renovated and repositioned in its place, leaving a view along the continuous space developed between the two upper floors. The reconversion involved a careful and gradual renovation or replacement of the various elements of the mill to meet the objective of preserving the beauty of the old construction.

Die Umnutzung dieser alten Mühle zum Wohnhaus neben einem Teich war eine radikale Maßnahme, die das Gebäude revitalisierte, aber seinen Charme bewahrte. Die Hauptaktion bestand darin, einen Innenhof zu schaffen, in den das Licht durch eine quer verglaste Einfassung und die Innenbelüftung eindringen konnte, um die konstante Feuchtigkeit, die das Haus bedrohte, zu reduzieren. Zu diesem Zweck wurde ein Streifen des Mittelteils „amputiert" und damit der ursprüngliche Abdruck des Gebäudes erhalten. Die bestehende Holzkonstruktion des Daches wurde demontiert, renoviert und an ihrer Stelle neu positioniert, so dass ein Blick auf den durchgehenden Raum zwischen den beiden Obergeschossen möglich war. Der Umbau umfasste eine sorgfältige und schrittweise Renovierung oder Erneuerung der verschiedenen Elemente der Mühle mit dem Ziel, die Schönheit des alten Gebäudes zu erhalten.

La reconversion en maison d'habitation de cet ancien moulin situé à côté d'un étang a été une action radicale qui a revitalisé le bâtiment tout en conservant son charme. L'action principale a consisté à créer une cour qui a permis à la lumière d'entrer par une enceinte vitrée transversale et une ventilation intérieure, nécessaires pour réduire l'humidité constante qui menaçait la maison. A cet effet, une bande de la partie centrale a été « amputée », préservant ainsi l'empreinte originale du bâtiment. La structure en bois du toit a été démontée, rénovée et repositionnée à sa place, permettant d'offrir une vue le long de l'espace continu développé entre les deux étages supérieurs. La reconversion a consisté en une rénovation ou un remplacement minutieux et progressif des différents éléments de l'usine afin de répondre à l'objectif de préserver la beauté de l'ancien bâtiment.

La reconversión en vivienda de este antiguo molino situado junto a un estanque supuso una actuación radical que revitalizó el edificio pero conservó su encanto. La principal actuación consistió en crear un patio que permitiese la entrada de luz a través de un cerramiento transversal acristalado y la ventilación interior, necesaria para reducir la humedad constante que amenazaba la casa. Para ello se «amputó» una franja de la parte central, preservándose así la huella original del edificio. La estructura de madera existente del techo fue desmontada, renovada y recolocada en su lugar, dejándose vista a lo largo del espacio continuo desarrollado entre las dos plantas superiores. La reconversión comportó una renovación cuidadosa y gradual o el reemplazo de los diversos elementos del molino para cumplir con el objetivo de preservar la belleza del antiguo edificio.

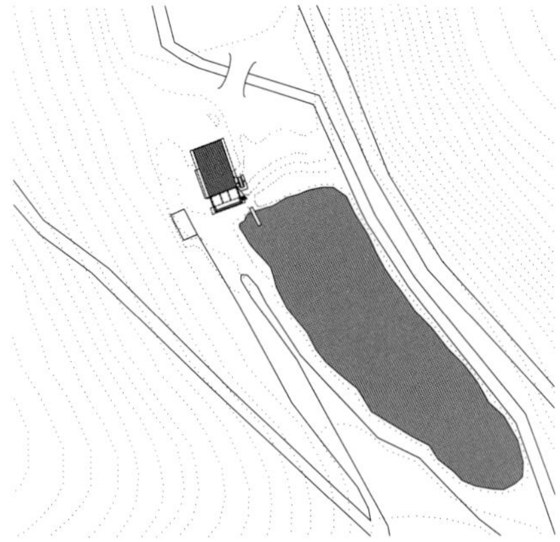

Site plan

Sketches

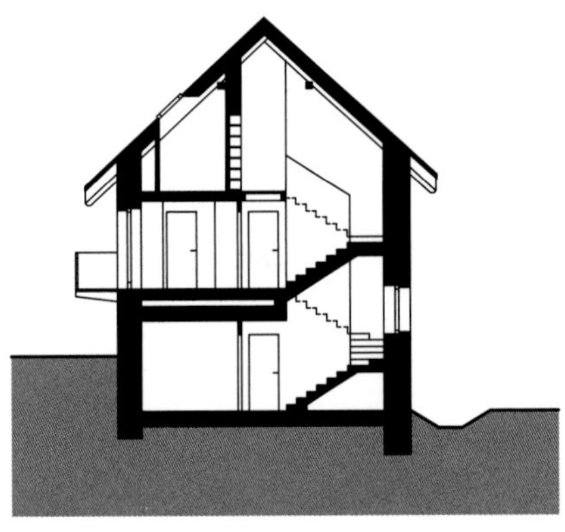

Section

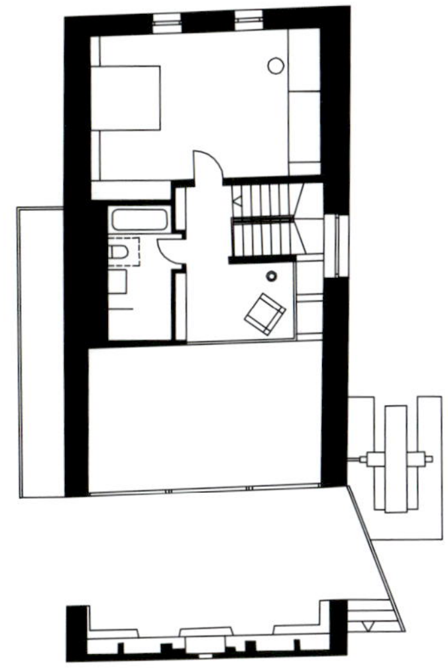

First floor plan

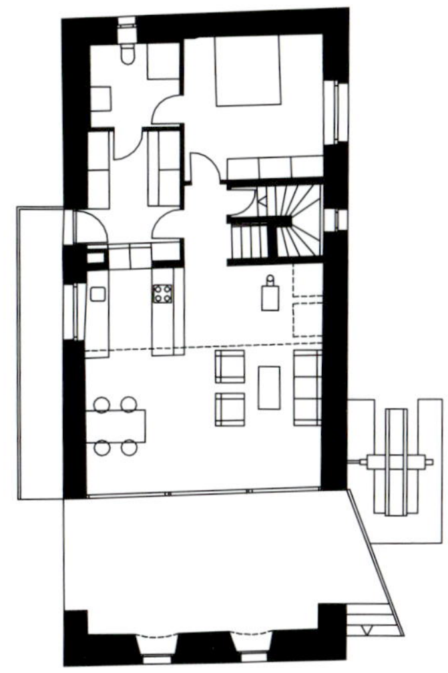

Ground floor plan

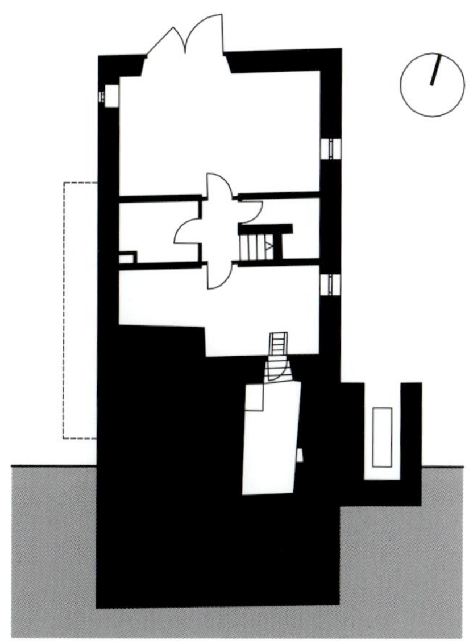

Basement plan

HOUSE ON WINDY PEAK

This traditionally designed house is situated on the top of the Ore Mountains. Its main nucleus, formed by the dining room, the living room and a small central porch, is located along the southwest façade and takes advantage of its excellent orientation through large windows that allows to enjoy the views and abundant sunlight. A lightweight one-storey staircase leads to the upper floor, where the bedrooms are located. The interior of the house is characterised by the use of wood and light colours, while the exterior is covered with dark-coloured planks characteristic of the region, obtained in an ecological way by heating the wood. The building is certified as a passive house thanks to the use of modern technology that controls the ventilation of the building, a heat pump and intelligent home systems.

Dieses traditionell gestaltete Haus liegt hoch oben im Erzgebirge. Der Kern, bestehend aus dem Esszimmer, dem Wohnzimmer und einer kleinen zentralen Veranda, liegt entlang der Südwestfassade und nutzt die hervorragende Ausrichtung durch große Fenster, die es den Bewohnern ermöglichen, die Aussicht und das reichliche Sonnenlicht zu genießen. Eine leichte, eingeschossige Treppe führt in das Obergeschoss, wo sich die Schlafzimmer befinden. Das Innere des Hauses zeichnet sich durch die Verwendung von Holz und hellen Farben aus, während das Äußere mit für die Region typischen dunklen Brettern bedeckt ist, die auf ökologische Weise durch Erwärmung des Holzes gewonnen werden. Das Gebäude ist dank des Einsatzes moderner Technik zur Steuerung der Lüftung des Gebäudes, einer Wärmepumpe und einer intelligenten Haustechnik als Passivhaus zertifiziert.

Cette maison de conception traditionnelle est située au sommet des Monts du Minerai. Son noyau principal, formé par la salle à manger, le salon et un petit porche central, est situé le long de la façade sud-ouest et profite de son excellente orientation à travers de grandes fenêtres qui vous permettent de profiter de la vue et de la lumière abondante du soleil. Un escalier léger d'un étage mène à l'étage supérieur, où se trouvent les chambres. L'intérieur de la maison se caractérise par l'utilisation de bois et de couleurs claires, tandis que l'extérieur est recouvert de planches de couleur foncée caractéristiques de la région, obtenues de manière écologique en chauffant le bois. Le bâtiment est certifié maison passive grâce à l'utilisation d'une technologie moderne qui contrôle la ventilation du bâtiment, une pompe à chaleur et une domotique intelligente.

Esta casa de diseño tradicional se sitúa en una cumbre de las montañas Ore. Su núcleo principal, formado por el comedor, la sala de estar y un pequeño porche central, se sitúa a lo largo de la fachada suroeste y aprovecha su excelente orientación mediante grandes ventanales que permiten disfrutar de las vistas y de una abundante entrada de luz solar. Una escalera ligera de un tramo conduce a la planta superior, donde se sitúan los dormitorios. El interior de la casa se caracteriza por el uso de la madera y los colores claros, mientras que el exterior se recubre con tablones de color oscuro característicos de la región, obtenidos de manera ecológica mediante el calentamiento la madera. El edificio está certificado como casa pasiva gracias al uso de moderna tecnología que controla la ventilación del edificio, una bomba de calor y una automatización inteligente del hogar.

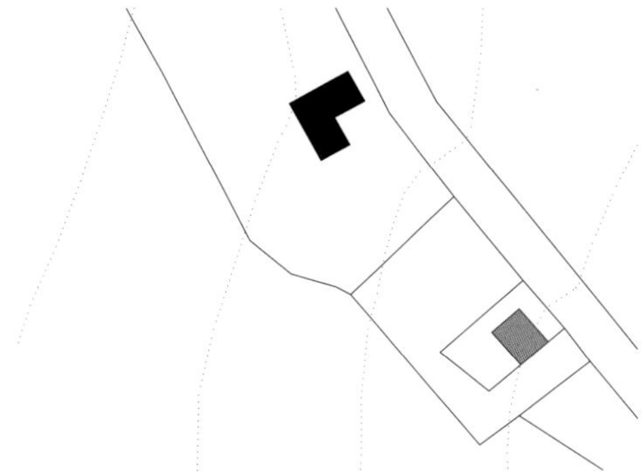

Site plan

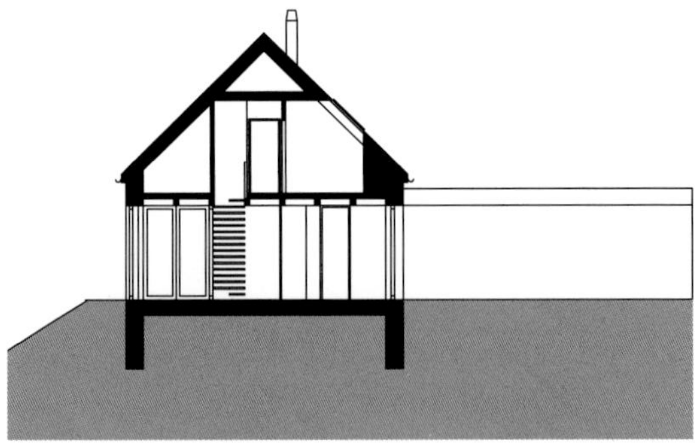

Section

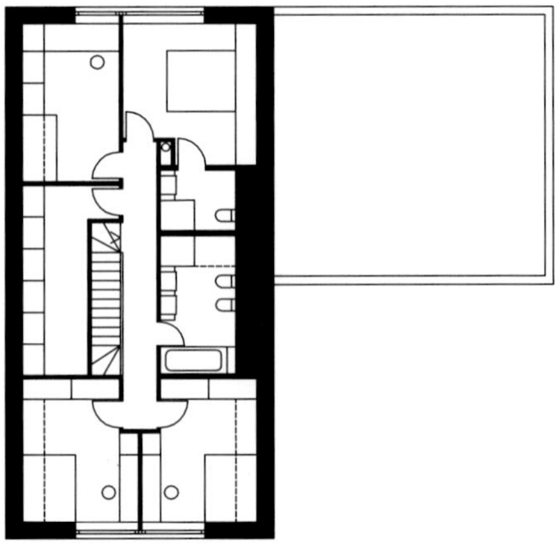

First floor plan

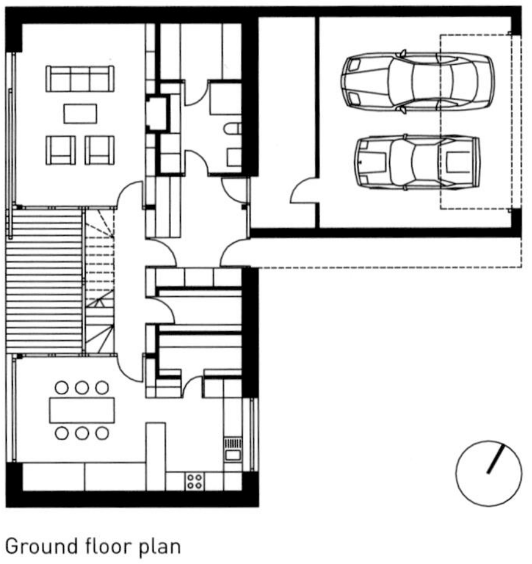

Ground floor plan

VSENORY

Situated in an old garden of a romantic villa, with beautiful views and sloping terrain, this house of strict right angles and white contrasts with the remains of the existing roundabout. Its design as a compact 4-storey tower minimises the footprint of the building, reduces costs and resolves level differences, as well as favouring the attainment of the passive house standards. Access from the street is via a metal structure that serves as a covered car park. The level of access and the common areas of the house form a single double-height space. The upper level houses the children's rooms. The lower level houses the main bedroom and the technical facilities. The composition of the façades converts the black window frames into frames of a changing nature.

Im alten Garten einer romantischen Villa mit wunderschöner Aussicht und Hanglage gelegen, kontrastiert dieses Haus mit strengen rechten Winkeln und Weiß mit den Resten des bestehenden Kreisverkehrs. Die Konstruktion als kompakter viergeschossiger Turm minimiert die Grundfläche des Gebäudes, reduziert die Fundamentkosten, löst Niveauunterschiede und begünstigt die Erreichung des Passivhausstandards. Der Zugang von der Straße erfolgt über eine Metallkonstruktion, die als überdachter Parkplatz dient. Die Zugangsebene und die Gemeinschaftsräume des Hauses bilden einen einzigen Raum doppelter Höhe. Im Obergeschoss befinden sich die Kinderzimmer und im Untergeschoss das Hauptschlafzimmer und die technischen Einrichtungen. Die Komposition der Fassaden verwandelt die schwarzen Fensterrahmen in Rahmen einer sich verändernden Natur.

Située dans un ancien jardin d'une villa romantique, avec de belles vues et un terrain en pente, cette maison aux angles droits et blancs stricts contraste avec les restes du rond-point existant. Sa conception en tour compacte de 4 étages minimise l'encombrement au sol du bâtiment, réduit les coûts de fondation et résout les différences de niveau, tout en favorisant l'atteinte de la norme de la maison passive. L'accès depuis la rue se fait par une structure métallique qui sert de parking couvert. Le niveau d'accès et les parties communes de la maison forment un seul espace à double hauteur. Le niveau supérieur abrite les chambres des enfants et le niveau inférieur abrite la chambre principale et les installations techniques. La composition des façades transforme les cadres de fenêtres noirs en cadres de nature changeante.

Situada en un antiguo jardín de una villa romántica, de hermosas vistas y terreno en pendiente, esta casa de estrictos ángulos rectos y color blanco contrasta con los restos de la glorieta existente. Su diseño como torre compacta de cuatro plantas minimiza la huella del edificio, reduce los costes de cimentación y resuelve las diferencias de nivel, además de favorecer la obtención del estándar de casa pasiva. El acceso desde la calle se realiza a través de una estructura metálica que sirve de aparcamiento cubierto. El nivel de acceso y las zonas comunes de la casa conforman un único espacio a doble altura. El nivel superior alberga las habitaciones de los niños y el nivel más inferior el dormitorio principal y las instalaciones técnicas. La composición de las fachadas convierte a los marcos negros de las ventanas en marcos de cuadros de una naturaleza cambiante.

Site plan

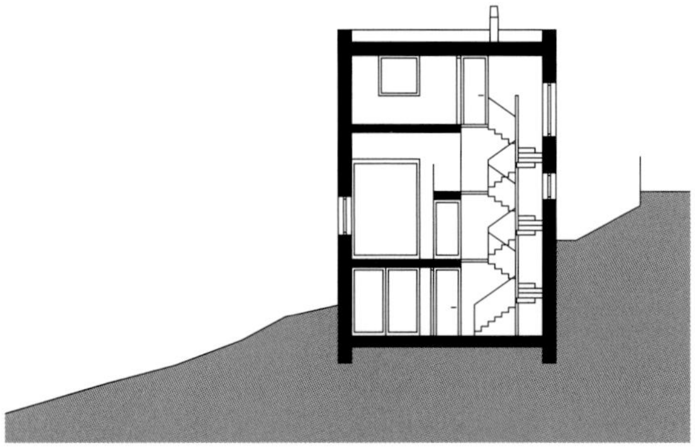

Section

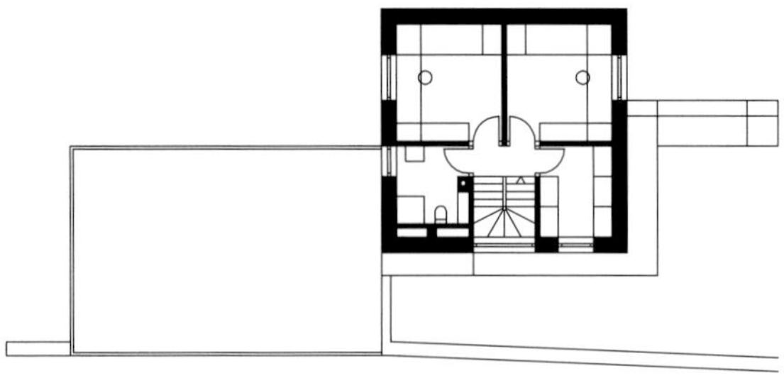

Level 1

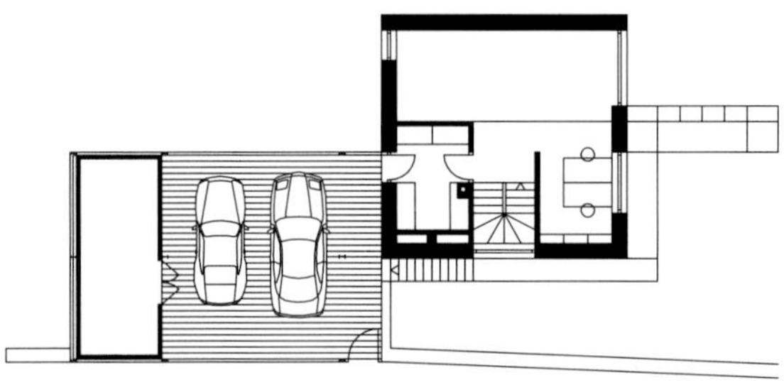

Street level

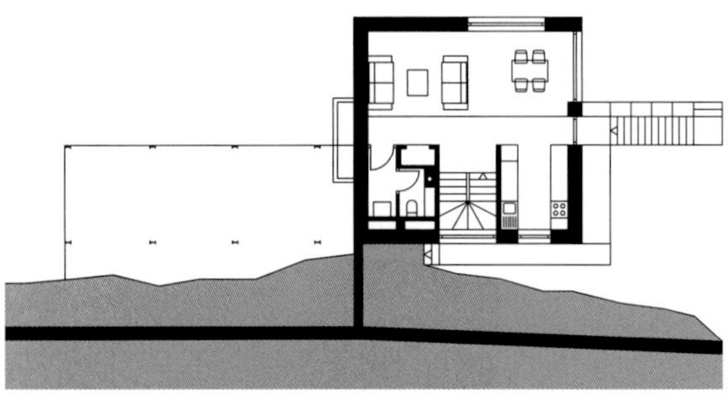

Level -1

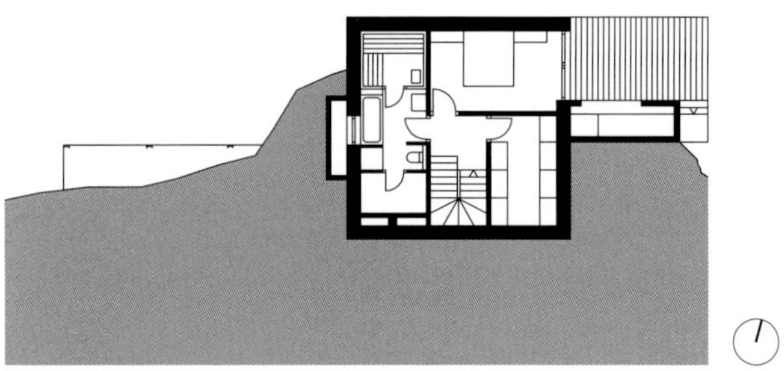

Level -2

STUDIO COMBO

Studio Combo is a young French architectural firm managed by Julien Labrousse & Jérome Friant. For the past two years, the agency has been developing projects with in-depth work on bioclimatic construction techniques and frugality issues.

Studio Combo est un jeune bureau d'architectes français dirigé par Julien Labrousse & Jérome Friant. Depuis deux ans, l'agence développe des projets avec un travail approfondi sur les techniques de construction bioclimatique et les problématiques de frugalité.

Studio Combo ist ein junges französisches Architekturbüro unter der Leitung von Julien Labrousse & Jérome Friant. In den letzten zwei Jahren hat die Agentur Projekte entwickelt, die sich intensiv mit bioklimatischen Bautechniken und Sparsamkeitsfragen befassen.

Studio Combo es un joven estudio de arquitectura francés dirigido por Julien Labrousse y Jérome Friant. Durante los últimos dos años, la agencia ha estado desarrollando proyectos con un trabajo profundo en técnicas de construcción bioclimática y problemas de frugalidad.

HOUSES ESTOSOTO CABO ESPICHEL

The objective of the project was to transform two buildings in ruins, in a process of conservation of the existing that redraws the volumes by means of a treated pine wood envelope and in which the surrounding landscape has not been altered to allow the houses to evolve in the natural context. The houses are 100% energy autonomous thanks to solar panels integrated into the vegetation. Heating and cooling are possible thanks to a heat exchanger. Grey water is treated and reused for agriculture.
The simple shapes and tones of locally produced wood used allow buildings to mix in different ways with the landscape, depending on the lights and seasons. Thanks to the varied shapes and heights of the windows, the spacious interiors enjoy views over the various landscapes of the area.

Ziel des Projekts war es, zwei Ruinen in Gebäude zu verwandeln, in einem Prozess der Erhaltung des Bestehenden, der die Volumen mit einer behandelten Kiefernholzhülle umzieht und in dem die umgebende Landschaft nicht verändert wurde, damit sich die Häuser im natürlichen Kontext entwickeln können. Die Häuser sind dank der in die Vegetation integrierten Solarmodule 100% energieautark. Heizen und Kühlen ist über einen Wärmetauscher möglich. Grauwasser wird aufbereitet und für die Landwirtschaft wiederverwendet. Die einfachen Formen und Töne des lokal produzierten Holzes ermöglichen es, dass sich die Gebäude je nach Licht und Jahreszeit auf unterschiedliche Weise mit der Landschaft vermischen. Dank der unterschiedlichen Formen und Höhen der Fenster genießen die geräumigen Innenräume einen Blick auf das abwechslungsreiche Landschaftsbild der Region.

L'objectif du projet était de transformer deux bâtiments en ruines, dans un processus de conservation de l'existant qui redessine les volumes au moyen d'une enveloppe en bois de pin traité et dont le paysage environnant n'a pas été modifié pour permettre aux maisons d'évoluer dans le contexte naturel. Les maisons sont 100 % autonomes en énergie grâce à des panneaux solaires intégrés à la végétation. Le chauffage et le refroidissement sont possibles grâce à un échangeur de chaleur. Les eaux grises sont traitées et réutilisées pour l'agriculture.
Les formes et les tons simples du bois produit localement permettent aux bâtiments de s'intégrer de différentes façons au paysage, selon les lumières et les saisons. Grâce à la variété des formes et des hauteurs des fenêtres, les intérieurs spacieux bénéficient d'une vue sur les différents paysages de la région.

El objetivo del proyecto fue transformar dos edificios en ruina, en un proceso de conservación de lo existente que redibuja los volúmenes mediante una envolvente de madera de pino tratada y en el que el paisaje circundante no ha sido alterado para permitir a las casas evolucionar en el contexto natural. Las casas son 100% autónomas energéticamente gracias a paneles solares integrados en la vegetación. La calefacción y la refrigeración son posibles gracias a un intercambiador de calor. Las aguas grises son tratadas y reutilizadas para la agricultura.
Las formas simples y los tonos de la madera de producción local utilizados permiten a los edificios mezclarse de diferentes maneras con el paisaje, dependiendo de las luces y las estaciones. Gracias a las variadas formas y alturas de las ventanas, los amplios interiores gozan de vistas sobre los diversos paisajes de la zona.

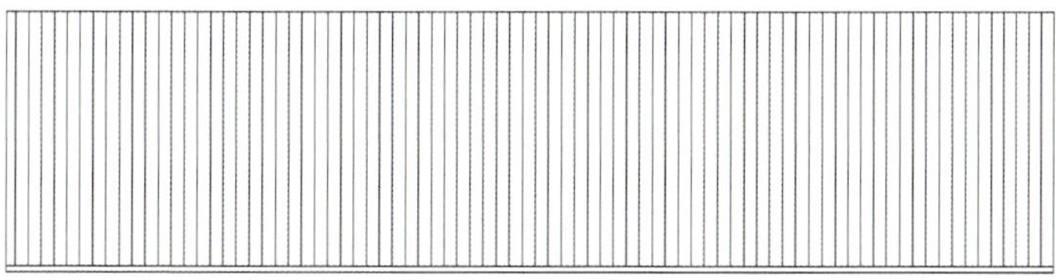

North elevation

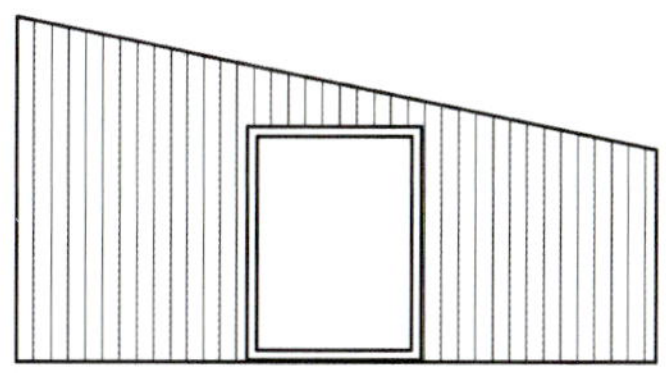

East elevation

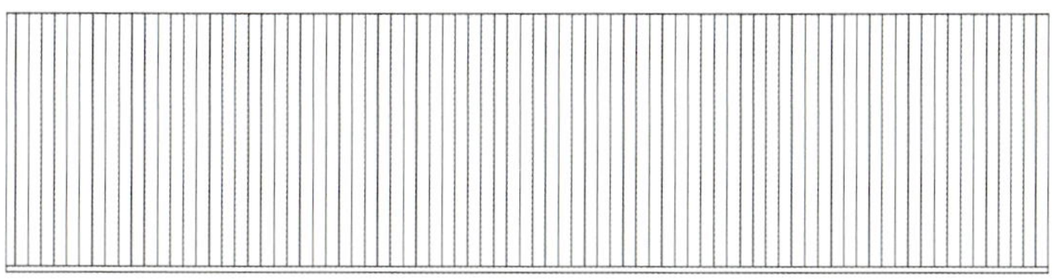

South elevation

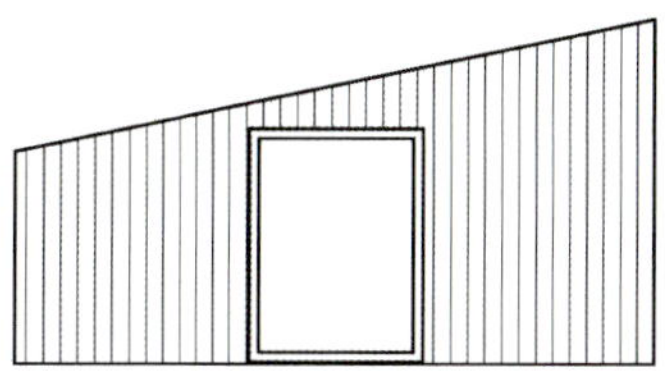

West elevation

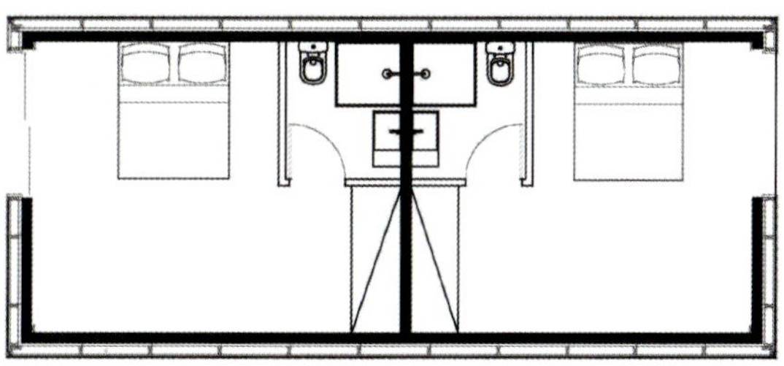

Ground floor plan

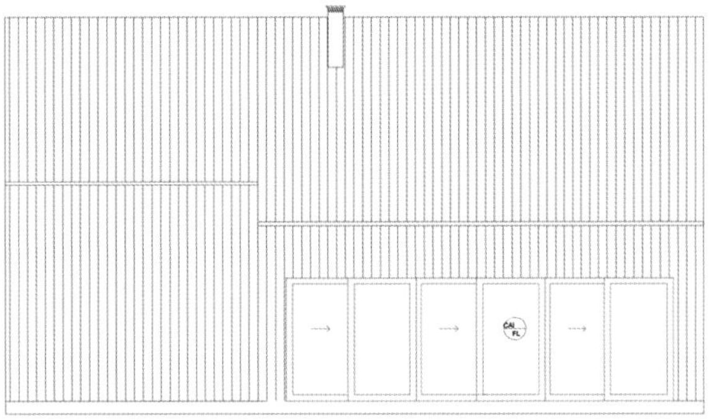

Northeast elevation. Front facade

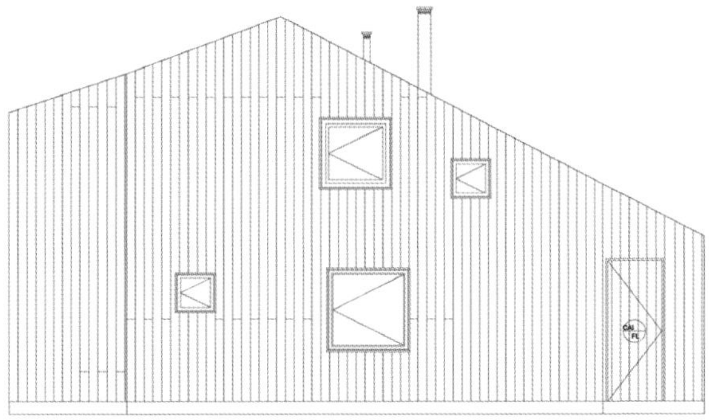

Southeast elevation

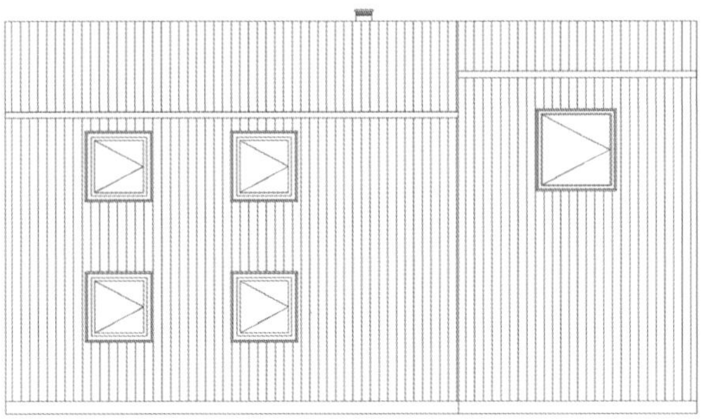

Southwest elevation

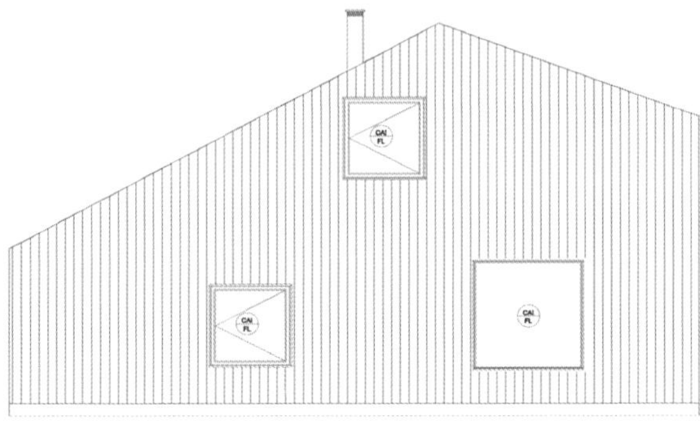

Northwest elevation

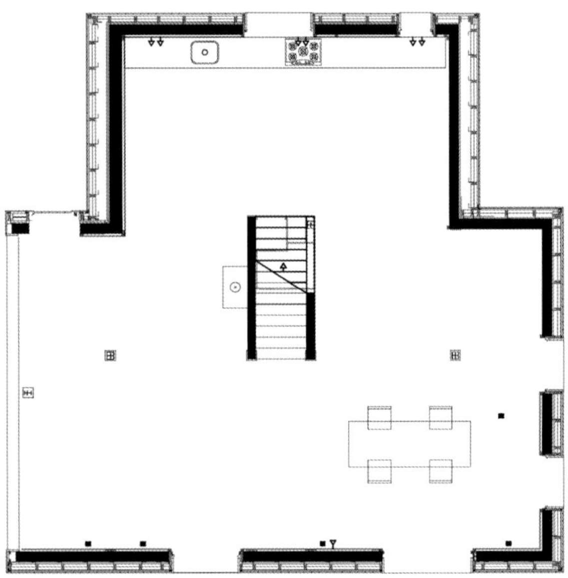

Ground floor plan

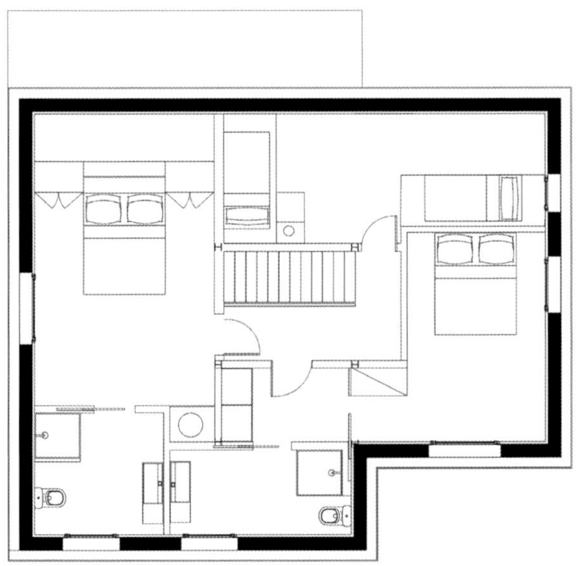

First floor plan

TEGNESTUEN LOKAL

Tegnestuen LOKAL is a young practice, established with the aim of creating sustainable architecture that respects our cultural heritage in order to support identity and diversity in a world that grows smaller day by day. We work with three subjects that combined create a holistic foundation for each project: Culture, People and environment.
Culture: We develop the historical layers so our architecture becomes a natural extension of Nordic architecture tradition and not a technological statement without root in its context.
People: We build for a sustainable lifestyle through a high degree of local community to ensure social, environmental and economic advantages. Community breeds security, is practical and ensures better use of resources.
Environment: We build buildings that have a positive effect on our local and global environment by ensuring local and renewable production and handling of energy, water and heat, but we also focus on the impact of our materials on the global environment.

Tegnestuen LOKAL est un jeune cabinet, établi dans le but de créer une architecture durable qui respecte notre patrimoine culturel afin de soutenir l'identité et la diversité dans un monde qui se réduit de jour en jour. Nous travaillons avec trois sujets qui, combinés, créent une base holistique pour chaque projet : culture, personnes et environnement.
Culture : Nous développons les couches historiques pour que notre architecture devienne un prolongement naturel de la tradition architecturale nordique et non une affirmation technologique sans racine dans son contexte.
Les gens : Nous construisons pour un mode de vie durable grâce à un haut degré de communauté locale afin d'assurer des avantages sociaux, environnementaux et économiques. La communauté engendre la sécurité, est pratique et assure une meilleure utilisation des ressources.
Environnement : Nous construisons des bâtiments qui ont un effet positif sur notre environnement local et mondial en assurant la production locale et renouvelable et la manipulation de l'énergie, de l'eau et de la chaleur, mais nous nous concentrons aussi sur l'impact de nos matériaux sur l'environnement mondial.

Tegnestuen LOKAL ist eine junges Unternehmen, das mit dem Ziel gegründet wurde, nachhaltige Architektur zu schaffen, die unser kulturelles Erbe respektiert, um Identität und Vielfalt in einer Welt zu fördern, die von Tag zu Tag kleiner wird. Wir arbeiten mit drei Themen, die zusammengenommen eine ganzheitliche Grundlage für jedes Projekt bilden: Kultur, Menschen und Umwelt.
Kultur: Wir entwickeln die historischen Schichten, so dass unsere Architektur zu einer natürlichen Erweiterung der nordischen Architekturtradition wird und nicht zu einem technologischen Statement ohne Wurzeln in ihrem Kontext.
Menschen: Wir bauen auf einen nachhaltigen Lebensstil durch ein hohes Maß an lokaler Gemeinschaft, um soziale, ökologische und wirtschaftliche Vorteile zu sichern. Die Gemeinschaft schafft Sicherheit, ist praktisch und sorgt für eine bessere Nutzung der Ressourcen.
Umgebung: Wir bauen Gebäude, die sich positiv auf unsere lokale und globale Umwelt auswirken, indem wir die lokale und erneuerbare Produktion und den Umgang mit Energie, Wasser und Wärme sicherstellen, aber wir konzentrieren uns auch auf die Auswirkungen unserer Materialien auf die globale Umwelt.

Tegnestuen LOKAL es un estudio joven, fundado con el objetivo de crear una arquitectura sostenible que respete el patrimonio cultural para apoyar la identidad y la diversidad en un mundo cada vez más pequeño. Trabajamos con tres conceptos que combinados crean una base holística para cada proyecto: la cultura, la gente y el medio ambiente.
Cultura: Desarrollamos las capas históricas para que nuestra arquitectura se convierta en una extensión natural de la tradición de la arquitectura nórdica y no en una afirmación tecnológica sin raíces en su contexto.
Gente: Construimos para lograr un estilo de vida sostenible a través de un alto grado de comunidad local que asegure ventajas sociales, ambientales y económicas. La comunidad fomenta la seguridad, es práctica y garantiza un mejor uso de los recursos.
Medio ambiente: Construimos edificios que tienen un efecto positivo en el entorno local y global, asegurando la producción renovable y el manejo de la energía, el agua y el calor. Nos centramos asimismo en el impacto de los materiales en el medio ambiente global.

TK-33

The focus of this house is to identify CO_2-heavy elements of the typical Danish house and replace them with eco-friendly alternatives in a contemporary formal language that resonates with the existing qualities of the town.
Concrete and brick building components of a typical house are replaced by a load bearing wooden structure, clad in a thin layer of tile shingles, which reduce emissions associated with the outer walls that usually account for 30 % of the total emissions during the construction phase. In addition, the façade system is C2C-certified allowing for reuse or gradual replacement and the distribution of the interior spaces allows for natural ventilation and a high degree of flexibility, extending the use of the house across owners.
Common areas are organized around the kitchen and expand into the natural landscape, aided by the height of the interior spaces.

Der Schwerpunkt dieses Hauses liegt darin, CO_2-belastete Elemente des typisch dänischen Hauses zu identifizieren und durch umweltfreundliche Alternativen in einer zeitgenössischen Formensprache zu ersetzen, die mit den bestehenden Qualitäten der Stadt übereinstimmt.
Beton- und Backsteinbauteile eines typischen Hauses werden durch eine tragende Holzkonstruktion ersetzt, die mit einer dünnen Schicht aus Fliesenschindeln verkleidet ist, die die Emissionen der Außenwände reduzieren, die in der Regel 30 % der Gesamtemissionen während der Bauphase ausmachen. Darüber hinaus ist das Fassadensystem C2C-zertifiziert, was eine Wiederverwendung oder einen schrittweisen Austausch ermöglicht. Die Verteilung der Innenräume schafft eine natürliche Belüftung und ein hohes Maß an Flexibilität, wodurch die Nutzbarkeit des Hauses für die Eigentümer erweitert wird.
Die Gemeinschaftsräume sind um die Küche herum organisiert und erstrecken sich in die Naturlandschaft, unterstützt durch die Höhe der Innenräume.

L'objectif de cette maison est d'identifier les éléments lourds en CO_2 de la maison danoise typique et de les remplacer par des alternatives écologiques dans un langage formel contemporain qui résonne avec les qualités existantes de la ville.
Les éléments de construction en béton et en brique d'une maison typique sont remplacés par une structure porteuse en bois, recouverte d'une mince couche de bardeaux de céramique, qui réduit les émissions associées aux murs extérieurs qui représentent habituellement 30 % des émissions totales pendant la phase de construction. De plus, le système de façade est certifié C2C, ce qui permet une réutilisation ou un remplacement progressif et la répartition des espaces intérieurs permet une ventilation naturelle et un degré élevé de flexibilité, prolongeant ainsi l'utilisation de la maison entre les propriétaires.
Les espaces communs sont organisés autour de la cuisine et s'étendent dans le paysage naturel, aidés par la hauteur des espaces intérieurs.

El objetivo de esta casa es identificar los elementos pesados de CO_2 de la típica casa danesa y reemplazarlos con alternativas ecológicas en un lenguaje formal contemporáneo que se haga eco de las cualidades existentes en la ciudad.
Los componentes de construcción de hormigón y ladrillo de una casa típica se sustituyen por una estructura de madera portante, revestida con una fina capa de tejas, que reducen las emisiones asociadas a las paredes exteriores, que suelen representar el 30 % de las emisiones totales durante la fase de construcción. Además, el sistema de fachada cuenta con la certificación C2C, lo que permite su reutilización o sustitución gradual, y la distribución de los espacios interiores permite una ventilación natural y un alto grado de flexibilidad, extendiendo el uso de la casa a todos los propietarios.
Las áreas comunes se organizan alrededor de la cocina y se expanden hacia el paisaje natural, ayudadas por la altura de los espacios interiores.

Elevation east

Elevation north

Elevation west

Elevation south

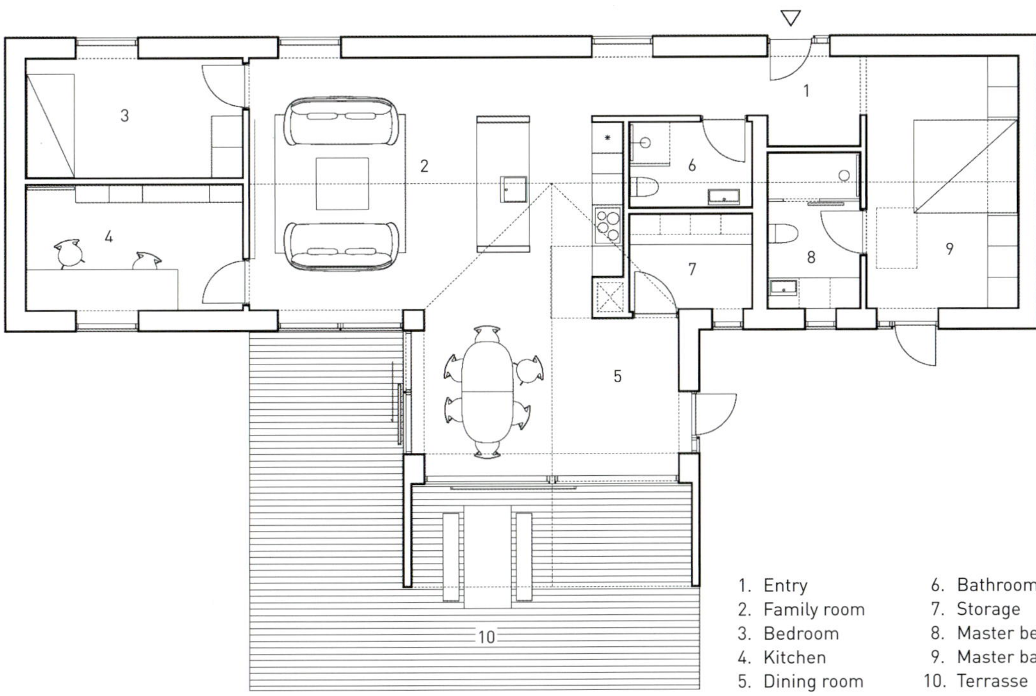

1. Entry
2. Family room
3. Bedroom
4. Kitchen
5. Dining room
6. Bathroom
7. Storage
8. Master bedroom
9. Master bathroom
10. Terrasse

Elevation south

Longitudinal section

TIM BENNETTON ARCHITECTS

In 2007, Tim Bennetton Architects was founded with the hope of designing homes that were both joyful and sustainable...that integrated interior and exterior to a high degree, and were appropriate for Queensland's subtropical climate. Since then, the design ethos of the studio has evolved over the years but the underlying interests have remained constant.
These include Tim's several years working with Gabriel and Elizabeth Poole (ongoing), collaboration with master craftspeople, his own fascination with landscape and sense of place/identity...and also his background in Civil/Structural Engineering. Queensland is almost unique in Australia for having its own vernacular domestic tradition (the 'Queenslander' houses). This tradition and the response to it informs a lot of the design work, particularly for renovation projects.
The studio is located in West End, a suburb of Brisbane, which while becoming 'gentrified' still retains its original energy, bohemian attitude, love of the arts and commitment to a sustainable planet.

En 2007, Tim Bennetton Architects a été fondé dans l'espoir de concevoir des maisons à la fois joyeuses et durables... qui intègrent l'intérieur et l'extérieur à un degré élevé, et qui conviennent au climat subtropical du Queensland. Depuis, la philosophie de conception du studio a évolué au fil des ans, mais les intérêts sous-jacents sont demeurés constants.
Il a travaillé plusieurs années avec Gabriel et Elizabeth Poole (en cours), a collaboré avec des maîtres artisans, a été fasciné par le paysage et le sens du lieu et de l'identité... ainsi que par son expérience en génie civil et structurel. Le Queensland est presque unique en Australie pour avoir sa propre tradition domestique vernaculaire (les maisons'Queenslander'). Cette tradition et la réponse qu'elle suscite sont à la base de nombreux travaux de conception, en particulier pour les projets de rénovation.

Le studio est situé dans le West End, une banlieue de Brisbane, qui, tout en devenant « gentrifiée », conserve son énergie originale, son attitude bohème, son amour des arts et son engagement pour une planète durable.

Im Jahr 2007 wurde Tim Bennetton Architects in der Hoffnung gegründet, Häuser zu entwerfen, die sowohl fröhlich als auch nachhaltig sind, die Innen- und Außenbereich in hohem Maße integrieren und dem subtropischen Klima von Queensland angemessen sind. Seitdem hat sich das Design des Studios im Laufe der Jahre weiterentwickelt, aber die zugrunde liegenden Interessen sind konstant geblieben.
Dazu gehören Tims mehrjährige Zusammenarbeit mit Gabriel und Elizabeth Poole (laufend), die Zusammenarbeit mit Meistern, seine eigene Faszination für Landschaft und Ortssinn ... und auch sein Hintergrund im Bauwesen. Queensland ist in Australien fast einzigartig, da es eine eigene einheimische Tradition hat (die Queenslander-Häuser). Diese Tradition und die Reaktion darauf prägt einen Großteil der Planungsarbeiten, insbesondere bei Renovierungsprojekten.
Das Studio befindet sich in West End, ei nem Vorort von Brisbane, der zwar „gentrifiziert" wird, aber dennoch seine ursprüngliche Energie, seine böhmische Einstellung, seine Liebe zur Kunst und sein Engagement für einen nachhaltigen Planeten bewahrt.

En 2007, Tim Bennetton Architects fue fundado con la esperanza de diseñar casas que fueran a la vez alegres y sostenibles.... que integraran el interior y el exterior en un alto grado, y que fueran apropiadas para el clima subtropical de Queensland. Desde entonces, el espíritu de diseño del estudio ha evolucionado a lo largo de los años, pero los intereses subyacentes han permanecido vigentes.
Estos incluyen los varios años de trabajo de Tim con Gabriel y Elizabeth Poole (en curso), la colaboración con maestros artesanos, su propia fascinación por el paisaje y el sentido de lugar/identidad... y también su formación en Ingeniería Civil y Estructural. Queensland es casi única en Australia por tener su propia tradición doméstica vernácula (las casas «Queensland»). Esta tradición y la respuesta a la misma influye mucho en el trabajo de diseño, especialmente en los proyectos de renovación.
El estudio está situado en West End, un suburbio de Brisbane, que aunque se está convirtiendo en un barrio «aburguesado», aún conserva su energía original, su actitud bohemia, su amor por las artes y su compromiso con un planeta sostenible.

YERONGA HOUSE

STRADBROKE HOUSE

YERONGA HOUSE

There were two main aims behind this renovation project. First, to solve problems commonly found in "Queenslander" timber houses: a dark and hot interior with poor ventilation and poor planning; and second to add a guest room and studio in the form of a new pavilion open towards the back garden. The project integrates the house into the landscape through new patios and stepped platforms that improve the relationship between interior and exterior. Sustainability was a priority for the clients. A new corridor through to the west side garden allows the interior to breathe, while a slatted awning regulates solar gain over that façade. Air conditioning was eliminated and natural ventilation and light entry was encouraged. Various water-sensitive urban design strategies are also incorporated, such as the permeable landscaped surfaces and the reuse of rainwater.

Mit diesem Renovierungsprojekt wurden zwei Hauptziele verfolgt. Erstens, um die in „Queenslander"-Holzhäusern üblichen Probleme zu lösen: ein dunkler und heißer Innenraum mit schlechter Belüftung und schlechter Planung; und zweitens, um ein Gästezimmer und ein Studio in Form eines neuen, zum Hintergarten hin offenen Pavillons hinzuzufügen. Das Projekt integriert das Haus in die Landschaft durch neue Terrassen und Stufenplattformen, die das Verhältnis von Innen und Außen verbessern. Nachhaltigkeit stand bei den Kunden im Vordergrund. Ein neuer Korridor durch den westlichen Seitengarten lässt den Innenraum atmen, während eine Lamellenmarkise den Sonneneintrag über diese Fassade reguliert. Die Klimaanlage wurde abgeschafft und die natürliche Belüftung und der Lichteintritt gefördert. Verschiedene wasserempfindliche städtebauliche Strategien werden ebenfalls einbezogen, wie z. B. die durchlässigen Landschaftsflächen und die Wiederverwendung von Regenwasser.

Ce projet de rénovation avait deux objectifs principaux. D'une part, pour résoudre les problèmes que l'on rencontre couramment dans les maisons en bois « Queenslander » : un intérieur sombre et chaud avec une mauvaise ventilation et une mauvaise planification ; d'autre part, pour ajouter une chambre d'amis et un studio sous la forme d'un nouveau pavillon ouvert sur le jardin arrière. Le projet intègre la maison dans le paysage par le biais de nouveaux patios et de plates-formes en gradins qui améliorent la relation entre l'intérieur et l'extérieur. La durabilité était une priorité pour les clients. Un nouveau couloir à travers le jardin ouest permet à l'intérieur de respirer, tandis qu'un auvent à lamelles régule le gain solaire sur cette façade. La climatisation a été éliminée et la ventilation naturelle et l'entrée de la lumière ont été encouragées. Diverses stratégies d'aménagement urbain sensibles à l'eau sont également intégrées, comme des surfaces paysagères perméables et la réutilisation de l'eau de pluie.

Este proyecto de renovación tenía dos objetivos principales. En primer lugar, para resolver los problemas que se encuentran comúnmente en las casas de madera «Queenslander»: un interior oscuro y caluroso con mala ventilación y mala planificación; y en segundo lugar, para añadir una habitación de huéspedes y un estudio en forma de un nuevo pabellón abierto hacia el jardín trasero. El proyecto integra la casa en el paisaje a través de nuevos patios y plataformas escalonadas que mejoran la relación entre interior y exterior. La sostenibilidad fue una prioridad para los clientes. Un nuevo corredor a través del jardín lateral oeste permite respirar al interior, mientras que un toldo de listones regula la ganancia solar sobre esa fachada. El aire acondicionado fue eliminado y se fomentó la ventilación natural y la entrada de luz. Se incorporan también diversas estrategias de diseño urbano sensible al agua, como las superficies ajardinadas permeables y la reutilización del agua de lluvia.

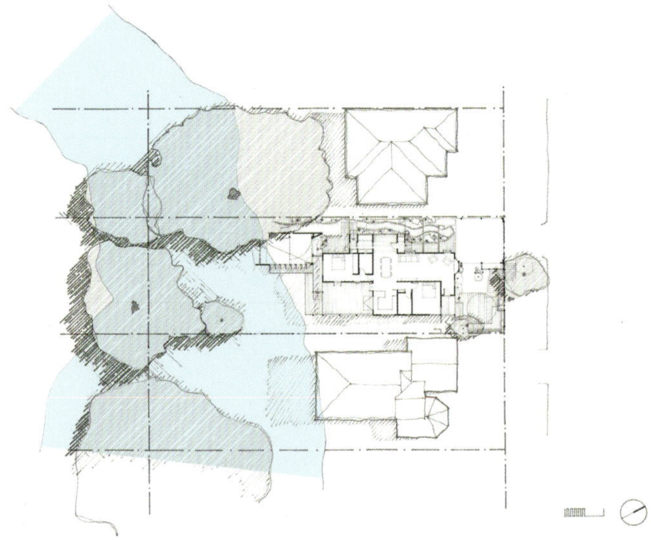

Site plan

Street elevation

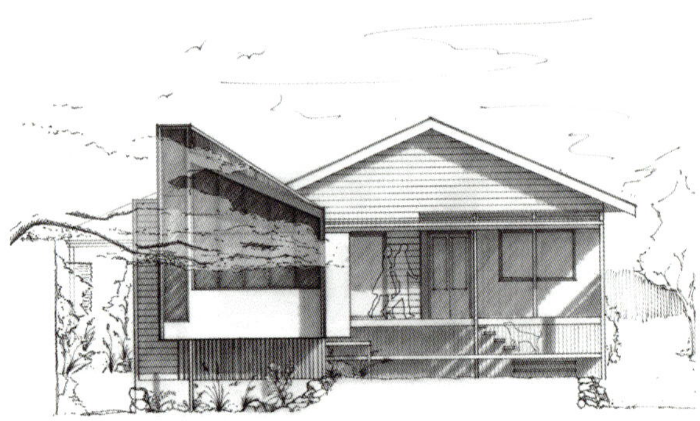

Rear elevation

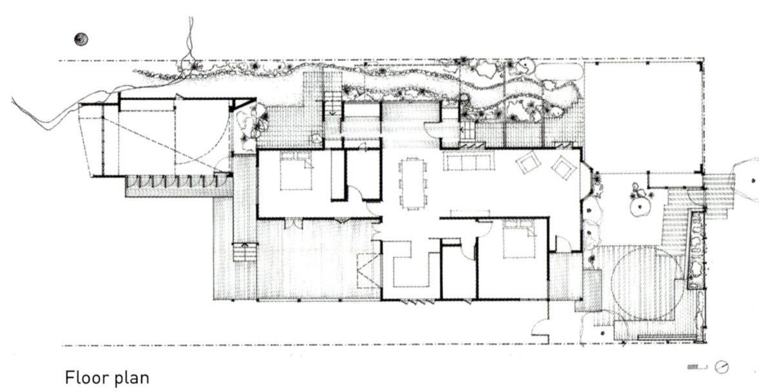

Floor plan

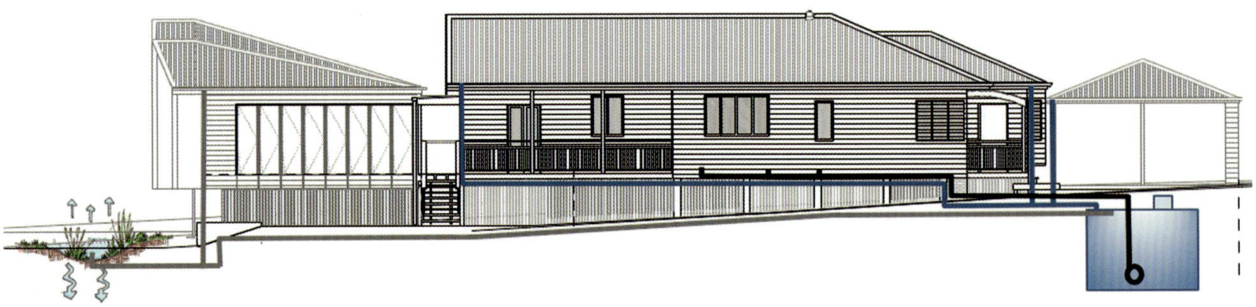

Water layout

STRADBROKE HOUSE

TIM BENNETON ARCHITECTS + GABRIEL & ELIZABETH POOLE DESIGN Co

Conceived as a permant camping 'beach cabin' on South Stradbroke Island, this house seems simple but is actually a sophisticated and committed response to sutainable living. Structured in two wings separated by a wide protected corridor and built with lightweight prefabricated systems, a series of structural porticos and the search for north orientation define its shape. The house is totally self-sufficient: water is collected on the roof and stored in tanks, some of which are reserved for fighting fires, electricity is obtained from photovoltaic panels and stored in batteries and a wastewater treatment system is incorporated.
The mobile capsules in children's bedrooms are an innovative response to the limits imposed by urban planning and capture the fun experience of camping under a tent.

Konzipiert unter dem Ideal einer „Strandhütte", manifestiert dieses scheinbar einfache, aber anspruchsvolle Haus auf einer Insel sein Engagement für nachhaltige Architektur. Strukturiert in zwei Flügeln, die durch einen breiten geschützten Korridor getrennt sind und mit leichten vorgefertigten Systemen gebaut wurden, definieren eine Reihe von strukturellen Portikus und die Nordorientierung ihre Form. Das Haus ist völlig autark: Auf dem Dach wird Wasser gesammelt und in Tanks gespeichert, von denen einige für die Brandbekämpfung reserviert sind, Strom aus Photovoltaikmodulen gewonnen und in Batterien gespeichert sowie eine Abwasseraufbereitungsanlage integriert.
Die mobilen Kapseln in Kinderzimmern sind eine innovative Antwort auf die städtebaulichen Grenzen und fangen das lustige Erlebnis des Campings unter einem Zelt ein.

Conçue sous l'idéal d'une « cabane de plage », cette maison en apparence simple mais sophistiquée, située sur une île, témoigne de son engagement pour une architecture durable. Structurée en deux ailes séparées par un large couloir protégé et construite avec des systèmes préfabriqués légers, une série de portiques structurels et la recherche de l'orientation nord définissent sa forme. La maison est totalement autosuffisante : l'eau est collectée sur le toit et stockée dans des réservoirs, dont certains sont réservés à la lutte contre les incendies, l'électricité est fournie par des panneaux photovoltaïques et stockée dans des batteries et un système de traitement des eaux usées est intégré.
Les capsules mobiles dans les chambres d'enfants sont une réponse innovante aux limites imposées par l'urbanisme et capturent l'expérience amusante du camping sous tente.

Concebida bajo el ideal de una «cabaña de playa », esta aparentemente simple pero sofisticada casa situada en una isla manifiesta su compromiso con la arquitectura sostenible. Estructurada en dos alas separadas por un amplio corredor protegido y construida con sistemas ligeros y prefabricados, una serie de pórticos estructurales y la búsqueda de la orientación norte definen su forma. La casa es totalmente autosuficiente: el agua se recoge en la cubierta y se almacena en tanques, algunos de ellos reservados para combatir incendios, la electricidad se obtiene de paneles fotovoltaicos y se almacena en baterías y se incorpora un sistema de tratamiento de aguas residuales.
Las cápsulas móviles que forman los dormitorios de los niños suponen una respuesta innovadora a los límites impuestos por la planificación urbana y capturan la divertida experiencia de acampar bajo una carpa.

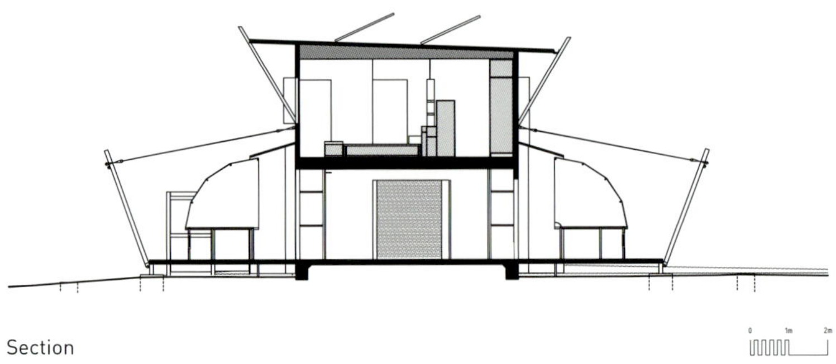

Section

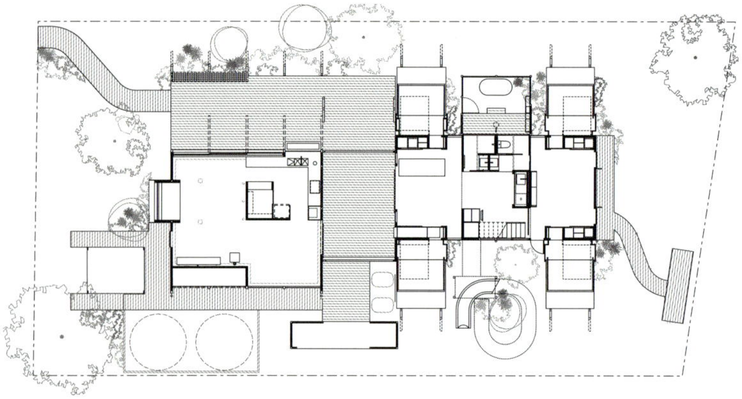

Lower floor plan

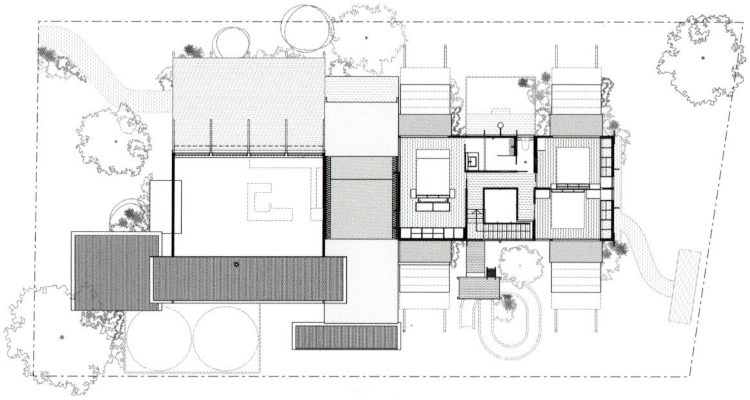

Upper floor plan

VTN ARCHITECTS

VTN Architects (Vo Trong Nghia Architects) is a leading architectural practice in Vietnam with offices in Ho Chi Minh City and Hanoi. More than 60 international architects, engineers and staff work closely on cultural, residential and commercial projects worldwide.
By experimenting with light, wind and water, and by using natural and local materials, VTN Architects employ a contemporary design vocabulary to explore new ways to create green architecture for the 21st century, whilst maintaining the essence of Asian architectural expression.
Vo Trong Nghia, principal and founding partner, studied architecture at the University of Tokyo before returning to Vietnam to establish VTN Architects in 2006. Through a series of award winning projects, Nghia has developed sustainable architectural design by integrating inexpensive, local materials and traditional skills with contemporary aesthetics and modern methodologies.

VTN Architects (Vo Trong Nghia Architects) est un cabinet d'architectes de premier plan au Vietnam avec des bureaux à Ho Chi Minh Ville et Hanoi. Plus de 60 architectes, ingénieurs et collaborateurs internationaux travaillent en étroite collaboration sur des projets culturels, résidentiels et commerciaux dans le monde entier.
En expérimentant avec la lumière, le vent et l'eau, et en utilisant des matériaux naturels et locaux, VTN Architects utilise un vocabulaire de design contemporain pour explorer de nouvelles façons de créer une architecture verte pour le 21ème siècle, tout en maintenant l'essence de l'expression architecturale asiatique.
Vo Trong Nghia, principal associé fondateur, a étudié l'architecture à l'Université de Tokyo avant de revenir au Vietnam pour fonder VTN Architects en 2006. Grâce à une série de projets primés, Nghia a développé une conception architecturale durable en intégrant des matériaux locaux peu coûteux et des compétences traditionnelles à l'esthétique contemporaine et aux méthodologies modernes.

VTN Architects (Vo Trong Nghia Architects) ist ein führendes Architekturbüro in Vietnam mit Büros in Ho Chi Minh City und Hanoi. Mehr als 60 internationale Architekten, Ingenieure und Mitarbeiter arbeiten weltweit eng mit Kultur-, Wohn- und Gewerbeprojekten zusammen.
Durch Experimente mit Licht, Wind und Wasser und die Verwendung natürlicher und lokaler Materialien nutzen VTN Architekten ein zeitgenössisches Designvokabular, um neue Wege zu finden, grüne Architektur für das 21. Jahrhundert zu schaffen und gleichzeitig die Essenz asiatischer Architektur zu bewahren.
Vo Trong Nghia, Geschäftsführer und Mitgründer, studierte Architektur an der University of Tokyo, bevor er 2006 nach Vietnam zurückkehrte, um VTN Architects zu gründen. In einer Reihe preisgekrönter Projekte hat Nghia nachhaltiges Architekturdesign entwickelt, indem es preiswerte, lokale Materialien und traditionelle Fähigkeiten mit zeitgenössischer Ästhetik und modernen Methoden kombinierte.

VTN Architects (Vo Trong Nghia Architects) es un estudio de arquitectura líder en Vietnam con oficinas en Ho Chi Minh City y Hanoi. Más de 60 arquitectos, ingenieros y personal internacional trabajan estrechamente en proyectos culturales, residenciales y comerciales en todo el mundo.
Experimentando con la luz, el viento y el agua, y utilizando materiales naturales y locales, los arquitectos de VTN emplean un vocabulario de diseño contemporáneo para explorar nuevas formas de crear arquitectura verde para el siglo XXI, manteniendo al mismo tiempo la esencia de la expresión arquitectónica asiática.
Vo Trong Nghia, socio principal y fundador, estudió arquitectura en la Universidad de Tokio antes de regresar a Vietnam para fundar VTN Architects en 2006. A través de una serie de proyectos premiados, Nghia ha desarrollado un diseño arquitectónico sostenible integrando materiales locales baratos y habilidades tradicionales con estética contemporánea y metodologías modernas.

STEPPING PARK HOUSE

HOUSE FOR TREES

BINH HOUSE

STEPPING PARK HOUSE

The design of this house turns it into an extension of the park next to which it is located. A great vacuum crosses diagonally the three floors of its volume, providing light and natural ventilation. Around this void, which contains the common spaces and incorporates circulation areas and natural elements such as plants and trees, the rooms are distributed as solid volumes. The green façades contribute to the continuity of the park inside the house and filter the intense tropical sun. This house is one of the projects in the "House for Trees" series, which seeks to draw attention to the important environmental problems generated by the scarcity of green spaces in Vietnamese cities. Its objective is the integration of green in projects at any scale, creating pockets of parks in the city and extending green buildings throughout the world.

Der Entwurf dieses Hauses macht es zu einer Erweiterung des Parks, in dessen Nähe es sich befindet. Ein großes Vakuum durchzieht diagonal die drei Stockwerke seines Volumens und sorgt für eine leichte und natürliche Belüftung. Um diesen Hohlraum, der die Gemeinschaftsräume enthält und Verkehrsflächen und natürliche Elemente wie Pflanzen und Bäume beherbergt, sind die Räume als feste Volumen verteilt. Die grünen Fassaden tragen zur Kontinuität des Parks im Inneren des Hauses bei und filtern die intensive tropische Sonne. Dieses Haus ist eines der Projekte der Reihe «House for Trees», die auf die wichtigen Umweltprobleme aufmerksam machen will, die durch die Knappheit von Grünflächen in vietnamesischen Städten entstehen. Ziel ist die Integration von Grün in Projekte jeder Größenordnung, die Schaffung von Parktaschen in der Stadt und die Ausweitung von Green Buildings auf der ganzen Welt.

La conception de cette maison en fait une extension du parc à côté duquel elle est située. Un grand vide traverse en diagonal les trois étages de son volume, apportant lumière et ventilation naturelles. Autour de ce vide, qui contient les espaces communs et incorpore des zones de circulation et des éléments naturels tels que des plantes et des arbres, les pièces sont distribuées en volumes solides. Les façades vertes contribuent à la continuité du parc à l'intérieur de la maison et filtrent l'intense soleil tropical. Cette maison est l'un des projets de la série « Maison pour les arbres », qui vise à attirer l'attention sur les problèmes environnementaux importants générés par la rareté des espaces verts dans les villes vietnamiennes. Son objectif est l'intégration de l'écologie dans des projets de toute envergure, en créant des poches de parcs dans la ville et en étendant les bâtiments verts à travers le monde.

El diseño de esta vivienda la convierte en una extensión del parque junto al que se ubica. Un gran vacío atraviesa en diagonal los tres pisos de su volumen, proporcionando luz y ventilación natural. En torno a este vacío, que contiene los espacios comunes e incorpora zonas de circulación y elementos naturales como plantas y árboles, las habitaciones se distribuyen como volúmenes sólidos. Las fachadas verdes contribuyen a dar continuidad al parque en el interior de la casa y tamizan el intenso sol tropical. Esta casa es uno de los proyectos de la serie «House for Trees», que intenta llamar la atención sobre los importantes problemas ambientales que genera la escasez de espacios verdes en las ciudades de Vietnam. Su objetivo es la integración del verde en proyectos a cualquier escala, creando bolsas de parques en la ciudad y extendiendo los edificios verdes por el mundo.

Elevation

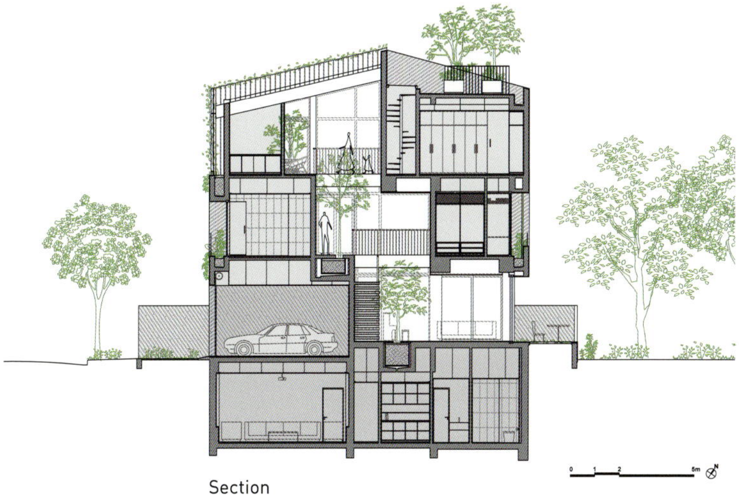

Section

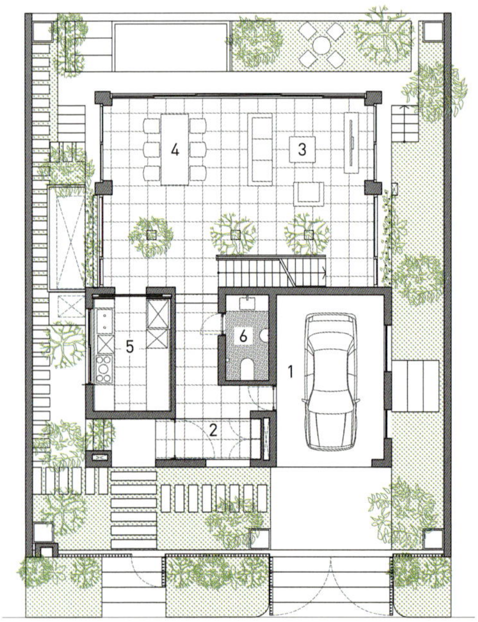

Ground floor plan

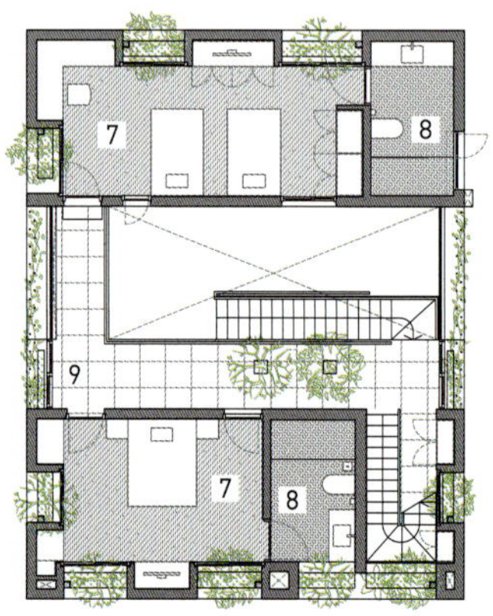

First floor plan

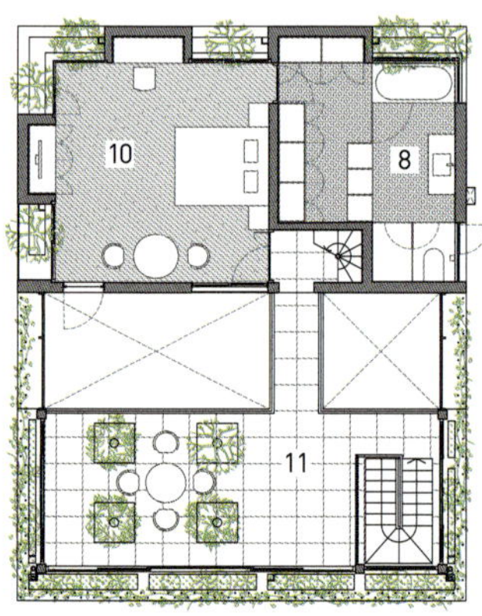

Second floor plan

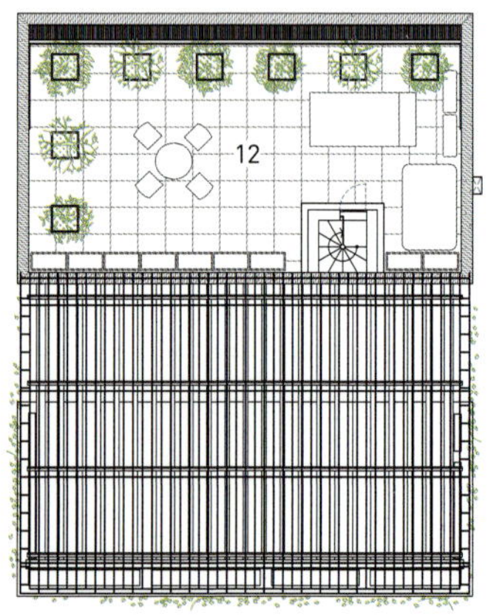

Roof plan

1. Garage
2. Entrance hall
3. Living room
4. Dining room
5. Kitchen
6. WC
7. Bedroom
8. Bathroom
9. Circulation
10. Master bedroom
11. Family room
12. Terrace

HOUSE FOR TREES

Under rapid urbanization, cities in Vietnam have diverged far away from their origins as rampant tropical forests. In Ho Chi Minh City, as an example, only 0.25 % area of the entire city is covered by greenery. As a result, new generations in urban areas are losing their connections with nature.
"House for Trees", a prototypical house within a tight budget of 155,000 USD, is an effort to change this situation. The aim of project is to return green space into the city, accommodating high-density dwelling with big tropical trees. Five concrete boxes, each houses a different program, are designed as "pots" to plant trees on their tops. With thick soil layer, these "pots" also function as storm-water basins for detention and retention, therefore contribute to reduce the risk of flooding in the city when the idea is multiplied to a large number of houses in the future.

Im Zuge der rasanten Urbanisierung haben sich die Städte Vietnams weit von ihren Ursprüngen in wilden tropischen Wäldern entfernt. In Ho Chi Minh City beispielsweise sind nur 0,25 % der gesamten Stadtfläche mit Grün bedeckt. Dadurch verlieren neue Generationen in städtischen Gebieten ihre Verbindung zur Natur.
«House for Trees», ein prototypisches Haus mit einem knappen Budget von 155.000 USD, ist ein Versuch, diese Situation zu ändern. Ziel des Projekts ist es, der Stadt Grünflächen zurückzugeben und hochverdichtete Wohnungen mit großen tropischen Bäumen zu beherbergen. Fünf Betonboxen, die jeweils ein anderes Programm beherbergen, sind als «Töpfe» zum Pflanzen von Bäumen auf ihren Dächern konzipiert. Mit einer dicken Bodenschicht fungieren diese Töpfe auch als Regenbecken für die Rückhaltung und tragen so dazu bei, das Überschwemmungsrisiko in der Stadt zu verringern, wenn die Idee in Zukunft mit einer großen Anzahl von Häusern multipliziert wird.

Sous l'effet d'une urbanisation rapide, les villes vietnamiennes se sont éloignées de leurs origines de forêts tropicales endémiques. A Ho Chi Minh Ville, par exemple, seulement 0,25 % de la superficie de la ville est couverte de verdure. En conséquence, les nouvelles générations des zones urbaines perdent leurs liens avec la nature.
« House for Trees », une maison prototype avec un budget serré de 155 000 USD, est un effort pour changer cette situation. L'objectif du projet est de restituer des espaces verts à la ville, en accueillant des habitations à haute densité avec de grands arbres tropicaux. Cinq boîtes en béton, abritant chacune un programme différent, sont conçues comme des « pots » pour planter des arbres sur leur cime. Avec une épaisse couche de sol, ces « pots » servent également de bassins de retenue et de rétention des eaux pluviales, contribuant ainsi à réduire le risque d'inondation dans la ville une fois que l'idée se sera répandue dans un grand nombre de maisons.

Tras una rápida urbanización, las ciudades de Vietnam se han alejado mucho de sus orígenes como bosques tropicales salvajes. En la ciudad de Ho Chi Minh, por ejemplo, solo el 0,25 % de la superficie de la ciudad está cubierta de vegetación. Como resultado, las nuevas generaciones nacidas en las zonas urbanas están perdiendo su conexión con la naturaleza.
La «House for Trees», una casa prototípica dentro de un presupuesto ajustado de 155 000 USD, es un esfuerzo para cambiar esta situación. El objetivo del proyecto es devolver el espacio verde a la ciudad, mezclando viviendas de alta densidad con grandes árboles tropicales. Cinco cajas de hormigón, cada una de las cuales alberga un programa diferente, están diseñadas como «macetas» para plantar árboles en sus copas. Estas «macetas» también funcionan como cuencos de aguas pluviales, contribuyendo a reducir el riesgo de futuras inundaciones en la ciudad.

Elevation

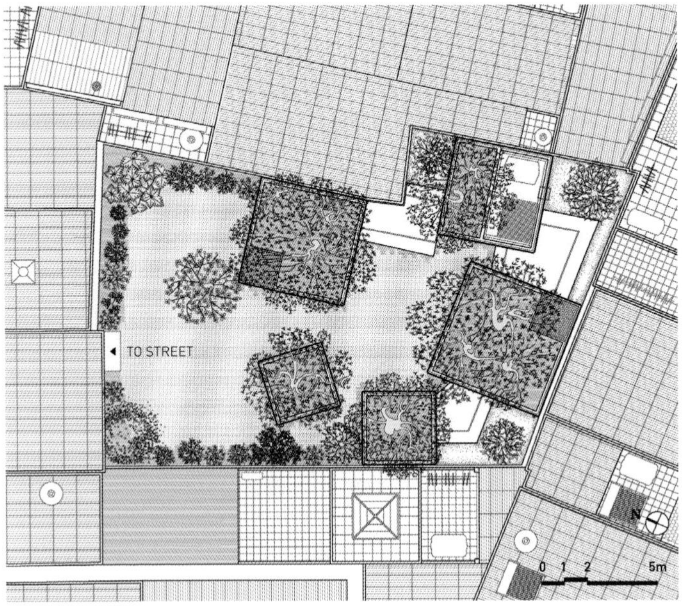

Site plan

First floor plan

Section A-A

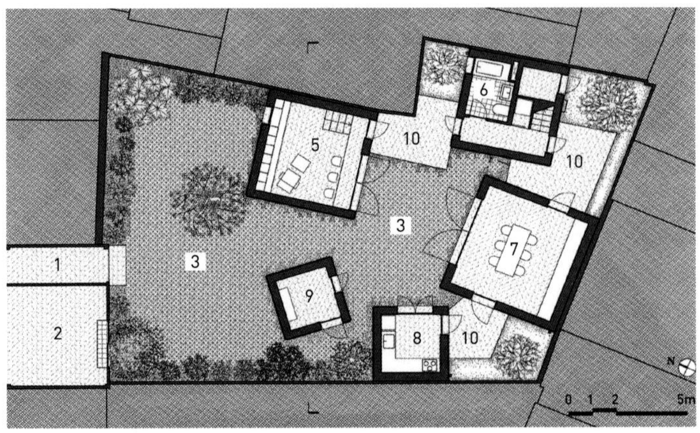

Ground floor plan

1. Approach
2. Storage
3. Front courtyard
4. Central courtyard
5. Library
6. Bathroom
7. Dining room
8. Kitchen
9. Altar room
10. Corridor
11. Bedroom
12. Bridge

BINH HOUSE

This project, also part of the "House for Trees" series, poses the challenge of creating an environment that allows a family of three generations to interact. Its scheme is composed of a series of alternately stacked volumes, delimited at the top by gardens with large trees and crop areas, and laterally by large glass openings. The layout of the resulting spaces creates lines of vision that favour the interrelation between the occupants and the entry of natural light, and generates a circulation of air that keeps the house always fresh. The arrangement of the stairs and service areas along a strip on the west side of the house limits the sun exposure of the most used areas. The use of sustainable materials in their construction significantly reduces operating and maintenance costs.

Dieses Projekt, das ebenfalls Teil der Reihe „Haus für Bäume" ist, stellt die Herausforderung dar, ein Umfeld zu schaffen, in dem eine Familie von drei Generationen interagieren kann. Das Schema besteht aus einer Reihe von abwechselnd gestapelten Volumen, die oben durch Gärten mit großen Bäumen und Ackerflächen und seitlich durch große Glasöffnungen begrenzt sind. Die Anordnung der entstehenden Räume schafft Sichtlinien, die die Wechselbeziehung zwischen den Bewohnern und dem Eintritt von natürlichem Licht begünstigen, und erzeugt eine Luftzirkulation, die das Haus immer frisch hält. Die Anordnung der Treppen und Servicebereiche entlang eines Streifens auf der Westseite des Hauses begrenzt die Sonneneinstrahlung auf die am häufigsten genutzten Bereiche. Die Verwendung nachhaltiger Materialien in ihrer Konstruktion reduziert die Betriebs- und Wartungskosten erheblich.

Ce projet, qui fait également partie de la série « Maison pour les arbres », pose le défi de créer un environnement qui permette à une famille de trois générations d'interagir. Son schéma se compose d'une série de volumes alternativement empilés, délimités en haut par des jardins avec de grands arbres et des zones de culture, et latéralement par de grandes ouvertures vitrées. L'agencement des espaces qui en résultent crée des lignes de vision qui favorisent l'interrelation entre les occupants et l'entrée de la lumière naturelle, et génère une circulation d'air qui garde la maison toujours fraîche. La disposition des escaliers et des aires de service le long d'une bande à l'ouest de la maison limite l'exposition au soleil des zones les plus utilisées. L'utilisation de matériaux durables dans leur construction réduit considérablement les coûts d'exploitation et d'entretien.

Este proyecto, enmarcado también dentro de la serie «House for Trees», plantea el reto de crear un entorno que permita interactuar a una familia de tres generaciones. Su esquema se compone de una serie de volúmenes apilados de forma alterna, delimitados en su parte superior por jardines con grandes árboles y zonas de cultivos, y lateralmente por grandes aberturas de vidrio. La disposición de los espacios resultantes crea líneas de visión que favorecen la interrelación entre los ocupantes y la entrada de luz natural, y genera una circulación de aire que mantiene la casa siempre fresca. La disposición de las escaleras y las áreas de servicio a lo largo de una franja del lado oeste de la casa limita la exposición al sol de las zonas con más uso. El uso de materiales sostenibles en su construcción reduce significativamente los costes operativos y de mantenimiento.

Site plan

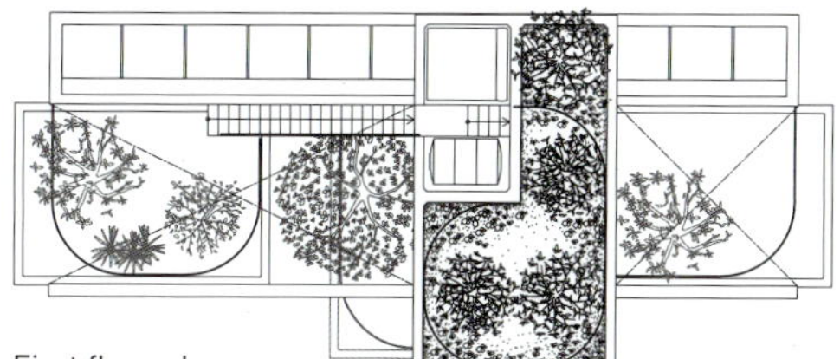

First floor plan

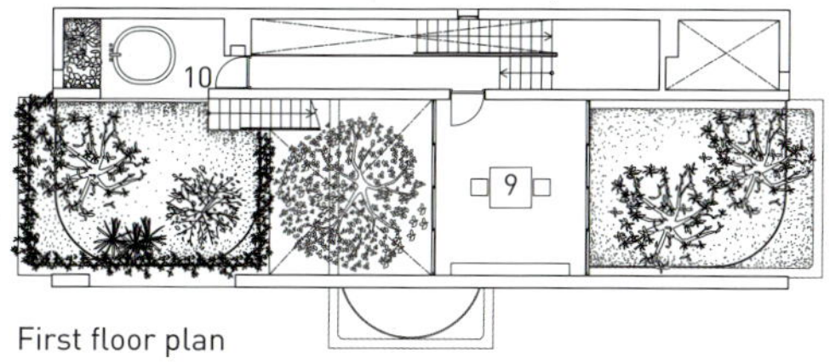

First floor plan

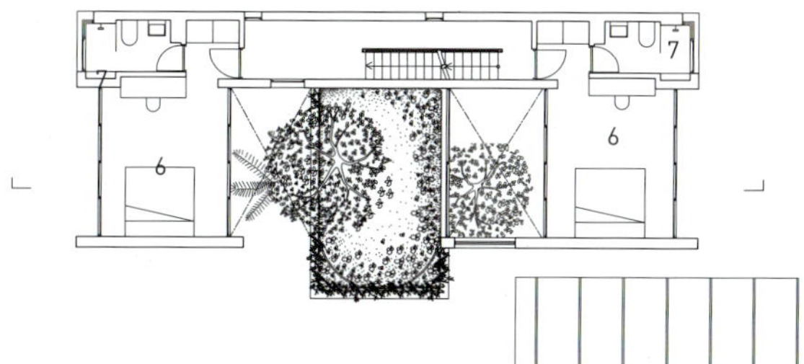

First floor plan

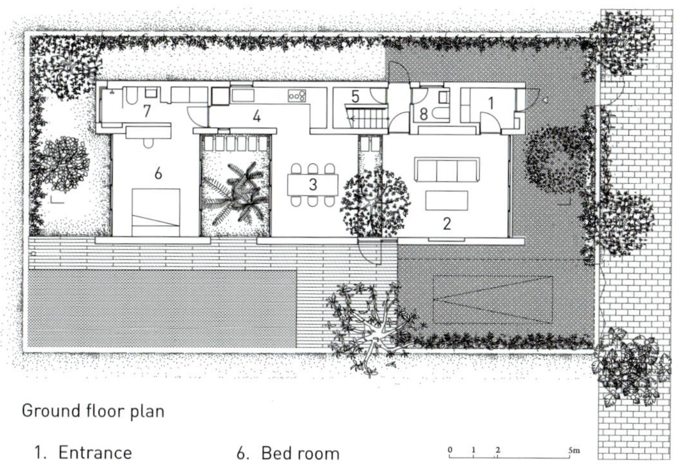

Ground floor plan

1. Entrance
2. Living room
3. Dining room
4. Kitchen
5. Storage
6. Bed room
7. Bed room
8. Powder room
9. Study room
10. Jacuzzi

WALLMAKERS

All our earlier settlements have always been made of natural materials. But the sad fact is that, today less than thirty percent of the world's population live in buildings made of earth, even though it is a more sustainable and durable material ; the blame of which may be solely placed on the advent of industrialisation and a widespread demand for "cement" houses". We, at Wallmakers have devoted ourselves to the cause of using mud and waste as the chief components, to make structures that are both, utilitarian and alluring.
Vinu Daniel completed his B. Arch in 2005 from The College of Engineering, Trivandrum. In 2007 he started Wallmakers. By 2008 he had received an award for a low cost, eco-friendly house from the 'Save Periyar' Pollution Control Committee for the house which was constructed for a cancer patient. Many such eye-openers in the course of his practice prompted him to resolve to devote his energies towards the cause of sustainable and cost-effective architecture.

Tous nos premiers établissements ont toujours été faits de matériaux naturels. Mais la triste réalité est qu'aujourd'hui, moins de trente pour cent de la population mondiale vit dans des bâtiments en terre, même s'il s'agit d'un matériau plus durable et durable, dont la seule responsabilité peut être attribuée à l'avènement de l'industrialisation et à la demande généralisée de « maisons en ciment ». Chez Wallmakers, nous nous sommes consacrés à la cause de l'utilisation de la boue et des déchets comme composants principaux, pour réaliser des structures à la fois utilitaires et séduisantes.
Vinu Daniel a terminé son B. Arch en 2005 au Collège d'ingénierie de Trivandrum. En 2007, il a créé Wallmakers. En 2008, il avait reçu un prix du Comité de lutte contre la pollution « Save Periyar » pour une maison peu coûteuse et respectueuse de l'environnement construite pour un patient atteint de cancer. Au cours de sa pratique, plusieurs de ces révélations l'ont poussé à se consacrer à la cause de l'architecture durable et rentable.

Alle unsere früheren Siedlungen wurden immer aus natürlichen Materialien gebaut. Aber die traurige Tatsache ist, dass heute weniger als dreißig Prozent der Weltbevölkerung in Gebäuden aus Lehm leben, obwohl es sich um ein nachhaltigeres und langlebigeres Material handelt; die Schuld daran liegt allein bei der Industrialisierung und einer weit verbreiteten Nachfrage nach „Zement-Häusern". Wir von Wallmakers haben uns der Sache verschrieben, Schlamm und Abfall als Hauptkomponenten zu verwenden, um Strukturen zu schaffen, die sowohl nützlich als auch verlockend sind.
Vinu Daniel schloss seinen B. Bogen 2005 am College of Engineering, Trivandrum, ab. Im Jahr 2007 startete er mit Wallmakers. 2008 erhielt er vom Umweltschutzausschuss „Save Periyar" eine Auszeichnung für ein preiswertes, umweltfreundliches Haus, das für einen Krebspatienten gebaut worden war. Viele dieser Augenöffner im Laufe seiner Praxis veranlassten ihn zu dem Entschluss, seine Energien für eine nachhaltige und kostengünstige Architektur einzusetzen.

Todos nuestros asentamientos anteriores siempre se han hecho con materiales naturales. Pero lo triste es que, hoy en día, menos del treinta por ciento de la población mundial vive en edificios hechos de tierra, aunque se trate de un material más sostenible y duradero; la culpa de ello puede atribuirse únicamente a la llegada de la industrialización y a una demanda generalizada de «casas de cement». Nosotros, en Wallmakers, nos hemos dedicado a la causa de utilizar el barro y los residuos como principales componentes, para crear estructuras que sean a la vez utilitarias y atractivas.
Vinu Daniel completó su B. Arch en 2005 en el Colegio de Ingeniería de Trivandrum. En 2007 comenzó a trabajar con Wallmakers. En 2008, el Comité de Control de la Contaminación «Save Periyar» le otorgó un premio por una casa de bajo coste y respetuosa con el medio ambiente que se construyó para un paciente con cáncer. Muchos de las cosas que fue descubriendo en el curso de su práctica le llevaron a decidir dedicar sus energías a la causa de la arquitectura sostenible y rentable.

DEBRIS HOUSE
RESIDENCE FOR MR. BIJU MATHEW

DEBRIS HOUSE

Sensitive to the nuances of the local context and to economic limitations, this home for a family of six uses recycled and eco-sensitive materials in its construction that overcome their limitations to create a building of great expressiveness. The image of the house is characterised by its walls of compacted earth from the excavation. However, it is the curvilinear wall that forms the small inner courtyard, built with the rubble from the previous building on the plot, which gives its name to the house and becomes its main element. Ecological measures such as a rainwater collection and recycling system, passive air circulation achieved through careful planning of the courtyard and façades or furniture built with recycled wood from boxes reinforce the project's commitment to society and the environment.

Sensibel für die Nuancen des lokalen Kontextes und die wirtschaftlichen Grenzen, verwendet dieses Haus für eine sechsköpfige Familie recycelte und ökologisch sensible Materialien in ihrer Konstruktion, die ihre Grenzen überwinden, um ein Gebäude von großer Ausdruckskraft zu schaffen. Das Bild des Hauses wird durch seine Wände aus verdichteter Erde aus dem Aushub geprägt. Es ist jedoch die kurvenförmige Wand, die den kleinen Innenhof bildet, der aus den Trümmern des vorherigen Gebäudes auf dem Grundstück gebaut wurde, das dem Haus seinen Namen gibt und zum zentralen Kern wird. Ökologische Maßnahmen wie ein Regenwassersammel- und Recyclingsystem, eine passive Luftzirkulation durch sorgfältige Planung des Innenhofes und der Fassaden oder Möbel aus Recyclingholz aus Kasten verstärken das Engagement des Projekts für Gesellschaft und Umwelt.

Sensitive to the nuances of the local context and to economic limitations, this home for a family of six uses recycled and eco-sensitive materials in its construction that overcome their limitations to create a building of great expressiveness. The image of the house is characterised by its walls of compacted earth from the excavation. However, it is the curvilinear wall that forms the small inner courtyard, built with the rubble from the previous building on the plot, which gives its name to the house and becomes its main element. Ecological measures such as a rainwater collection and recycling system, passive air circulation achieved through careful planning of the courtyard and façades or furniture built with recycled wood from boxes reinforce the project's commitment to society and the environment.

Sensible a los matices del contexto local y a unas limitaciones económicas, esta vivienda para una familia de seis personas emplea materiales reciclados y ecosensibles en su construcción que superan sus limitaciones para crear un edificio de gran expresividad. La imagen de la casa se caracteriza por sus muros de tierra compactada procedente de la excavación. Sin embargo, es el muro curvilíneo que conforma el pequeño patio interior, construido con los escombros del anterior edificio de la parcela, el que da nombre a la casa y se convierte en su núcleo central. Medidas ecológicas como un sistema de recolección y reciclaje de agua de lluvia, la circulación de aire pasiva lograda mediante la planificación cuidadosa del patio y de las fachadas o el mobiliario construido con madera reciclada de cajas refuerzan el compromiso del proyecto con la sociedad y el medio ambiente.

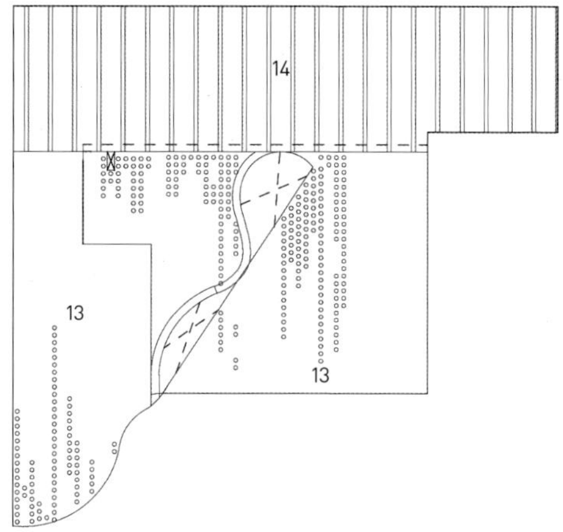

Roof plan

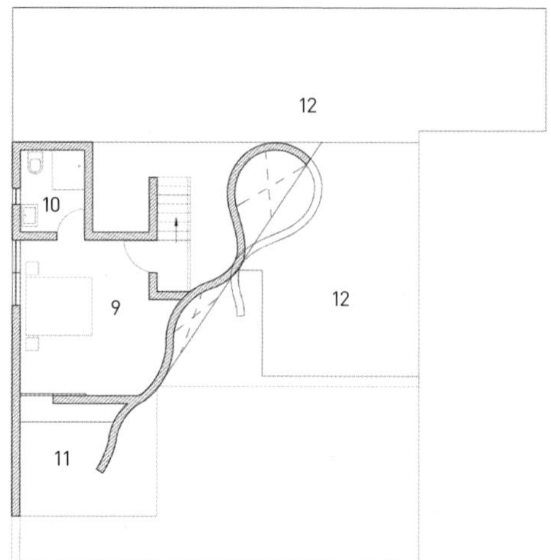

First floor plan

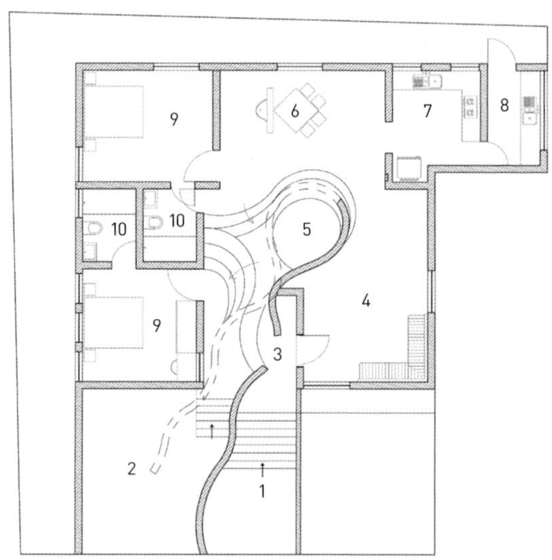

Ground floor plan

1. Entrance
2. Car porch
3. Sitout
4. Drawing room
5. Courtyard
6. Dining area
7. Kitchen
8. Work area
9. Bedroom
10. Toilet
11. Balcony
12. Terrace
13. Coconut shell filler
14. Ferrocement shell roof

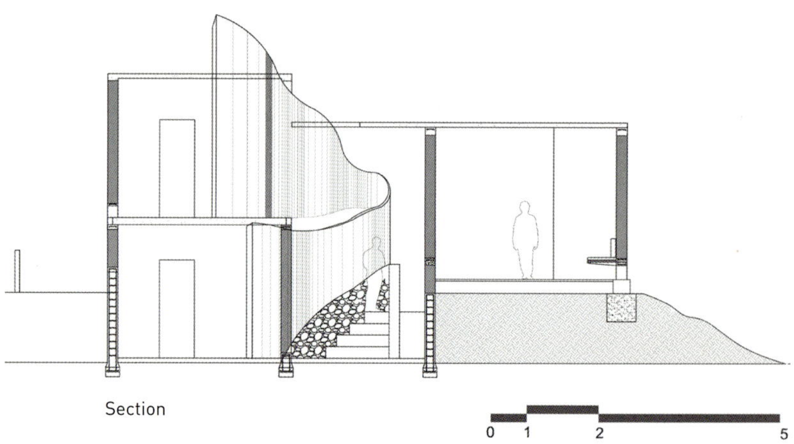

Section

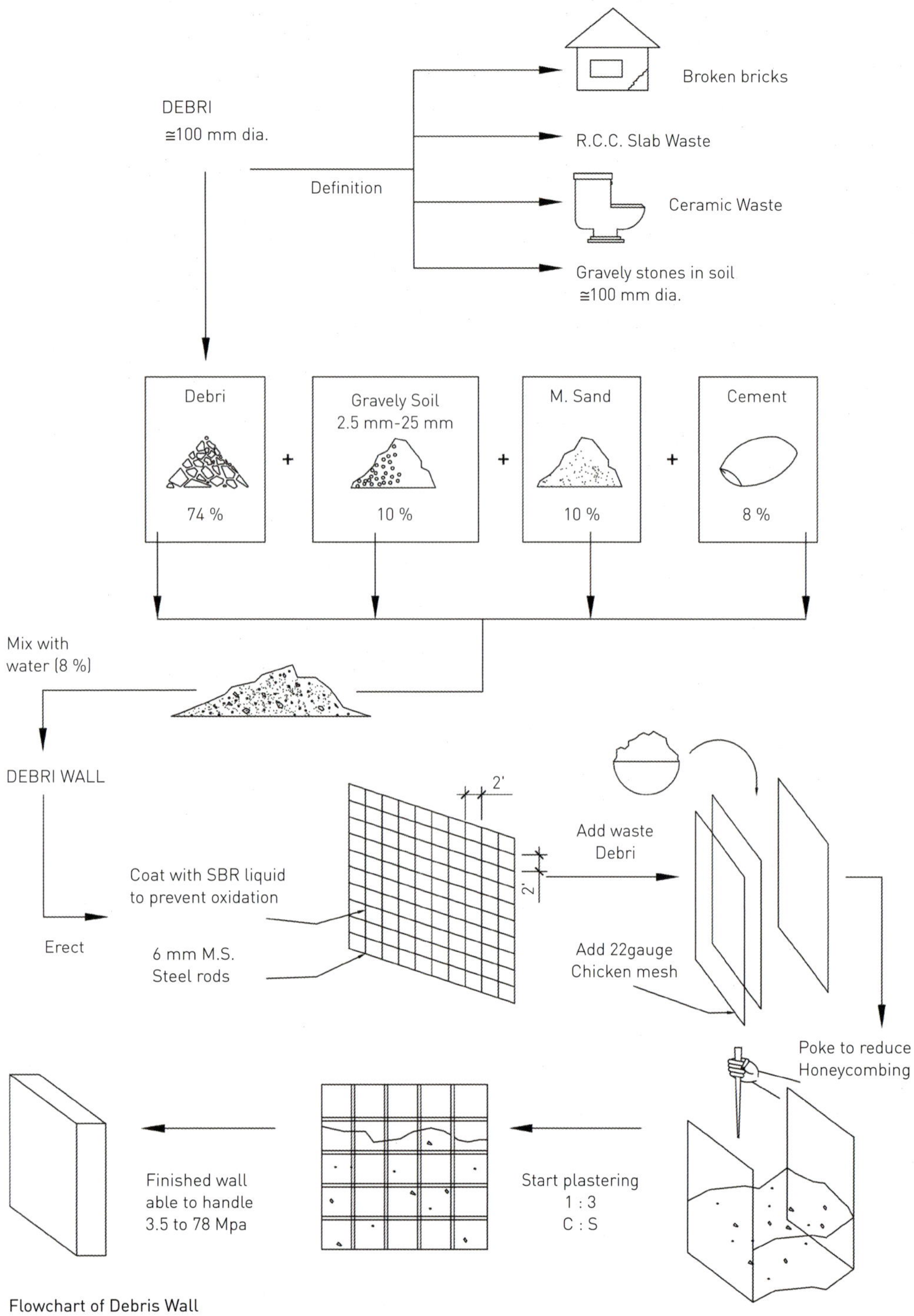

Flowchart of Debris Wall

WARREN BENBOW ARCHITECTS

Warren Benbow Architects are a small rural micro-practice living and working in the Welsh Marches, the ancient borderland between England and Wales. Formed by partners Dean Benbow and Emily Warren in 1999 we work mainly in the field of housing but also undertake restoration, conversion, education and cultural projects.
Our work attempts to be sustainable both in terms of its desire to minimise energy usage and maximise respect for the environment. It is also rooted in a sense of place and the use of materials and forms that sustain deep seated local cultural connections. In this way we hope our best work helps sustain a way of life that is being encroached on by the bland conformity of much mass produced building.
We have won RIBA Regional Design Awards in 2014 and 2018 RIBA Regional Sustainability Award in 2018 and were finalists for the Passivhaus Trust Awards 2018.

Warren Benbow Architects est un petit cabinet rural qui vit et travaille dans les Welsh Marches, l'ancienne frontière entre l'Angleterre et le Pays de Galles. Formés par les associés Dean Benbow et Emily Warren en 1999, nous travaillons principalement dans le domaine du logement, mais nous entreprenons également des projets de restauration, de conversion, d'éducation et de culture.
Notre travail s'efforce d'être durable, à la fois dans sa volonté de minimiser la consommation d'énergie ainsi que de maximiser le respect de l'environnement. Elle est également enracinée dans un sens du lieu et dans l'utilisation de matériaux et de formes qui entretiennent des liens culturels locaux profondément enracinés. De cette façon, nous espérons que notre meilleur travail aidera à maintenir un mode de vie qui agit comme contrepoids à la fadeur de la conformité de la plupart des bâtiments produits en série.
Nous avons remporté les RIBA Regional Design Awards en 2014 et 2018 et le RIBA Regional Sustainability Award en 2018 et avons été finalistes pour les Passivhaus Trust Awards 2018.

Warren Benbow Architects sind ländliches Kleinunternehmen, beheimatet in den Walisischen Marken, dem alten Grenzgebiet zwischen England und Wales. Gegründet von den Partnern Dean Benbow und Emily Warren im Jahr 1999, arbeitet es hauptsächlich im Bereich Wohnen, führt aber auch Restaurierungs-, Umbau-, Bildungs- und Kulturprojekte durch.
Unsere Arbeit versucht, nachhaltig zu sein, sowohl in Bezug auf den Wunsch, den Energieverbrauch zu minimieren, als auch darin, den Respekt vor der Umwelt zu maximieren. Sie speist sich darüber hinaus aus einem Gefühl des Ortes und der Verwendung von Materialien und Formen, die tief lokal verwurzelte kulturelle Verbindungen aufrechterhalten. Auf diese Weise hoffen wir, dass unsere beste Arbeit dazu beiträgt, eine Lebensweise aufrechtzuerhalten, die durch die fade Konformität vieler massenproduzierter Gebäude beeinträchtigt wird.
Wir haben die RIBA Regional Design Awards 2014 und den RIBA Regional Sustainability Award 2018 gewonnen und waren Finalist für die Passivhaus Trust Awards 2018.

Warren Benbow Architects es un pequeño estudio rural que vive y trabaja en las Marcas Galesas, antigua frontera entre Inglaterra y Gales. Formado por los socios Dean Benbow y Emily Warren en 1999, trabajamos principalmente en el campo de la vivienda, pero también llevamos a cabo proyectos de restauración, conversión, educación y cultura.
Nuestro trabajo pretende ser sostenible tanto en su voluntad de minimizar el consumo de energía como de maximizar el respeto por el medio ambiente. También tiene sus raíces en el sentido del lugar y en el uso de materiales y formas que sostienen conexiones culturales locales profundamente arraigadas. De esta manera esperamos que nuestro mejor trabajo ayude a respaldar un estilo de vida que está siendo invadido por la insulsa conformidad de la producción en masa de edificios.
Hemos ganado los premios RIBA Regional Design Awards en 2014 y 2018 RIBA Regional Sustainability Award en 2018 y fuimos finalistas de los Passivhaus Trust Awards 2018.

HOPE VIEW HOUSE

The project was born as a landscape intervention that followed the pattern of the surrounding area: wooded on the upper hills, meadows in the lower area and the house hidden in the meeting line of both.
The building is presented as a stone wall 80 m long and extends towards the top of the site in a series of terraces. An opening 20 m long and 2.2 m high in this south-facing wall concentrates most of the glazing in the house. A porch with columns in front of this opening attenuates excess solar gain while becoming the main architectural element of the design.
Designed to Passivhaus standards, the house's equipment includes a geothermal heat pump, mechanical ventilation with heat recovery and photovoltaic panels and generates more energy than it uses.

Das Projekt entstand als Landschaftsintervention, die dem Muster der Umgebung folgte: bewaldet auf den oberen Hügeln, Wiesen im unteren Bereich und das Haus versteckt in der Begegnungslinie beider.
Das Gebäude ist als 80 m lange Steinmauer dargestellt und erstreckt sich in einer Reihe von Terrassen zur Grundstücksspitze. Eine 20 m lange und 2,2 m hohe Öffnung in dieser nach Süden ausgerichteten Wand konzentriert den Großteil der Verglasung im Haus. Eine Veranda mit Säulen vor dieser Öffnung dämpft den überschüssigen Sonneneintrag und wird gleichzeitig zum wichtigsten architektonischen Element des Entwurfs.
Das nach Passivhausstandard konzipierte Haus ist mit einer Erdwärmepumpe, mechanischer Lüftung mit Wärmerückgewinnung und Photovoltaikmodulen ausgestattet und erzeugt mehr Energie als es verbraucht.

Le projet est né d'une intervention paysagère qui a suivi le modèle de la région environnante : boisées sur les hautes collines, prairies dans la partie basse et la maison cachée dans la ligne de rencontre des deux.
Le bâtiment se présente sous la forme d'un mur de pierre de 80 m de long et s'étend vers le haut du site en une série de terrasses. Une ouverture de 20 m de long sur 2,2 m de haut dans ce mur orienté plein sud concentre l'essentiel du vitrage de la maison. Un porche avec des colonnes devant cette ouverture atténue l'excès de gain solaire tout en devenant l'élément architectural principal de la conception.
Conçu selon les normes Passivhaus, l'équipement de la maison comprend une pompe à chaleur géothermique, une ventilation mécanique avec récupération de chaleur et des panneaux photovoltaïques et génère plus d'énergie qu'elle n'en utilise.

El proyecto nació como una intervención paisajística que siguiese el patrón de la zona que la rodea: arbolado en las colinas superiores, prados en la zona inferior y la casa escondida en la línea de encuentro de ambos.
El edificio se presenta como un muro de piedra de 80 m de largo y se extiende hacia la parte superior del terreno en una serie de terrazas. Una abertura de 20 m de largo y 2,2 m de alto en este muro orientado a sur concentra la mayor parte del acristalamiento de la casa. Un porche con columnas situado frente a esta abertura atenúa el exceso de ganancia solar, a la vez que se convierte en el principal elemento arquitectónico del diseño.
Concebida bajo los estándares Passivhaus, el equipamiento de la casa incluye una bomba de calor geotérmica, ventilación mecánica con recuperación de calor y paneles fotovoltaicos y genera más energía de la que utiliza.

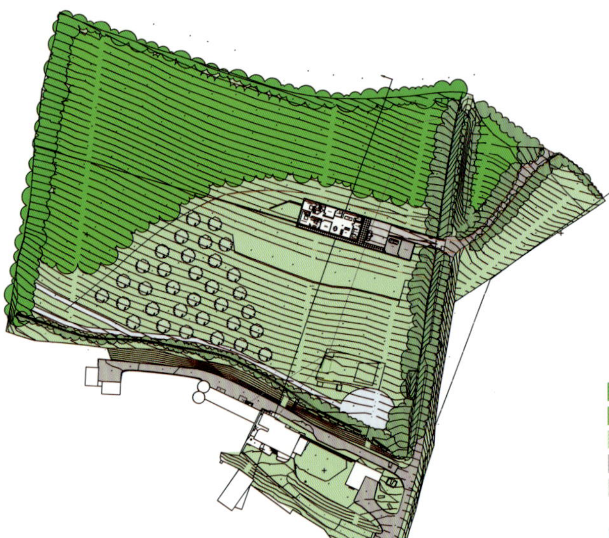
Existing mature trees and hedges
New tree planting
Wildflower meadow planting
Existing tarmac driveway
New gravel driveway and parking (resin bonded gravel to sloped sections)
New drainage ditch and pond (flood protection for adjacent properties)

Site plan

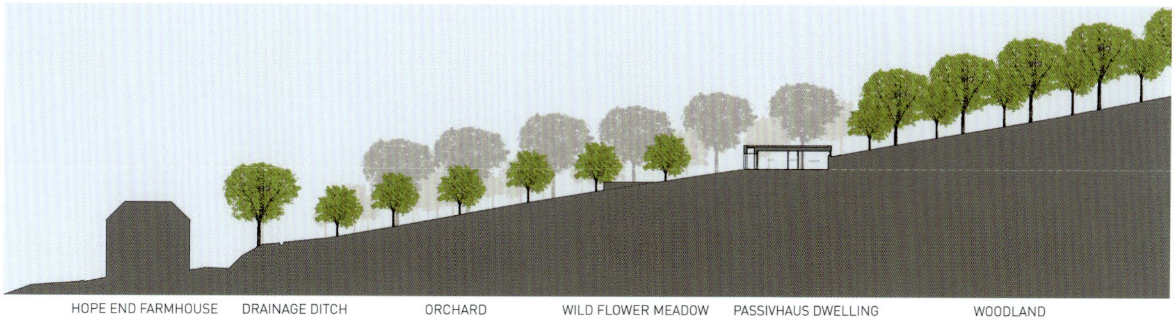

Site section

South elevation

East elevation

West elevation

Site section D-D

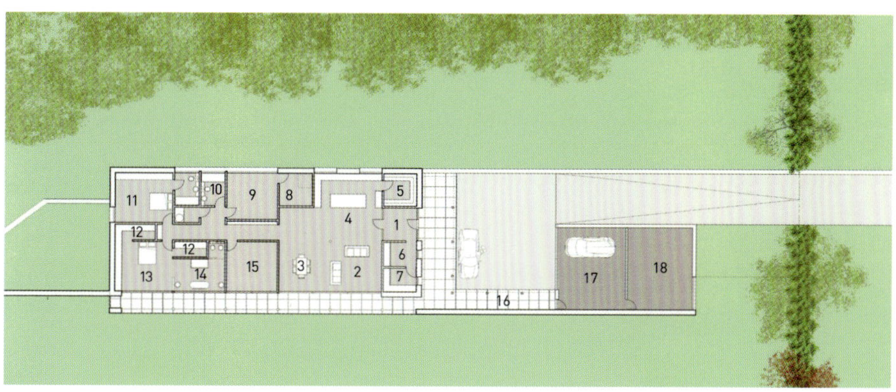

1. Entrance
2. Living
3. Dining
4. Kitchen
5. Pantry
6. Coats lobby
7. Utility
8. Plant room
9. Yoga room
10. Family bathroom
11. Guest bedroom
12. Walk in wardrobe
13. Master bedroom
14. En suite
15. Office or bedroom
16. Covered link to garage
17. Garage
18. Workshop

Ground floor plan

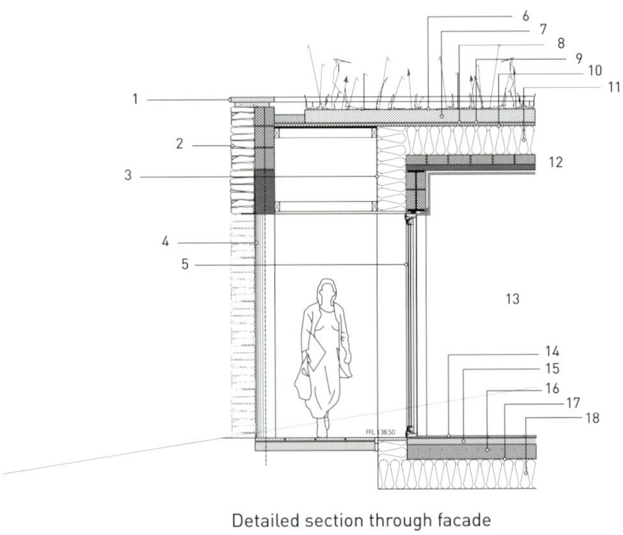

Detailed section through facade

1. Cut stone coping
2. Locally sourced stone
   Laid coursed
   Stonework only partially bedded
   On rear half only to create voids
   for plant
   Growth in facework
3. Insulation zone
4. Polished concrete columns to framed opening
5. Triple glazed passivhaus a rated doors and windows
6. Wildflower planting to roof
7. Soil sub-base growing medium
8. Protection fleece filter
9. Reservoir board
10. Single ply membrane
11. Insulation zone
12. Beam and block structural deck
13. Living
14. Tiled floor finish over
15. Screed containing underfloor heating pipes over
16 Concrete raft foundation over
17. DPM over
18. Insulation zone

CAKE

DIRECTORY

AKA Architects

www.aka-architects.com.au

Apple Crate Schack

Architects: AKA architects
Project team: Andrew Kerr, Geoff Clark
Location: Flowerpot, Tasmania, Australia
Construction period: 2 years, 9 months (due to wait for milled timber boards to dry season)
Total built area: 61 m^2 enclosed; 20 m^2 decks; 20 m^2 patio
Photo credits: © Jordan Davis
Awards: 2018 Houses Awards Shortlist: Sustainability
General contractor: R. B. Edwards & Son
Consultants: Aldanmark Consulting Engineers; Holdfast Building Surveyors; GEO Environmental Solutions (on-site waste water); Hobart Building Assessment Services (thermal performance rating); Southern Planning (bushfire hazard assessment)

Altamarea Arquitectura

www.alta-marea.cl

Casa Rios

Architects: Altamarea Arquitectura
Project team: Gonzalo Herreros Montero
Location: Punta de Lobos, Pichilemu
Construction period: 2016-2017
Total built area: 160 m^2
Photo credits: © Felipe Cantillana
General contractor: Altamarea Constructora

Casas MQ

Architects: Altamarea Arquitectura
Project team: Gonzalo Herreros Montero
Location: Punta de Lobos, Pichilemu
Construction period: 2015-2016
Total built area: 290 m^2
Photo credits: © Felipe Cantillana
General contractor: Altamarea Constructora

Casa WB

Architects: Altamarea Arquitectura
Project team: Gonzalo Herreros Montero
Location: Cahuil, Pichilemu
Construction period: 2016
Total built area: 70 m^2
Photo credits: © Felipe Cantillana
General contractor: Altamarea Constructora

Architects Uncharted

www.facebook.com/ArchitectsUncharted

Chien House

Architects: Architects Uncharted
Project team: Chien, Chi-Shen
Location: Taoyuan, Taiwan
Construction period: January 2013 - August 2014
Total built area: 263 m^2
Photo credits: © Chien, Chi-Shen
Awards:
-2017 TID Award
-2017 Golden Pin Award
-2018 K-design Award

The Wheel

Architects: Architects Uncharted
Project team: Chien, Chi-Shen
Location: Taichung, Taiwan
Construction period: April 2018 - July 2018
Total built area: 157.71 m^2
Photo credits: © Chien, Chi-Shen / Tsai Shan
Awards:
-2018 London Design Awards
-2018 New York Design Awards
-2018 Architecture MasterPrize
-2018 IDA Design Awards
-2018 A' Design Award
-2019 iF Design Award
-2019 TID Award
General contractor: Windstar Studio

atelier RISTING

www.atelierRISTING.com

Glass Cabin

Architects: atelierRISTING llc
Project team: Steven R. Risting, AIA, LEED AP
Location: Northeast Iowa
Construction period: October 2015 – July 2018
Total built area: 104 m^2
Photo credits: © Steven and Carol Risting
Awards:
-2018 American Institute of Architects (AIA) INDIANA design award – Citation Award
-2019 American Institute of Architects (AIA) INDIANAPOLIS design award – Honor Award
-2019 American Institute of Architects (AIA) INDIANAPOLIS design award – Sustainability Award
General contractor: Steven Risting
Suppliers: Modern Building Products, Pella Windows and Doors, Lil' Bit of Country Stoves & Fireplaces (JØtul F350 wood stove), Midwest PermaColumn, Cali Bamboo (cork flooring)

Bio Architects

bio-architects.com

DD77

Architects: Ivan Ovchinnikov, Olga Sandakova
Project Team: DublDom
Location: Moscow
Construction period: 2019
Total built area: 120 m^2
Photo credits: © Artem Lasovsky (www.artlasovsky.com), Ivan Ovchinnikov
General contractor: DublDom

Bridge House

Architects: Ivan Ovchinnikov
Location: Tula Region, Russia
Construction period: 2018
Total built area: 117 m^2
Photo credits: © Artem Lasovskiy, Ivan Ovchinnikov

Broissin M. Arch. Gerardo Broissin

www.broissin.com

Irekua Anatani House

Architects: Broissin
Partner in Charge: M. Arch. Gerardo Broissin
Project leader: Arq. Adrian Tellez
Project team: Arq. Adrian Tellez (project leader), M. Arch. Gerardo Broissin, Arq. Mauricio Cristóbal, Arq. Alejandro Rocha, Arq. Adrian Tellez, Arq. Thelma Blake, Arq. Luis Alberto Barrera
Location: Avándaro, Estado de México
Construction period: 2015-2017
Total built area: 700 m^2
Photo credits: © Alexandre d' La Roche
Awards:
-IDA Design Award, Gold Medal in New Residential Building. United States, 2017
-A'Design Award, Gold Medal in Architecture, Building and Structure Design. Italy, 2017
-Architecture Masterprize, Bronze Medal in Green Architecture. United States, 2016
General contractor: Miguel Campero
Suppliers: Furniture: Marina Pani
Consultants: Structural Engineering: Ing. Humberto Girón

Delin Arkitektkontor

www.delinarkitektkontor.se

Lundnäs House

Architect: Buster Delin
Project team: Buster Delin
Location: Arbrå, Hälsingland, Sweden
Construction period: 2009-2015
Total built area: 80 m^2 including patio
Photo credits: Patric Johansson
Awards: 1st award, Design S 2016
General contractor: Buster Delin
Suppliers: Local

Villa Raku

Architect: Buster Delin
Project team: Buster Delin
Location: Risvägen 54, Nacka, Sweden
Construction period: 2014-2016
Total built area: 240 m^2
Photo credits: Karin Björkquist
Awards:
-Stadsbyggandsutmärkelsen 2015 (Awarded as best villa in Nacka 2015)
General contractor: Blomdahls Byggservice AB

Equipo de Arquitectura

www.equipodearquitectura.com.py

Caja de Tierra

Architects: Equipo de Arquitectura
Project team: Horacio Cherniavsky and Viviana Pozzoli
Location: Asunción, Paraguay
Construction period: 2017-2018
Total built area: 45 m^2
Photo credits: © Leonardo Méndez, Federico Cairoli, Lauro Rocha
Awards: Frame Awards Small Office of the Year, Bienal de Arquitectura de Quito 2018 Finalist
Structural engeneering: Emilio Richer
Rammed earth consultant: Yago García-Enríquez

Casa Patios

Architects: Equipo de Arquitectura + José Cubilla
Project team: Horacio Cherniavsky, Viviana Pozzoli and José Cubilla
Location: Asunción, Paraguay
Construction period: 2016-2017
Total built area: 450 m^2
Photo credits: © Leonardo Méndez, Federico Cairoli, Lauro Rocha
Structural engeneering: Enrique Granada + Emilio Richer

Estudio Valdés

www.estudiovaldes.cl

Galpón Ranco

Architects: Estudio Valdés
Project Team: Arquitecto a cargo: Alberto Cruz Elton, Carlos Ignacio Cruz Elton, Arquitecto colaborador: Isabel De La Fuente Recabarren
Location: Lago Ranco, Región Los Ríos, Chile
Construction period: 2015
Total built area: 138 m^2 useful and 54 m^2 terrace
Photo credits: © Felipe Díaz Contardo
Suppliers: Palo Pintao (www.palopintao.cl)

Finne Architects

www.finne.com

Mazama House

Architects: Finne Architects
Project Team: Nils Finne (Design Principal), Chris Hawley (Project Manager / Architect)
Location: Mazama, Washington, USA
Construction period: 2012-2015
Total built area: 409 m^2
Photo credits: © Benjamin Benschneider

Awards:
2015 Canadian Wood Council Award
General contractor:
Rimmer and Roeter, Wenatchee
Consultants: Monte Clark Engineering, structural engineers

Port Ludlow House

Architects: Finne Architects
Project Team:
Nils Finne, Design Principal
Chris Hawley, Project Manager / Architect
Location: Port Ludlow, Washington, USA
Construction period: 2010-2012
Total built area: 228 m^2
Photo credits: © Benjamin Benschneider
Awards: 2015 CONTEMPORIST award for most popular house in Pacific Northwest
General contractor: Rob Gruye
Consultants: SSF engineers, structural engineering

GHA Giordano Hadamik Architects

www.gha4u.com

Villa Nemes

Architects: Giordano Hadamik Architects GHA, Arch. Daniele Giordano, Dipl. Ing. Nadine Hadamik
Planning + Health and safety:
Arch. Roberto Ferraro
Structure: Ing. Daniele D'IGNOTI
Mechanical electrical engineer:
Moroni Penna Ingegneri
Geologist: Dott. Giorgio Ligorini
Survey: Geom. Pastorelli Antonio
Completion:
April 2015
Building area: house 200 m^2; garage 45 m^2; pool 50 m^2
Location: Imperia, Italy
Contractor: Saguato Silvano & C. SAS
Photo credits: © GHA
Awards:
-Winner: The Plan Award 2017 - Category: Villa
-Winner: Design Competition: Live outside the box 2015
-Winner: Build Award 2017: Best International Interior Design Studio - Germany
-Winner: Build Award 2017: Housing Development Project of the Year 2017
-Awarded: CID Award 2017: Special Recognition International
-Awarded: Top 20 architectures 2016 on Archilovers
-Shortlisted: Kitchen Design Special Contest - The Plan 2018
-Longlisted: WAN AWARD House of the year 2016

Grieve Gillett Andersen

www.ggand.com.au

Crayon House

Architect: Grieve Gillett Andersen
Project team: Dimitty Andersen, Tim Fenton, Sam Jeyaseelan, Garth Davos
Location: Goodwood, South Australia, Australia
Construction period:
August 2015 – April 2016
Total built area: 200 m^2
Photo credits: © Sam Noonan
Awards:
-The John S Chappel Award for Residential Architecture Houses (New), Australian Institute of Architects;
-Award for Sustainable Architecture, Australian Institute of Architects
General contractor: Craig Speziali
Suppliers: Fielders (metal cladding), Sculptform (timber cladding)
Consultants: CRW Engineers (Structural and Civil Engineering)
WAX Design (Landscape Architecture)

Goolwa Beach House

Architect: Grieve Gillett Andersen
Project team: Steve Grieve, Adam Sickerdich, Garth Davos
Location: Goolwa Beach, South Australia, Australia
Construction period:
April 2011 – February 2012 (including demolition of existing building and site works)
Total built area: 288 m^2
Photo credits: © Peter Barnes
Awards:
-Award for Sustainable Architecture, Australian Institute of Architects
-Commendation for Residential Architecture, Australian Institute of Architects
General contractor:
Mobbs Construction
Suppliers: Revolution Roofing
Consultants: Wallbridge Gilbert Aztec (Structural Engineering)

Hartree + Associates Architects

www.hartree.com.au

Arthouse Swanbourne

Architects:
Hartree + Associates Architects
Location: Swanbourne, Western Australia, Australia
Construction period:
Jan 2016 – Feb 2018
Total built area: 780 m^2
Photo credits: © Robert Frith
Awards:
-Australian Institute of Architects WA Chapter - Residential Architecture – Houses (New) – 2019 Architecture Award
General contractor:
Gransden Construction

Goldtree House

Architects:
Hartree + Associates Architects
Location: East Fremantle, Western Australia, Australia
Construction period: February 2017 – December 2017
Total built area: 400 m^2
Photo credits: © Robert Frith
Awards: Australian Institute of Architects WA Chapter - Residential Architecture – Houses (Alterations & Additions) – 2018 Architecture Award
General contractor: Hollycrest Pty Ltd

Juri Troy Architects

www.juritroy.com

L-House

Architect: Juri Troy Architects
Project team: Juri Troy; DI Jürgen Schretzmayer; DI Timea Kos
Location: Purkersdorf, Austria
Construction period:
October 2017 - September 2018
Total built area: 143 m^2
Photo credits: © Juri Troy
General contractor: Herbitschek GmbH
Suppliers:
-Lights: Georg Bechter Licht GmbH
-Windows: JOSKO
Structural consultant:
Dr. Pech Ziviltechniker GmbH

House under the Oaks 2

Architect: Juri Troy Architects
Project team: Juri Troy; Jürgen Schretzmayer
Location: Eichgraben, Austria
Construction period: 2018
Total built area: 143 m^2
Photo credits: © Juri Troy
General contractor: Fa. Berger
Suppliers:
-Windows: Janko
-Baumeister Steinberger
-Sun protection: Hella
Consultants: ZMP GmbH (Structure)

Streckhof with destillery

Architect: Juri Troy Architects
Project team: Juri Troy, Angelo Ferrara, Timea Kos
Location: Weingraben, Austria
Construction period:
April 2017 – August 2018
Total built area: Built up area: 95 m^2
Floor area: 137 m^2
Photo credits: © Juri Troy
General contractor: m^2 Architekten, DI Georg Marterer (Local construction management)
Suppliers:
-Roof: Holzbau KAST GmbH, Gols; Rathmanner GmbH, Neutal
-Masonry: Baumeister Pfnier & Co GmbH, Oberpullendorf
-Lights: Georg Bechter Licht, Langenegg
-Furniture and doors: Kattun Tischler, St. Martin an der Raab
-Flooring: Malerwerkstatt Gerold Ulrich, Satteins
-Windows: Fensterbau ZECH, Götzis
Consultants: Höhenberger Engineering-ZT-GmbH (structural)

kt814 architecture

www.kt814.com

SoFa (South Face)

Architects: kt814 architecture
Project team: Rich Assenberg, Nathan Gray – kt814
Location: Teton County, Wyoming, USA
Construction period: 2014-2015
Total built area: Main floor 173 m^2, second floor 184 m^2, garage 76 m^2
Photo credits: © David Agnello, kt814
General contractor:
Jackson Hole Contracting
Suppliers:
-Tulikivi – Fireplace – TU 2200
-Thermodor - Appliances
-Runtal - Wall-mounted radiators
-Raupanel – Radiant floor systems
-LiveRoof – Modular green roof system
-Zola Windows – Exterior windows and doors - Thermo Clad Pine windows
-Lamilux – Skylight
-Montana Timber Products - Douglas fir exterior siding
-HellaShade – Exterior motorized solar blinds
Consultants: MJ Structural Engineers, SaGe Mechanical Engineeers, Agrostis Landscape Architects

House of Fir

Architects: kt814 architecture
Project Team: Nathan Gray, Rich Assenberg – kt814
Location: Teton County, Wyoming, USA
Construction period: 2015 -2016
Total built area: 297 m^2 (232 m^2 habitable – 65 m^2 garage)
Photo credits: David Agnello
General contractor: Everett Building
Suppliers:
-Montigo – Fireplace - P52
-Thermodor - Appliances
-Mitsubishi - Wall-mounted multi-zone heat-pump
-Mr Steam - Steam shower
-MTI – Bathtub - Andrea 23 Tub w/ Sculpted Finish
-Zola Windows – Exterior windows and doors - Thermo Clad Pine windows
-Sonneman – Lighting - Stix LED pendant

-Montana Timber Products - Douglas fir exterior siding
-MechoShade – Interior solar shades – ElectroShade motorized shade system
-Zehnder – ERV
-Rubio Monocoat – Interior wood finishes
Consultants:
Structural Engineer: MJ Structural Engineers
Landscape Architects: Agrostis Inc.
Mechanical Engineers: JTEC, Inc.
Civil Engineers: Valley West Engineering

LAMZ Arquitectura

www.lamzarquitectura.com

Cabaña Teitipac

Architects: Luis Alberto Martínez Zúñiga (LAMZ Arquitectura)
Project team: Romeo Ayuso, Francisco López, Óscar Acevedo
Location:
San Antonio Teitipac, Oaxaca, México
Construction period: 2018
Total built area: 185 m²
Photo credits: © Lorena Darquea
General contractor: LAMZ Arquitectura
Consultants: Eduardo Fernández

LTD Architectural Design Studio

www.ltdarch.co.nz

Back Country House

Lead Architects: David Maurice
Project location: Puhoi, New Zealand
Completion Year: 2016
Gross Built Area (square meters or square foot): 164 m²
Photo credits: © Jo Smith (www.josmithphotographer.co.nz)
Other participants:
Markplan consulting Ltd (Engineer)

MWArchitekten

www.MWArch.org

Hillside Douplex

Architects: MWArchitekten
Project team: Lukas Mähr, Carmen Wurz
Location: Schützenstrasse 3, 6845, Hohenems, Austria
Construction period: 01.2018 – 01.2019
Total built area: 250 m²
Photo credits: © Adolf Bereuter
General contractor:
Berchtold Holzbau Wolfurt
Suppliers: PREFA, SILESTONE, Stiebel Eltron, Roto
Consultants: Engineer: Mader + Flatz Baustatik ZT GmbH

Natrufied

www.natrufied.com

Bosvilla

Architects: Natrufied Architecture
Project team: Boris Zeisser with Anja Verdonk and Klaas J de Jong
Location:
Bergen (NH), the Netherlands
Construction period: 2017-2018
Total built area: 400 m²
Photo credits: © Christian Richters, Berlin/Boris Zeisser, Bergen
General contractor: J.M. Putter, Uitgeest, with Elektropartner, Heerhugo-waard and TBG techniek, Beverwijk
Suppliers: Garden: Van Haneghem Tuin en Landschap, Heiloo
Interior: DIS studio, Amsterdam
Consultants:
Structural engineer: Pieters Bouwtechniek, Delft
M+E engineer: Duurzaam aan de Zaan, Marken-Binnen

Pfenniger & Asociados

www. pfennigerarquitectura.cl

Casa Holmes Fuentealba

Architects: Pfenniger & Asociados
Project team:
Francis Pfenniger & Valeria Verlezza
Location: Yutuy – Chiloé - Chile
Construction period: 2014
Total built area: 155 m²
Photo credits: © Carlos Hevia Riera, Lorena González V., Benjamín Holmes
Awards: Seleccionada en Bienal de arquitectura de Chile 2014
General contractor: Benjamín Holmes Ch.
Consultants: Francis Pfenniger

Sebastián Calero Larrea Daniel Moreno Flores

www.sebastiancalerolarrea.com

www.danielmorenoflores.blogspot.com

El Camarote

Architect: Sebastián Calero Larrea
Project team: Miguel Calero Castro (architectural design)
Location: Conocoto, DMQ
Construction period: 2016
Total built area: 165 m²
Photo credits: © JAG Studio, Sebastián Calero Larrea
Illustrations: Carlos Valverde
Awards:
-Selected project and publication. XXI Bienal Panamericana de Quito -2018
-Nominated project (Ecuador). Mies Crown Hall Americas Prize 2016/2017
-Honorific mention. Young Architects in Latin America. Collateral Event of the 16th International Architecture Exhibition. La Biennale di Venezia
General contractor: Sebastián Calero Larrea
Consultants: Ing. Patricio Cevallos (structural engineering), Orlando Rojas (wood systems), Marco Mullo (master builder), Luis Morales (electric system)

El Carrizal

Architects: Sebastián Calero Larrea, Daniel Moreno Flores
Project team: Santiago Egas, Luis Fernando Taco, Roberto Alban, Ana María Aguilar, Gustavo Aguirre, Mateo Torres, Gabriela Loaiza, José López, Tatiana Chávez, Ernesto Landazuri, David Donoso, Juan López, Juan Fernando Moreno, Mercedes Cano, Rafael Cáceres, Ñeca, Pete y los escaladores.
Location: La Morita, DMQ
Construction period: 2014–2015
Total built area: 210 m²
Photo credits: © Federico Cairioli, Andrés Villota, Roberto Albán, JAG Studio
Photo architects: Marie Combette
illustrations: Carlos Valverde
Vegetable filters illustration:
Marie Combette
General contractor: Sebastián Calero Larrea + Daniel Moreno Flores
Suppliers: Ferretería Cano Lastra
Consultants:
Ing. Patricio Cevallos (structural engineering), Paulina Lasso (water treatment system), Rafael Cáceres (system of knots and cables), Fabián Tenorio (master builder), Luis Morales (electric system)

Sparks Architects

www.sparksarchitects.com

Valley House

Architects: Sparks
Project team: Dan Sparks, Tommy Vuletic
Location: Montville, Queensland, Australia
Construction period: 2016
Total built area: 256 m²
Photo credits:
© Christopher Fredrick Jones
Awards:
-AIA Queensland Residential Architecture Houses Award Montville Residence
-AIA Sunshine Coast Award For Residential Architecture Commendation Montville Residence
-Australian Design Review Second Most Popular Project Montville Residence
-National Houses Award Shortlisted Montville Residence
General contractor: Jaicon Constructions

Tent House

Architects: Sparks
Project name: Tent House
Architects: Sparks
Project team: Tent - Dan Sparks, Michael Cornish, Alex Keen
Location: Noosa Hinterland, Queensland, Australia
Construction period: 2012
Total built area: 230 m²
Photo credits:
© Christopher Fredrick Jones
Awards:
-AIA Sunshine Coast Award for Project of the Year
-AIA Queensland State Award for Residential Architecture
-AIA National Awards "People's Choice"
-National "Houses" Award Commendation
General contractor:
Jaicon Constructions
Suppliers: Fabritecture
Consultants: Fabritecture

Steendijk

www.steendijk.com
Instagram: @steendyk

Bellbird Retreat

Architects: Steendijk
Project team: Brian Steendijk, Shaun Crossman, Timo Lueck
Location: Killarney, Queensland, Australia
Construction period: completed 2018
Total built area: 67 m²
Photo credits: © Christopher Frederick Jones, Brian Steendyk, Craig Hodges
Awards:
-Architecture Masterprize - international winner - residential architecture
-World Architecture News 2018 Award - international winner - small spaces
-World Architecture Festival 2019- shortlist
Dezeen Awards - shortlist
Australian Institute of Architects State Awards:
-winner - Robin Dods Award for Residential Architecture - Houses (New)
-winner - Colorbond Award for Steel Architecture
-winner - Award for Sustainable Architecture
-Australian Steel Institute 2018 Award - national winner- small projects
General contractor: EA&PJ Bell
Suppliers: Breezway, Gjames, EMBASSYliving, Austral, Claypave, Beacon Lighting
Consultants: Westera Engineers

Stempel & Tesař architekti

www.stempel-tesar.com

Renovation of mill and conversion into housing

Architects: Stempel & Tesar architects
Project Team: Ján Stempel, Jan Jakub Tesař, Aleš Herold
Location: Slapy, Czech Republic
Construction period: 2014-2017
Total built area: 241
Photo credits: © Filip Šlapal
Awards:
Czech Architecture award – finalist 2018
General contractor: Tepkom l.c.

House on Windy Peak

Architects: Stempel & Tesar architects
Project team: Ján Stempel, Jan Jakub Tesař, Aleš Herold
Location: Mníšek, Ore Mountain, Czech Republic
Construction period: 2014-2018
Total built area: 198 m²
Photo credits: © Filip Šlapal
General contractor: self-help
Suppliers: TERMO l.c.
Consultants: František Štěpán

Tower Home

Architects: Stempel & Tesar architects
Project team: Ján Stempel, Jan Jakub Tesař, Aleš Herold, Lenka Mlíkovská
Location: Všenory, Czech Republic
Construction period: 2014-2016
Total built area: 164 m²
Photo credits: © Filip Šlapal
Awards: Czech Architecture award – nomination 2017; Passive house 2017
General contractor: self-help

Studio Combo

www.studio-combo.fr

Houses Estosoto Cabo Espichel

Architects: Studio Combo
Julien Labrousse & Jérome Friant
Project team: Julien Labrousse, Ines Poncet, Alfredo Luvison
Location: Estrada Nacional 379 CCI 1207- Azóia 2970-181 Sesimbra, Portugal
Delivery date: 2019
Total built area: 204 m²
Photo credits: © Guillaume Guerin
Consultants: b2s ingenierie

Tegnestuen LOKAL

www.tegnestuenlokal.dk

TK-33

Architects: Tegnestuen LOKAL
Project team: Christopher Carlsen, Morten Bang
Location: Tikøb, Denmark
Construction period: 2016
Total built area: 130 m²
Photo credits: © Peter Jørgensen, Jan Ove Christensen
Suppliers: Kompromemt

Tim Bennetton Architects

www.timbennetton.com.au

Yeronga House

Architects: Tim Bennetton Architects
Project Team: Tim Bennetton, Ryan Bunn
Location: Yeronga, Queensland, Australia
Construction period: 2016-2017
Total built area: 150 m²
Photo credits: © Shantanu Starick
Awards:
-Shorlist – House Alteration and Addition over 200 m² (Houses, 2018)
-Sustainable Architecture – State Shortlist (Australian Institute of Architects, 2018)
-Sustainable Architecture – State Commendation (Australian Institute of Architects, 2018)
-Residential Architecture – State Award (Australian Institute of Architects, 2018)
General contractor: Greg Thornton Constructions (Greg Thornton)
Suppliers: Barry Hamlet - Studio Steel (Custom awnings, gutters, window hoods)
Des Shield – D&C Shield Pty Ltd (Cabinetmaker)
Stewart Anderson (Landscape Contractor)
Consultants: AD Structure – (Engineer)
Water Technology – Steve Clark – (Stormwater Landscape Design)
Building Certification Consultants – (Building Certifier)

Stradbroke House

Architects: Tim Bennetton Architects in association with Gabriel Poole, www.gabrielpoole.com.au
Project Team: Tim Bennetton, Gabriel Poole, Elizabeth Poole, Simon Martin, Barry Hamlet
Location: South Stradbroke Island, Queensland, Australia
Construction period: 2015-2016
Total built area: 284 m²
Photo credits: © Mindi Cooke, Harry Frith
Awards:
-House of the Year – Gold Coast Region (Australian Institute of Architects, 2018)
-Sustainable Architecture – State Shortlist (Australian Institute of Architects, 2018)
-Robin Dods Award for Residential Architecture (House of the Year, Queensland) (Australian Institute of Architects, 2018)
General contractor: Charles Warren Constructions (Charles Warren)
Suppliers:
-Barry Hamlet: Studio Steel (Structural steel, punkah fan, fold out bed structures – including design input)
-Des Shield: D&C Shield Pty Ltd (Cabinetmaker)
-Steven Clegg: Steven Clegg Design (Landscape Design)
-Mike Murray: Creative Canvas (Canvas Awnings, covers for fold out sleeping rooms)
-Elizabeth Poole – colours, artworks
Consultants: Rod Bligh, Bligh Tanner – (Structural Engineer)
Building Certification Consultants – (Building Certifier)

VTN Architects (Vo Trong Nghia)

www.votrongnghia.com

Stepping Park House

Architects: VTN Architects (Vo Trong Nghia Architects)
Principal architects: Vo Trong Nghia, Hidetoshi Sawa
Project architects: Nguyen Van Thien
Status: completed 2018
Location: Ho Chi Minh City, Vietnam
Site area: 252 m²
GFA: 475 m²
Photo credits: © Hiroyuki Oki
Contractor: Wind and Water House JSC

House for trees

Architects: VTN Architects (Vo Trong Nghia Architects)
Principal architects: Vo Trong Nghia, Masaaki Iwamoto, Kosuke Nishijima (3 principals)
Architects: Nguyen Tat Dat
Contractor: Wind and Water House JSC
Status: Built in 04.2014
Program: Private house
Location: Tanbinh, Ho Chi Minh City
GFA: 226 m² (226.50)
Footprint: 111.66 m²
Site area: 474.32 m²
Client: Individual
Photo credits: © Hiroyuki Oki

Bihn house

Architects: VTN Architects (Vo Trong Nghia Architects)
Principal architects: Vo Trong Nghia
Design team: Masaaki Iwamoto, Chiang Hsing-O, Nguyen Tat Dat, Nguyen Duy Phuoc, Takahito Yamada
Office credit: VTN architects (Vo Trong Nghia Architects)
Status: Built in 03.2016
Program: Private house
Location: Ho Chi Minh, Vietnam
Site area: 321.6 m²
Footprint: 136 m²
GFA: 233 m²
Contractor:
Wind And Water House JSC
Photo credits: © Hiroyuki Oki, Quang Dam

Wallmakers

www.wallmakers.org

Debris House
Residence for Mr. Biju Mathew

Architect's Firm: Wallmakers
Location: St. Peter's Junction, Patanamthitta, Kerala, India
Completion Year: 2015
Gross Built Area: 194 m²
Lead Architects: Vinu Daniel, Archana Nambiar, Jinsy Ann Rajan, Shobitha Jacob, Melvin Davis, Vijith, Abdul Aseeb, Sagar Kudtarkar, Dawal Dasari, Suhaas, Shekkizar, Srivarshini JM
Masonry contractors:
P.S. Suresh – Shivranjini Constructions, Pondicherry
Fabrication team:
Kunjumon James - J.K steels
Mep: Unni Krishnan, Sajith Lal
Photo credits: © Anand Jaju

Warren Benbow Architects

www.warrenbenbow.com

Hope View House

Architects: Warren Benbow Architects
Project team: Dean Benbow & Emily Warren
Location: Cradley, Herefordshire, England, UK
Construction period:12 months, January 2016 - January 2017
Total built area: 440 m²
Treated Floor Area (for passivhaus purposes 256 m²)
Photo credits: © Lisa Lodwig
Awards:
-RIBA Regional Award 2018 RIBA Regional
-Sustainability Award 2018 Finalist UK Passivhaus Awards 2018
General contractor: Covenhope Construction Ltd.
Suppliers:
Polished concrete - Midlands Flooring
Doors & Windows - Internorm
Roof - Alwitra ICB
Stone - Birch Hill Pennant Quarry
Consultants:
Structural Engineer Allan Pearce at Pearce Edwards
Landscape Consultant Mackley Davies
Passivhaus Advisor Nick Grant at Elemental Solutions
Services Alan Clarke
Passivhaus Assessor Kym Mead